Truth in Philosophy

Truth in Philosophy

BARRY ALLEN

HARVARD UNIVERSITY PRESS
Cambridge, Massachusetts
London, England
1993

This book is printed on acid-free paper, and its binding materials have been chosen for strength and durability.

Library of Congress Cataloging-in-Publication Data
Allen, Barry, 1957–
    Truth in philosophy / Barry Allen.
        p.   cm.
    Includes index.
    ISBN 0–674–91090–7 (alk. paper)
    1. Truth.   I. Title.
BD171.A3855 1993
    121—dc20   92–35722
                    CIP

For Richard Rorty

εἷς μύριοι, ἐὰν ἄριστος ᾖ.

Heraclitus

Contents

Abbreviations

Derrida

G   *Of Grammatology*, trans. Gayatri Chakravorty Spivak (Baltimore: Johns Hopkins University Press, 1976).

L   *Limited Inc* (Evanston: Northwestern University Press, 1989).

M   *Margins of Philosophy*, trans. Alan Bass (Chicago: University of Chicago Press, 1982).

SP   *Speech and Phenomena*, trans. David B. Allison (Evanston: Northwestern University Press, 1973).

Foucault

DP   *Discipline and Punish*, trans. Alan Sheridan (New York: Vintage, 1979).

HS   *The History of Sexuality*, vol. 1: *Introduction*, trans. Robert Hurley (New York: Vintage, 1980).

PF   "The Ethics of Care for the Self as a Practice of Freedom," in *The Final Foucault*, ed. J. Bernauer and D. Rasmussen (Cambridge: MIT Press, 1988).

PK   *Power/Knowledge: Selected Interviews and Other Writings, 1972–1977*, ed. C. Gorden (New York: Pantheon, 1980).

PPC   *Politics, Philosophy, Culture: Interviews and Other Writings, 1977–1984*, ed. L. D. Kritzman (Oxford: Blackwell, 1988).

SP   "The Subject and Power," in H. Dreyfus and P. Rabinow, *Michel Foucault: Beyond Structuralism and Hermeneutics*, 2d ed. (Chicago: University of Chicago Press, 1983).

Heidegger

BP   *The Basic Problems of Phenomenology*, trans. Albert Hofstadter (Bloomington: Indiana University Press, 1982).

BW   *Basic Writings*, ed. David Farrell Krell (New York: Harper &

Row, 1977) ("On the Essence of Truth" and "Letter on Humanism").

EGT   *Early Greek Thinking*, trans. David Farrell Krell and Frank A. Capuzzi (New York: Harper & Row, 1975).

MF   *The Metaphysical Foundations of Logic*, trans. Michael Heim (Bloomington: Indiana University Press, 1984).

PLT   *Poetry, Language, Thought*, trans. Albert Hofstadter (New York: Harper & Row, 1971).

SZ   *Sein und Zeit*, 15th ed. (Tübingen: Max Niemeyer, 1979); *Being and Time*, trans. John Macquarrie and Edward Robinson (New York: Harper & Row, 1962). The margin of the translation carries the German pagination, to which I refer.

TB   "Time and Being," in *On Time and Being*, trans. Joan Stambaugh (New York: Harper & Row, 1972). *Zur Sache des Denkens*, 2d ed. (Tübingen: Max Niemeyer Verlag, 1976).

WT   *What Is Called Thinking?* trans. J. Glenn Gray (New York: Harper & Row, 1968). *Was Heißt Denken?* 3d ed. (Tübingen: Max Niemeyer Verlag, 1971).

William James

M   *The Meaning of Truth* (Cambridge, Mass.: Harvard University Press, 1978).

P   *Pragmatism* (Cambridge, Mass.: Harvard University Press, 1978).

Nietzsche

B   *Beyond Good and Evil*, trans. Walter Kaufmann (New York: Vintage, 1966).

EH   *Ecce Homo*, trans. Walter Kaufmann (New York: Vintage, 1967).

GM   *On the Genealogy of Morals*, trans. Walter Kaufmann (New York: Vintage, 1967).

PN   *The Portable Nietzsche*, ed. and trans. Walter Kaufmann (New York: Viking, 1954) (*Thus Spoke Zarathustra, Twilight of the Idols, Antichrist*).

WP   *The Will to Power*, trans. Walter Kaufmann and R. J. Hollingdale (New York: Vintage Books, 1967).

Wittgenstein

NB   *Notebooks, 1914–1916*, 2d ed., trans. G. E. M. Anscombe (Chicago: University of Chicago Press, 1979).

PG   *Philosophical Grammar*, trans. Anthony Kenny (Berkeley: University of California Press, 1978).

PI   *Philosophical Investigations*, 3d ed., trans. G. E. M. Anscombe (Oxford: Blackwell, 1967). References are to numbered sections of Part I or page numbers of Part II.

RFM   *Remarks on the Foundations of Mathematics*, rev. ed., trans. G. E. M. Anscombe (Cambridge, Mass.: MIT Press, 1978).

TLP   *Tractatus Logico-Philosophicus*, trans. D. F. Pears and B. F. McGuinness (London: Routledge & Kegan Paul, 1961).

What is philosophy today—philosophical activity, I mean—if it is not . . . the endeavor to know how and to what extent it might be possible to think differently, instead of legitimating what is already known? . . . it is entitled to explore what might be changed, in its own thought . . . to learn to what extent the effort to think one's own history can free thought from what it silently thinks, and so enable it to think differently.

FOUCAULT

Prologue

On a huge hill,
Cragged, and steep, Truth stands, and hee that will
Reach her, about must, and about must goe.

John Donne

Truth is the Philosopher's value *par excellence*. For Heraclitus, "Thinking well is the greatest excellence and wisdom: to act and speak what is true, perceiving things according to their nature." Plato's Socrates says, "I renounce the honors sought by most men and, pursuing the truth, I shall endeavour both to live and, when death comes, to die, as good a man as I possibly can be. And I exhort all other men . . . to enlist in this contest which excels all others." After Heraclitus and Socrates, after Plato and the Stoics, what distinguishes the *philosophoi* is that unlike others who claim to be wise, their path to wisdom passes through the *askesis* or discipline of truth. That, Plato says, we must "seek always and altogether, on pain of being an imposter without part or lot in true philosophy."[1]

In Plato's allegory, we begin life as prisoners chained to the walls of a cave. We see only shadows and, knowing no better, take them for realities, until our contentment is unsettled by a glimpse outside and a vision of true being. Yet the story leaves unclear what motive it is that leads the philosophical hero to escape from the realm of deception or, later, to return in order to disenchant the others. The good of all this seems to go without saying.[2]

Nietzsche was the first to draw attention to this omission. "Consider both the earliest and most recent philosophers: they are all oblivious of how much the will to truth itself first requires justification; here there is a lacuna in every philosophy . . . truth [is] not *permitted* to be a problem at all" (*GM*3.24). Philosophers have long wondered whether we really know the truth, but few seriously ask whether we should want it at all. What value does *true* add to *believed?* Why the privilege of truth despite opinion, despite appearances, despite the utility, pleasure, or security one may need forgo for the sake of truth? "Here," Nietzsche says, "I touch on my problem, on our problem, my unknown friends . . . in us the will to truth becomes conscious of itself as a *problem*" (*GM*3.27).

This problem—the problem of truth's value, its relation to well-being or the good—belongs to a historical discourse of truth in philosophy from Heraclitus to Heidegger. In what follows I describe this discourse, sketching its history and identifying its oldest presuppositions. My aim in this is to show how these presuppositions can be criticized and how truth looks from a perspective that does not confirm or reproduce them.

I begin with a historical introduction. What I call the classical philosophy of truth is an ensemble of four interdependent ideas in ancient philosophy (Greek and Christian) concerning truth's relation to nature, language, being, and the good. Together they define the historical discourse on truth I call *onto-logic*. The first principle of onto-logic is that the "logical" possibility of sentential truth-value derives from the "ontological" possibility of beings that "are what they are," that have an identity of their own. For onto-logic, truth is *true to* such beings; it takes its measure from what is, whose nature truth discloses.

In Part One, I look at versions of onto-logic first in Greek and Christian sources, then in modern philosophy. But it is not my intention to write the history of Western truth. The historical studies in Part One merely establish some context for the discussion of six philosophers which follows: Nietzsche and William James (Part Two); and Heidegger, Derrida, Wittgenstein, and Foucault (Part Three).

Part Two is entitled "Nietzsche's Question." As I have indicated, the question concerns the good of truth. Nietzsche was the first philosopher to take this seriously as a problem. "The will to truth requires a critique — let us thus define our own task — the value of truth must for once be *experimentally called into question*" (*GM*3.24). I discuss the results of the experiment in Chapter 3.

It is convenient to pass from Nietzsche to William James. For both, there is no impressive difference between truth "itself" and what passes for true in practice; for both, what passes for true has nothing to do with adequation to a transcendent order of Being, fixed and closed forever. We admire and evaluate as true those beliefs which enlarge predictability and facilitate action by increasing control. For James, this practical value is "the good in the way of belief" and "the meaning of truth." Yet unlike Nietzsche he never seriously questions truth's claim to the highest value, which he tries instead to reconstruct around a New World center.

Foucault takes up Nietzsche's question and sharpens it, making truth visible as a power in the political government of conduct. But I do not pass directly to Foucault. The classical harmony of truth and the good is supported by a chorus of onto-logical assumptions concerning nature, being, identity, and difference. This solidarity has to be elucidated, its presuppositions exposed and destroyed, before it is possible to consider the ethical and political questions around truth in what seems to me the right light. That is why after a discussion of Nietzsche and James in Part Two I set aside the question of truth's value and devote most of Part Three to a critical study of onto-logic.

Heidegger too is a critic of truth's onto-logic, in particular of the idea that the essence of truth is its correspondence to reality. My discussion of Heidegger in Chapter 5 can be read as a commentary on his alternative, which he summarizes in the formula "The essence of truth is freedom" (*BW*.125). The chapter on Derrida which follows begins with a look at his revisionary appropriation of Saussure's theory of signs, analyzing its critical implications for both the onto-logical tradition and Heidegger's revision of classical truth. For a reason that I explain there, however, I am not content to rest the case against onto-logic with Heidegger and Derrida. In Chapter 7, on Wittgenstein, I explain what I think is the strongest case against the interpretation of truth in terms of adequacy or correspondence. Wittgenstein is useful for this because although he did not know it his *Tractatus Logico-Philosophicus* recapitulates the oldest assumptions of the discourse on truth in philosophy, and because although he did not understand his later work in this way it contains ideas for a fundamental objection to the onto-logic of correspondence. This is the argument "from nature to history" mentioned in the title of Part Three.

From Wittgenstein, I return to Nietzsche's question in a discussion of Foucault. The faith that truth cannot fail to be, if not the lamp of liberation, then at least neutral among parties requires the assumption that where there is truth (the real article), a statement is made to be true by something like nature, or being, or the way the world is. As long as this assumption finds favor among philosophers we must misunderstand the relationship between the existence of truth and the exercise or actuality of power. Assume that truth's essence is "correspondence to reality," and any ethically or politically sensitive control exercised through the use of truth, or through what passes for true, must be interpreted as effects of an interfering, falsifying factor, like propaganda, ideology, or distorted communication. But the truth is otherwise. Differences between true and false do not exist apart from the practice in which these values are produced and evaluated and statements made to circulate as true, as known or probable, as information, news, results, and so on. Only here have statements currency, the capacity to circulate, to penetrate practical reasoning, to be taken seriously, to *pass* for the truth. These practical conditions situate truth amid all the major asymmetries of social power, undermining its status as a common good.

In making this argument I use the notion of *passing for true.* A statement passes for true when, whether by the authority of its source, or by formally sustaining evaluation for truth, or by any other means (for example, mass media advertising), it passes from a source to a receiver, successfully soliciting belief, penetrating practical reasoning, and thus to an infinitely variable degree modifying the subjective representation of options and necessities for belief and choice. This is an example of the effect Foucault terms *government.* A closer look at this idea in Chapter 8 sets the stage for the argument "from being to politics" with which I conclude.

I discuss the work of these six authors in the light of two philosophical questions about truth. First, what is the objection to a correspondence theory of truth? Almost everyone has heard that there is supposed to be something wrong with this, but what exactly?

As the studies of Part One confirm, what has always been at stake in the history of this idea is the value of adequacy: Truth is ministerial, vicegerent, responsive to what is, from which it takes its measure. On this interpretation, the occasional truth in speech or thought presupposes the more originally determinate *being* or self-identical *presence* of the things whose being as they are makes truths true. Against this I argue (Chapter 7) that the identity and difference of things are as thoroughly conditioned by the historical circumstances of practice as the identity and difference of signs, symbols, or languages. The essence of truth therefore cannot not be adequacy or correspondence. For on the one hand what is said is often true, plain true. But on the other hand nothing "is what it is" regardless of the historical discourse that refers to it. So whatever "there is" when there is truth in speech, there is nothing whose nature or presence makes what we say true. A statement is not made to be true by the corresponding presence of anything whatever. Statements are not *made* to be true at all; instead, they are made to circulate, to pass for true.

This is not to say that "passing" is what makes a statement true or that "true" should be defined as warranted assertability. The only sense in which truth is "determined" is when a given statement is evaluated for truth and sustains that evaluation. Since this does not always happen on every occasion when something true is said, not all truths are "determined" to be true. Even when truth *is* determined (that is, evaluated, verified), *what* determines it (a technique for producing truth) does not "make" a statement true by endowing it with the essential true-making attribute. There is no such thing. The difference between truth and falsehood is not made by the presence or absence of a unique attribute. It is a mistake to think truth "itself" is a unit or principle of natural unity whose character (correspondence, coherence, assertability, or whatever) can be expected to enter into an explanation of why some statements are true and others not.[3]

My argument does not concern truth's essence or formal definition at all but rather its existence, to which the practical possibility of evaluation is indispensable. This is not the banal observation that apart from speakers there would be no statements true or false. My claim is that apart from these contingent practical conditions, *nothing else* "determines" the difference between being true or false. There is nothing more to the "determination" of truth-values than the determin*ability* that first comes with the language-game that makes their estimation a practical possibility, and there is nothing more to the truth (the "being true") of the occasional truth than the historical fact that there is an economy of knowledge in which what is said passes for true.

The way I frame the objection to a correspondence theory of truth eventually leads me to a second question, Nietzsche's question concerning truth's value. This question is independent of the first one, to the extent that a philosopher who believed in truth-as-correspondence might still raise and presumably answer it. But Nietzsche's question cannot be avoided if one frames the objection to correspondence as I do. For my argument relieves truth of a relationship to Nature and Being that has held sway in philosophy since antiquity. One cannot disturb this relationship and not expect implications for broad ethical and political questions concerning the use of truth, to which Chapter 8 provides no more than an introduction.

PART ONE

===

Historical Introduction

Unum, verum, bonum—the old favourites deserve their celebrity. There *is* something odd about each of them. Theoretical theology is a form of onomatolatry.

J. L. Austin

1 *Classical Philosophy of Truth*

> Do you think that wisdom is anything other than the truth in which the highest good is perceived and held fast?
>
> St. Augustine, *On Free Choice of the Will* II.ix

Aristotle defines truth for classical philosophy: "to say of what is that it is, and of what is not that it is not, is true."[1] This seems simple, but it is important to see that it is not. The formula synthesizes three distinct and in no way obvious or unobjectionable assumptions, assumptions which prove decisive for the career of truth in philosophy.

First, the priority of nature over language, culture, or the effects of historical experience. One can say of *what is* that it is just in case there exists a *what* which is *there*, present, with an identity, form, or nature of its own.

Second, the idea that truth is a kind of sameness, falsity a difference, between what is said and what there is. In another formula Aristotle says, "he who thinks the separated to be separated and the combined to be combined has the truth, while he whose thought is in a state contrary to the objects is in error" (1051b). To be true, *what* you think separated must be *what is* separated—that is, they must be the same (the same form or *eidos*). To accommodate the priority of nature, however, truth has to be a secondary sort of sameness: according to the classical metaphor, the imitation of original by copy. It is up to us to copy Nature's originals, whose identity and existence are determined by causes prior to and independent of local convention.

Thus a third feature of classical truth: the secondary and derivative character of the signs by which truth is symbolized and communicated. Classical truth subordinates the *being* (the existence and identity) of signs (linguistic or otherwise) to the natural, physical, finally given presence of the nonsigns they stand for.

Here are three ideas I collect under the description "classical philosophy of truth." I shall elaborate on them before I take up a fourth theme, which concerns the good of truth. These three already situate truth in relation to *nature, being,* and *language.*

The Truth of Nature

It is characteristic of Greek philosophy to think of truth as something that a statement has because of something else's being one way and not another. Truth's value consists in its adequacy to this "something else"—to beings that are there by nature, and the modifications and interferences they undergo. It is usual to speak of nature as the aggregate of natural things. Yet in both English and Greek there is an earlier usage from which this derives, according to which "nature" means not an aggregate but a principle or source *(archē)* residing in the things themselves and responsible for their characteristic behavior. As Collingwood observes, "When a Greek writer contrasts *phusis* [nature] with *technē* (i.e. what things are when left to themselves with what human skill can make of them) or *phusis* with *bia* (how things behave when left to themselves with how they behave when interfered with) he implies that things have a principle of growth, organization, and movement, in their own right and that this is what he means by their nature; and when he calls things natural he means that they have such a principle in them."[2]

Some things exist not by (their) nature, but only through something else—for example, qualities, places, and artifacts. But there would be no qualities or places apart from the natural beings that own and occupy them, and while carpenters work on wood and navigators work the sea, these acts modify determinations more original, beings that are in the end simply *there,* present, given for thought and action. Aristotle calls what is originally present or there by (its) nature a substance *(ousia)*. Not everything that exists is a substance, but nothing exists apart from substances, and while individual substances like you and me are corruptible, what is veritably substantial in what is, what is actually there by (its) nature—these natures or forms themselves—are eternal elements in the intelligible gathering-together *(logos)* of a static yet tensed (enduring, permanently present) natural order *(kosmos)*.

Temporal presence figures again in the Greek idea that *to be* entails a determinate identity which a being owns, as it were, precisely because it *is* a being and because a being has to be "identical to itself." Etienne Gilson writes of Plato, "he never tires of repeating, really to be is to be 'its own self according to itself: *auto kath auto*' . . . there is no difference whatsoever between being and self-identity . . . to be is 'to be the same.'" That is, to be one and the same, this one or that, for a while. This seems also to be the force of Aristotle's contention that being and unity "are the same and are one thing in the sense that they are implied in one another" (1003b). The being of a being, here determined as unity, holds elements together and makes a thing one, the same, self-identical, for precisely as long as it lasts. Greek ontology thus thinks of being in terms of identity and identity as self-identity, a unity or unification proper to the thing itself, its own nature. For classical metaphysics, the so-called principle of identity ($A = A$) is no bare tautology. Heidegger aptly describes it as "a principle of being that reads: To every being as such there belongs identity, the unity with itself." He continues: "What the principle of identity, heard in its fundamental key, states is exactly what the whole of Western European thinking thinks—and that is: the unity of identity forms a basic characteristic of the being of beings."[3]

To be a being, on this interpretation, is to possess a durable identity, original or derived. Some entities own their identity, being what they are by their own nature *(ousia, substances)*. Others (qualities, places, and so on) are renters, deriving their being (their identity and existence) from a relationship to the original owners, the substances, the aristocrats of Greek ontology. The connection between being and truth now comes into view. Plotinus remarks, "if we can say of each and every thing what it is, it is owing to its unity as well as to its identity." Beings, merely because they are, have something *to* them, identities which are their own. This "self-identical being" is the ground of classical truth. It is because beings are "identical to themselves" that there is something about them to get right. The self-identity of a being is thus, as it were, nature's own criterion of truth. No doubt this is why Augustine speaks of a truth in things prior to the truth of speech or thought. In a sentence that has been repeated for centuries, he says, "The true is that which is" *(verum est id quod est)*. Writing well before the recovery of the Aristotelian corpus in the West, Anselm says, "Everyone speaks of the truth of signification, but very few consider the truth which is in the essence of things." Matthew of Aquasparta, a follower of Bonaventure and medieval Augustinianism amid the Aristotelianism of the late thirteenth century, argues that "if there were no truth in the thing, there would be no truth in the understanding, since the truth of the thing is the cause of that."[4]

Thomas Aquinas tried to correct this line. Recalling Aristotle's remark that "falsity and truth are not in things . . . but in thought" (1027b), he says: "Although the truth of our intellect is caused by the thing, yet it is not necessary that the essence of truth should be there primarily, any more than the essence of health should be primarily in medicine rather than in the animal . . . the being of the thing, not its truth, is the cause of truth in the intellect."[5] Yet even as he discredits the truth of things, Thomas confirms the older Greek idea that considered in relation to intellect, *to be* is to be *true-making*. This is an elementary determination of the being of beings, for Plato and Aristotle as much as Augustine and the Scholastics. If there is truth, if it exists at all, we owe this to the beings whose *being* (unity, identity, self-sameness) lets them last for a while, thus giving us something to get right or be true to. But now I have begun a new theme (truth and being) whose development I shall postpone until I say something of truth in signs.

The Truth of Signs

Aristotle begins *De Interpretatione* with a statement of the proper order among nature, the soul, and the linguistic sign:

> Now spoken sounds are symbols (*sumbola*) of affections in the soul, and written marks symbols of spoken sounds. And just as

written marks are not the same for all men, neither are spoken sounds. But what these are in the first place signs (*semia*) of—affections in the soul—are the same for all; and what these affections are likenesses (*homeiomata*) of—actual things—are also the same. (16a)

Two ideas with an essential historical and theoretical reference to this text have governed Western thought on language and language's signs. First, linguistic conventionality: Languages are more like laws or fashions than stellar motion or organic growth. Later, Aristotle defines a noun or name *(onoma)* as "a spoken sound significant by convention."[6] Second, a secondary sign: Speech is before writing, images before speech, things before images. Nature comes before convention, being before representation. At the end of Aristotle's series (writing, speech, affection, thing) we reach a permanently present natural form whose being or self-identical presence is the ontological presupposition of signs, knowledge, and truth.

Following Aristotle's lead, Western work on language and its signs from the Stoics to Locke subordinates these typically "conventional" or "arbitrary" contrivances to beings whose identity and existence is autonomous of the language that names them. The identity of a given sign (*what* sign it is) is determined by the identity of the nonsign it stands for, and language is first of all an apparatus for naming and predication. It is as if signs cannot be signs apart from something that is emphatically not itself another sign. In relation to this more original being, the identity and existence of signs are derivative, secondary, dependent, accidental.

I shall look into this idea further in Chapter 6, where I discuss Saussure's theory of the linguistic sign. I should note here that for Aristotle the truth-value (true or false) of a proposition is as secondary and derived as the identity of a sign. "It is not because we think truly that you are pale, that you *are* pale," he says, "but because you are pale, we who say this have the truth" (1051b). Elsewhere, he says that "the being of a man carries with it the truth of the proposition that he is, and the implication is reciprocal; for if a man is, the proposition wherein we allege that he is is true, and conversely, if the proposition wherein we allege that he is is true, then he is." Being and truth are reciprocal, perhaps, but ontologically asymmetrical: "The true propo-sition, however, is in no way the cause of the being of the man, but the fact of the man's being does seem somehow to be the cause of the truth of the proposition, for the truth or falsity of the proposition depends on the fact of the man's being or not being" (14b).

The Truth of Being

Heidegger remarks that "in ontological problematics, being and truth have from time immemorial been brought together if not entirely identified" (*SZ*.228). He thinks this is a kind of hint. There is, how-ever, reason to think it is an originally meaningless accident of histori-cal grammar. *To be* is spoken in many ways, but for Aristotle "it is obvious that of these the what-something-is, which signifies the sub-stance, is the first" (1028a). In a study of the Greek verb "be" *(einai)*, Charles Kahn shows the priority of its use as a predicating copula and the corresponding insignificance of the difference between existing and not existing. "Both of them," he writes of Plato and Aristotle, "system-atically subordinate the notion of existence to predication, and both tend to express the former by means of the latter. In their view *to be* is to be a definite kind of thing." In contrast to *what* something is, the factor of existing, if it appears at all, appears secondary and of no dis-tinct significance. For both, "existence is always *einai ti,* being some-thing or other, being something definite. There is no concept of exis-tence as such." This is not to say that Aristotle, for instance, is oblivious of the difference between what a thing is and its existence. Joseph Owens observes, "Aristotle does not for an instant deny exis-tence. He readily admits it in Being *per accidens.* But he does not seem even to suspect that it is an act worthy of any special consideration, or that it is capable of philosophical treatment."[7]

Kahn also describes a so-called veridical use of the Greek "be" ac-cording to which it "must be translated by 'is true,' 'is so,' 'is the case,' or by some equivalent phrase." He remarks that "instead of existence . . . it was another use of *to be* that gave Parmenides and Plato their philosophical starting point: the veridical use of *esti* and *on* for 'the facts' that a true statement must convey. Thus the Greek concept of Being takes its rise from . . . this notion of *what is* as whatever distinguishes truth from falsehood . . . doctrines of Being first arose in Greece in connection with the question: what must reality be like for knowledge and informative discourse to be possible and for statements and beliefs of the form *X is Y* to be true?" To ask what reality must be *like* for sentences to be true implies that truth in sentences is their being like what is. Kahn writes, "the pre-philosophic conception of truth in Greek . . . involves some kind of correlation or fit between what is said or thought, on one side, and what is or what is the case or the way things are on the other side." As veridical, the Greek *esti* "poses a relation between a given descriptive content and the world to which it refers or which it purports to describe . . . truth depends on some point of similarity or agreement between the two." Truth, in Greek, is the virtue of a discourse that subordinates itself to what is, assuming second hand the same form as the beings whose being makes the discourse true. "If we bear in mind the structure of the veridical use of the verb, we will easily see how the philosophers' interest in knowledge and truth, taken together with this use of 'to be,' immediately leads to the concept of Being as . . . the facts that make true statements true."[8]

This must have seemed obvious to a linguistically homogeneous culture whose copula verb also had the force of "to be true," while suppressing the difference between predication and existence. The path to truth as correspondence was opened by this fortuitous lexical contingency. What began as a meaningless assimilation survived the Greek language as a metaphysician's platitude: Truths are true because of what there is. The assimilation of truth and being lives on in the assumption that possible predication and possible existence are the same. Even philosophers as seemingly far removed from Greek metaphysics as Hume and Wittgenstein assume that the criterion of what can *be* is what can be *said*. For Hume, "Whatever is distinct, is distinguishable; and whatever is distinguishable, is separable by the thought or imagination . . . and may be conceiv'd as separately existent, and may exist separately, without any contradiction or absurdity." A fragment of Parmenides' poem *On Nature* reads: "for it is the same thing to think and to be." Although he certainly did not know it, Wittgenstein seems almost to paraphrase this in the *Tractatus:* "A thought contains the possibility of the situation of which it is the thought. What is thinkable is possible too" (*TLP*.3.02). There is no difference for these philosophers between *can be thought (imagined, said)* and *can be*. Logic is the common measure. Of course, this would be appropriate if truth were an assimilating adequacy to beings. In that case, a logically consistent predication would owe its possibility of being true to the ontological possibility of the thing whose being would make it true. Possibilities of truth and possibilities of being would therefore be the same. I use the term *onto-logic* for this ontological interpretation of truth-value as "made" or "determined" by the being of beings (any beings whatever). I also use the term more broadly for the classical understanding of truth, being, nature, and language in which this technical interpretation of truth is historically embedded.[9]

I disagree with Kahn on one point. Referring to "the convergence or interdependence of the concepts of predication, existence, and truth" in Greek, he says: "If we may rightly regard this fact as a kind of historical accident . . . it is surely a happy accident, a lucky chance, which . . . facilitated the work of the Greek philosophers by bringing together 'by chance' concepts which properly belong together in any general theory of language and the world." If he believes in this "properly belonging together," it is curious that Kahn should elsewhere cite from a study of "Being" in classical Chinese to the effect that there is no concept of being which languages are well or ill equipped to present: "the functions of 'to be' depend upon a grammatical rule for the formation of the sentence, and it would be merely a coincidence if one found anything resembling it in a language without this rule." What propriety, then, to the Greek assimilation of "be" and "be true"? If another language lacks this feature it is different, but not for that a less propitious language for seeking or speaking the truth about truth. The idea that truth requires from philosophy a "general theory of language and the world" is itself "a kind of historical accident." Any intuition to the effect that when a statement is true it is so *because* a being is as it is, is an artifact of this history, whose arbitrary and accidental origin should undercut any probative force, in philosophical argumentation, for this so-called correspondence intuition.[10]

Aristotle's formula for truth is far from self-evident or trivial. It passes for a platitude perhaps, but thoughtlessly. That does not mean there are no platitudes about truth. Here are three.

Truth is conserved in valid inference. Wittgenstein might have called this a grammatical remark. It is a kind of rule coordinating the use of the words "true" and "valid inference." It is a norm for the use of language, contingent but prescribed.

The predicate "is true" is not interchangeable salva veritate *with the predicate "is believed."* There is nothing logically impossible in saying "Socrates believes *S*" (or "Everybody believes *S*") and also "*S* is not true." Nor is the term "true" logically interchangeable with pragmatic predicates like "useful" or "expedient," although the critical implications this is supposed to have against the pragmatic philosophy of truth have been exaggerated (as I show in Chapter 4).

The sentence "Snow is white" is true if and only if snow is white. Likewise for any other true-or-false sentence. Some say this shows that the predication of truth to a sentence merely has the effect of canceling the quotation marks you need in order to refer to it, leaving the original sentence, unadorned and unqualified. In Quine's phrase, truth is disquotation. He thinks this insight is enough to make an ignominious end of correspondence. But it is a mistake to suppose that Tarski's semantic conception of truth, which strictly applies only to rigorously formalized calculi, can either displace or elucidate the metaphysical and moral analogies of onto-logic, and it is this historical discourse, not a spontaneous intuition, which is responsible for the idea that truth is one, and that its oneness has something to do with correspondence.[11]

Quine is right, though, to think that with Tarski there is an end of something. After Tarski it is unlikely that logic will have anything interesting to say to philosophy about truth. Certainly logic cannot be expected to cast light on the enigmatic relationship between truth and being. Tarski explains a method for defining a truth-predicate in a canonically formalized system. More precisely, the method yields a recursive definition of *satisfaction,* which is then used to define truth (for that system). The important point, however, is that this "satisfaction" is altogether different from the classical rightness of fit. For instance, whatever "satisfies" one true sentence also satisfies any other however different, so that whatever satisfies "Snow is white" also satisfies "Grass is green" (assuming both are true sentences in an appropriate logical system). There is no provision in Tarski's logic for different beings to make semantically different truths true. I should add that calling the systems for which a Tarski-style truth-predicate can be defined *languages* is so far merely an esoteric metaphor, although this has not stopped theorists from assuming that the study of these systems casts light on the nature of the so-called natural languages, themselves mere synchronic abstractions from local, historical discourse. Altogether, then, this suggests that the more authoritative Tarski's methods become in logic, the less logic will have to say to philosophy about truth.[12]

The Good of Truth

"Of all things good," Plato says, "truth holds the first place among gods and men alike." Conversely, "deception in the soul about realities, to have been deceived, and to be blindly ignorant, and to have and to hold falsehood there, is what all men would least of all accept and . . . loathe it most of all."[13] I shall say something about what later antiquity and modern thought make of this, but first I want to look in the opposite direction, back to Heraclitus. Here are six of the extant fragments:

> It is wise, listening not to me but to the *logos,* to agree that all things are one. (XXXVI/50)
>
> To the soul belongs a *logos* that increases itself. (CI/115)
>
> You will not find out the limits of the soul by going, even if you travel over every way, so deep is its *logos.* (XXXV/45)
>
> The ordering (*kosmos*), the same for all, no god nor man has made, but it ever was and will be: fire everliving, kindled in measures and in measures going out. (XXXVII/30)
>
> Speaking with understanding they must hold fast to what is shared by all, as a city holds to its law, and even more firmly. For all human laws are nourished by a divine one. It prevails as it will and suffices for all and is more than enough. (XXX/114)
>
> Although this *logos* holds forever, men fail ever to comprehend, both before hearing it and once they have heard. Although all things come to pass in accordance with this *logos,* men are like

the untried when they try such words and works as I set forth, distinguishing each according to its nature and telling how it is. (I/1)

Heraclitus does three things in these texts. First, he assimilates soul and cosmos by a *logos* common (the same) to both, a *logos* which measures the soul's depth and increase even as it gathers all things into a *kosmos,* an "ordering the same for all." Second, he thinks of this gathering-together as the operation of *law,* yet a law beyond the differences of cities, a *logos* beyond the conventional differences of languages, beyond all differences, immanently divine, common to all, in accordance with which "all things come to pass." Finally, *untried* he calls men who have not attempted to "distinguish each according to its nature and tell how it is." Knowing the truth becomes the summit of *aretē,* excellence. With this we are, as Kahn observes, "a long way from the Homeric conception of *aretē* as the warrior's virtue and valour and skill in combat . . . To identify truthful speech as the highest excellence is to take up an uncompromising position on an issue where the traditional Greek attitude was . . . ambivalent."[14]

While nothing in the extant fragments anticipates Aristotle's definition, there are doxographic and philosophic reasons to link this primordial discourse of *logos* to the Greek work on truth. The philosophic reason is that the idea of truth as an imitative, assimilating adequation requires the commensurability of what is thought or said and what is. As one cannot compare the color of two things unless both are colored, so one cannot have a true-making assimilation (or a falsifying discrepancy) between speech or thought and what is without something common. This is supplied by *logos.* The soul is measured by the *logos* it shares with the measure that gathers all things into a *kosmos.* This common measure gives what is distinctive to the human being (*zōon logon echon*) a power to distinguish each thing according to its nature and tell how it is.

In this respect, Aristotle seems Heraclitean. In *De Anima* he says, "the soul is in a way all beings."—In what way?—When one perceives a stone "it is not the stone that is in the soul, but its form *(eidos)*" (431b). The soul is in a way *the same* as all beings because it can assimilate itself to any form. Elsewhere Aristotle links form and *logos* through *phusis*, nature, which he defines as "shape *(morphē)* or form *(eidos)* according to *logos*" (193a). This double linking of form—on one side to nature and being, on the other to *logos*, language, reason, and measure—recurs in later work on truth. For instance, in Kant's so-called highest principle of synthetic judgment: "the conditions of a possible experience in general are at the same time conditions of the possibility of objects of experience."[15] This makes the transcendental logic of possible experience the same as the onto-logic of what there is to be perceived, to be known, to get right. And though Wittgenstein joked about being a philosophy professor who had never read Aristotle (which is no doubt true), the idea recurs in his *Tractatus Logico-Philosophicus*. There he goes so far as to define "logical form" as "the form of reality," reiterating the idea that thought and being share a common *logos:* "A gramophone record, the musical thought, the written notes, and the sound waves all stand to one another in the same internal relation of depicting that holds between language and the world. A logical structure *(logische Bau)* is common to them all" *(TLP*.4.014).

At least one ancient source links truth and *logos* in Heraclitus. Sextus Empiricus (who probably had texts now lost) says that Heraclitus "proposed *logos* as the criterion of truth," and that "the *logos* which he declares to be judge of truth is not any ordinary sort but the *logos* which is shared or common *(koinos)* and divine . . . According to Heraclitus it is by drawing in this *logos* in respiration that we become intelligent." Hegel was persuaded of this report's authenticity. He describes the Heraclitean *logos* as "the measure, the rhythm, that runs through the being of everything," and as "the principle of thought, as it is the principle of the world." "This whole," he says, "the universal and divine understanding in unity with which we are logical, is, according to Heraclitus, the essence of truth."[16]

It is not known whether Parmenides wrote before or after Heraclitus, yet he teaches a kindred contempt for opinion, polemically opposing "the motionless heart of well-rounded Truth" to "the opinions of mortals, in which there is no true reliability." As Collingwood observes, for Parmenides truth is not "immanent in belief, as a kind of leaven leavening the lump of error. Belief is mere belief and consequently sheer error. Truth is quite different from it, and is under no obligation to come to terms with it." Truth has an excellence *(arete)* all its own, and like a hero it can be tested. Truth is what stands up to the *elenchus,* to rigorous dialectical interrogation. The true is what withstands this torment, what survives this hard-hitting test of truth.[17]

Among Greeks it was understood that one must torture slaves to test the truth of their claims. Demosthenes says: "Now you consider torture *(basanos)* the most reliable of all tests both in private and in public affairs. Wherever slaves and free men are present and facts have to be found, you do not use the statements of the free witnesses, but you seek to discover the truth by applying torture to the slaves. Quite properly, men of the jury, since witnesses have sometimes been found not to give true evidence, whereas no statements made as a result of torture have ever been proved to be untrue."[18]

The Roman Law tradition explicitly defines torture by reference to truth. Ulpian (third century c.e.) writes: "By torture *(quaestio)* we are to understand the torment and suffering of the body in order to elicit the truth." The thirteenth-century jurist Azo writes: "Torture is the inquiry after truth by means of torment." And Bocer in the seventeenth century: "Torture is interrogation by torment of the body . . . for the purpose of eliciting the truth." As these texts suggest, up to the eighteenth century what Beccaria called this "infamous crucible of truth" was indispensible to the juridical determination of truth. Philosophers too, from Parmenides down, have found torment an apt metaphor for the test of truth. Plato suggests that sometimes the best way to get the truth is "to put the statement itself to a mild degree of torture." Diderot translates this into an image of modern inquiry: "we must attach ourselves solely to our object and torment it, so to speak, until the phenomena have been so linked that once one of them is given, all the others follow." Whether it is for the sake of a truth we want to know (as when witnesses or phenomena are interrogated), or against heretics who oppose the truth we already know, Western thinking has traditionally rationalized torture as a necessary instrument for truth.[19]

A century or more after Heraclitus and Parmenides, Plato declares truth nourishing to our minds "even as [to] the mind of a god." Every soul "that has a care to receive her proper food" longs to come "into touch with the nature of each thing by that part of the soul to which it belongs to lay hold on that reality, the part akin to it"—the part that is common, the same. "Through that . . . [we] truly live and grow, and find surcease from travail, but not before." Without Plato's metaphorics, the Sophist Isocrates probably speaks for many of his contemporaries when he says "truthful, legal, and just speech is the reflection of a good and trustworthy soul." Likewise Aristotle, for whom "falsehood is in itself mean and culpable, and truth noble and worthy of praise" (1127a). *Eudaimonia,* our fullest good, extends "just so far as contemplation does, and those to whom contemplation more fully belongs are more truly happy, not as a mere concomitant but in virtue of the contemplation; for this in itself is precious" (1178b).[20]

This evaluation of truth is widely shared among pagan and Christian thinkers throughout late antiquity. Already in the Gospel of John there is a visible effort to connect the good of truth to the object of Christian worship: "The truth will set you free" (8:32); "I am the way, and the truth, and the life" (14:6); "he who acts in truth comes into the light" (3:21). Conversely, Satan "has never based himself on truth; the truth is not in him" (8:44). It has been said that in this Gospel Plato and Isaiah meet.[21] From the second century, Christian thought oscillates between two attitudes toward philosophy. Sometimes it is repudiated (what has Athens to do with Jerusalem?), yet Patristic authors also searched their libraries of Heraclitus, Plato, and the Stoics for analogies and anticipations of what they called *their* Logos. Thus Tertullian: "God made this universe by his word and reason and power. Your philosophers are also agreed that the artificer of the universe seems to be *Logos.*" Justin Martyr believes the Greeks "spoke well in proportion to the share [they] had of the seminal *Logos.*" For Clement, the study of philosophy becomes "a preparation, paving the way for him who is perfected in Christ." The claim to have the truth could also be a stratagem to get pagan philosophers to take Christians seriously. Justin writes, "We claim to be acknowledged not because we say the same things as these writers [Greek philosophers] said, but because we say true things." His disciple Tatian declares: "The soul, O Greeks, is not immortal; if it knows not the truth, it dies."[22]

The Stoics, the most inventive philosophers of late antiquity, were an important link in the Christian appropriation of classical truth. In what is probably an early and therefore possibly a "Socratic" dialogue, Plato has Socrates argue that since wisdom is the only unqualified good, and since we all desire to be happy, "what seems to be necessary, you see, is that every man in every way shall try to become as wise as possible." Elsewhere, he has Socrates teach that while appearances cause dangerous confusion, with wisdom comes knowledge of the truth, and with that the power to compensate for and thus cancel everything misleading in the false deliverances of sense. Knowledge, by "revealing the true state of affairs," allows "the soul to live in peace and quiet and abide in the truth, thus saving our life." To seek *eudaimonia* in a wisdom born of the discipline of truth becomes a leading idea of Stoic philosophy. Cicero informs us that "all disorders are, they think, due to judgment and belief . . . disorder is the characteristic of deception *(errorem)* . . . This deception, as being the root of all evil, philosophy promises to drag out utterly." He says Stoics teach that "the Chief Good consists in applying to the conduct of life a knowledge of the working of natural causes, choosing what is in accord with nature and rejecting what is contrary to it." Thus the great value of knowing the truth: "He who is to live in accordance with nature must base his principles upon the system and government of the entire world. Nor can anyone judge truly of things good and evil, save by a knowledge of the whole plan of nature."[23]

St. Augustine would know Stoic philosophy from his careful study of Cicero if not more directly. He explicitly rejects the Socratic-Stoic idea that falsity is the first cause of disorder in the soul. "We sin from two causes: either not seeing what we ought to do, or not doing what we see ought to be done; of these two the former is due to ignorance, the latter to weakness." Yet error is always bad in Augustine's book, "hideous and repulsive just in proportion as it appears fair and plausible when we utter it or assent to it." Truth remains good without qualification: "If anyone should propose to himself so to love truth, not only truth which is in contemplation but likewise that which is in true propositions . . . I know not whether he could be said wisely to err in anything." "Add truth to life and you get happiness."[24]

St. Anselm speaks of a rightness *(rectitudo)* of fit that is both the essence of truth and an ethical rightness of action in the thinking of true thoughts: "whoever thinks that that which is is, thinks as he should, and consequently the thought is right." A century later the accent shifts to a rightness whose model is no longer the apostles, saints, and martyrs, but science according to Aristotle. "Thirteenth- and fourteenth-century thinkers . . . began to speak about 'science' as if it were the only worthy form of human thought . . . The idea of 'science' and the desire to be 'scientific' shaped the scholasticism of the thirteenth century and it signaled it as something new in the medieval West."[25]

An idea of scientific inquiry, Aristotle's or any other, had to overcome a long-standing suspicion of curiosity. Tertullian declared, "After Christ, we have no need for curiosity." For Augustine, "three kinds of vice, that is, carnal pleasure, pride, and curiosity *(curiositas)*, comprehend all sins." He speaks contemptuously of "some individuals who, having abandoned virtue and not knowing what God is . . . busy themselves with intense and eager curiosity, exploring that mass of matter we call the world." By the eleventh century, Peter Damien stands in a long line of ecclesiastical skepticism about the value of knowledge which, he says, "bears sorrow. For we know that the knowledge that each of us has consists in recalling our years in the bitterness of our soul, and in lamenting our own sins with teeming rivers of tears." In a statement that must have contributed to the climate of suspicion against philosophy leading to the condemnations of 1277, Boethius of Dacia, one of the so-called Averroists or radical Aristotelians at Paris in the early 1270s, writes: "there is no sin in understanding and theorizing . . . But the action of the philosopher is such a contemplation of truth. Therefore, it is easier for the philosopher to be virtuous than for another . . . Whoever does not lead such a life does not live rightly." According to one source, the first of the 219 propositions condemned by Tempier, Bishop of Paris, in 1277 reads: "That there is no more excellent state than to study philosophy."[26]

Truth continued to receive the praise of early modern Europe. For instance, Francis Bacon: "The Inquirie of Truth, which is the Lovemaking, or Wooing of it; The knowledge of Truth, which is the Presence of it; and the beleefe of Truth, which is the Enjoying of it; is the

Soveraigne Good of humane Nature." The mid-seventeenth-century Port Royal Logic teaches that "Men who relate their lives and actions to eternal things can be said to have a worthy goal—a real and enduring one. All other men love vanity and nothingness and run after falsity and error." Later, Spinoza proves that "in an absolute sense . . . we [cannot] find contentment in anything but truth."[27]

A strong English line after Bacon reaffirms his evaluation of truth. For instance, Locke: "I know there is truth opposite to falsehood, that it may be found if people will, and is worth the seeking, and is not only the most valuable, but the pleasantest thing in the world." Also John Balguy: "our maker . . . has made us capable of Truth, Virtue, and Happiness . . . So great is, or will be, the Harmony among them, that they may rather be looked upon as one and the same End, than as distinct and several." And Richard Price: "the preference of Truth must arise in every intelligent mind," while "every degree of illumination which we can communicate must do the greatest good. It helps prepare the minds of men for the recovery of their rights and hasten the overthrow of priestcraft and tyranny." Back on the Continent, for Beccaria history is one "vast sea of errors . . . The happy time has not yet arrived in which truth shall be the portion of the greatest number, as error has heretofore been." Writing while in hiding from the Revolutionary police, Condorcet sees nothing more "welcome to the philosopher [than] this picture of the human race freed from all its chains, released from the domination of chance, and from that of the enemies of its progress, advancing with a firm and sure step in the path of truth, virtue, and happiness."[28]

There is irony in Bacon's criminal record, for it was he who first separated truth from virtue. "My way of discovering sciences goes far to level men's wits, and leaves but little to individual excellence." After Bacon, it would be possible for an indifferent or even wicked man to possess the truth. Tradition opposed this. For Augustine, "the causes of things . . . [can] only be comprehended by a purified mind"; Hugh of St. Victor declares unpraiseworthy "learning stained by a shameless life." But when Bacon envisions the advancement of learning in corporate terms, as a great social enterprise, personal virtue becomes as irrelevant to scientific knowledge as spiritual fulfillment is unlikely. The aim of knowledge is not the illumination of isolated minds but the perfection of humanity. The ideal relationship between mind and nature is not eternal contemplation but historical domination. Truth has no value apart from a serviceability that can be measured in terms of the calculated use of forces. Bacon knows very well that he is revising values. In *Novum Organum* (1620), he writes:

> Another objection will without doubt be made . . . They will say that the contemplation of truth is more dignified and exalted than any utility or extent of effects; but that our dwelling so long and anxiously upon experience and matter, and the fluctuating state of particulars, fastens the mind to earth, or rather casts it down into an abyss of confusion and disturbance, and separates or removes it from a much more divine state, the quiet and tranquility of abstract wisdom.

"We willingly assent to their reasoning," he says, "and are most anxious to accept the very point they hint at and require."

> For we are founding a real model of the world in the understanding, such as it is found to be, not such as man's reason has distorted. Now this cannot be done without dissecting and anatomizing the world most diligently . . . Truth, therefore, and utility, are here perfectly identical *(ipsissimae res).*[29]

It would be wrong to represent the modern period as one long encomium to truth. Montaigne was perhaps the first to place a question mark here. "Knowledge is a great and very useful quality . . . But yet I do not set its value at that extreme measure that some attribute to it, like Herillus the philosopher, who placed in it the sovereign good, and held that it was within its power to make us wise and content. That I do not believe, nor what others have said, that knowledge is the mother of all virtue, and that vice is produced by ignorance."

Hans Blumenberg observes a variation on this skeptical theme in Voltaire. "Already in Antiquity for the Skeptics and now for the Enlightener the multiplicity of philosophical schools provokes the suspicion that they were all equally dogmatic."

Voltaire turns noticeably away from the Cartesian assumptions of the early Enlightenment, which assumed that the connection between physics and ethics, between science and the conduct of life, between theory and practice, was a relation of conditionality: that the completion of the knowledge of nature will provide *everything* that must secure the acceptance and permanence of a *morale définitive* [Descartes] that is adequate to reality . . . The observation of the history of science in his [Voltaire's] time—the indecision, which to him was incomprehensible, between Cartesianism and Newtonianism—had exposed the realm of theory as a reign of dogmatic intolerance . . . The great surprise is that theological dogmatics is only a special case of the need to have precise knowledge about what is invisible—whether it be vortexes or gravitation, the Trinity or grace—and not to allow anyone to make different assertions about it. And this on account of the assumption that absolutely *everything* depends on the truth, or even on *one* truth.[30]

Two other modern tendencies contribute to the revision of traditional assumptions about truth's value: Hume's utilitarian anti-representationalism and the critical philosophy of Kant. Their respective efforts to press skepticism as far as it can be, and to transcend the opposition between skeptics and dogmatists in the name of the progress of reason, let neither thinker tolerate happy platitudes about our aptitude for truth. Hume's *Enquiry Concerning Human Understanding* (1748) is the *locus classicus* for the "usual objection" against correspondence theories of truth—that since any effort to confirm the correspondence of perception or belief must lead to more perceptions and beliefs, there is no rational basis for supposing that perceptions *represent* anything at all or that their truth consists in a correspondence to something that is not itself another perception. (I return to this "usual objection" in the Epilogue.) Bacon was still capable of distinguishing between what is merely useful and what is really true. Against the Copernican system, he writes: "it is not merely calculations or predictions that I aim at, but philosophy . . . not what is in accordance with the phenomena, but what is found in nature herself, and is actually and really true." Locke cleaves to the same distinction, as I show in Chapter 2. But for Hume there is nothing to "accord" with except phenomena, and nothing to guide us in this except feeling.[31]

For Kant, humanity's title to the truth of being is far from self-evident. If truth is what the best, most objective, and scientific judgments have in common, then the content of truth has nothing to do with the supposedly "noumenal" being of the things we naively suppose experience to disclose, but is determined instead by our passivity, finitude, and animal need for order. Yet Kant accepts "the nominal definition of truth, that it is the agreement of knowledge with its object," and this had to have contributed to the plausibility of transcendental idealism. Mind makes nature, but still it is *nature* that is made, "constituted" by the act that endows judgment with objectivity and determines the content of truth. Kant is no less certain than Heraclitus that this ordering of perceptions, this *kosmos,* is governed by a *logos* which transcends the merely local differences of history and power.[32]

2 *Modern Truth*

No more useful inquiry can be proposed than that
which seeks to determine the nature and scope of
human knowledge . . . This investigation should be
undertaken at least once in life by anyone who has
the slightest regard for truth.

Descartes, *Rules for the Direction of the Mind* VIII

I wish that for once we could at least get the right
feeling about how compelling idealism is.

Jakob Beck, *Explanatory Abstract
of the Critical Writings of Professor Kant,
Prepared in Consultation with the Same* (1796)

If I move from antiquity to modern Europe, it is not because there was
no important work on truth in the meantime. But it is not my intention
to write the history of truth in philosophy. I turn to the modern period
because I wish to show how the reception of Greek skepticism, beginning in the sixteenth century, propels a metaphysical revision of classical truth. The new prestige of skeptical dialectic in the seventeenth and
eighteenth centuries (I mean the seriousness with which skeptical argumentation is received, not its approbation) had the effect of making
subjectivity newly central to the philosophy of truth, and this gave idealism a kind of inevitability. To speak of this as revisionary implies
that the result is a singular variation in a history of versions, and that
with its variants it shares the thematic unity of some common assumptions.

Descartes represents the problem of skepticism as if it arose by a
kind of natural movement of critical reason. But rational and by no
means uncritical thinkers before and after Descartes have been unim-

pressed (or merely amused) by skeptical argumentation. Neither Plato nor Aristotle seriously doubts that human beings can have the truth and can be reasonably certain of it. Although doubt about this does acquire serious sense for later Greek philosophy, skepticism fell into oblivion before the Christian period and did not contribute to the subsequent development of the problem of truth until its recovery in the Renaissance. Yet by the time of Descartes the situation is entirely different. Evidently something happened to make it impossible for philosophy to be indifferent to skepticism.[1]

A starting point for understanding the change is with Luther in the sixteenth century. By mid-century the reformation of Western Christianity was well under way. For political as much as theological reasons, the mechanisms devised centuries earlier for the suppression of heresy (mendicant orders, inquisitions, monastic reform) were of no avail; Protestants and Catholics merely denounced and burned each other as heretics. Furthermore, it is part of the definition of heresy in canon law that it is not merely an error but one so susceptible of reasoned refutation that to persist in it after correction (this persistence is the second part of the definition of heresy) betrays the heretic's willfulness and egregious pride. It is therefore unlikely that Catholic theologians would have used skeptical arguments against heretics even if they had possessed them. But Luther was in this respect new and different. In his answer to the Diet of Worms he maintained that "unless I am convicted of error by the testimony of Scriptures or (since I put no trust in the unsupported authority of Pope or of councils, since it is plain that they have often erred and often contradicted themselves) by manifest reasoning . . . I cannot and will not recant anything."[2] The theological tactics effective against earlier heretics would be unavailing; something altogether different was required. It so happened that the dissemination of Greek manuscripts which had begun in Italy in the fifteenth century had recently brought the skeptical works of Sextus Empiricus to the attention of some high-placed friends of the Church, who took up the idea that Pyrrhonian dialectic might be useful against the reformers. If there is a problem of skepticism in modern philosophy, it is because of this improbable alliance a generation before Descartes.

Richard Popkin shows how "a skeptical attitude arose among certain thinkers, primarily as a defense of Catholicism," and how a skeptical defense of the faith "was to dominate the French Counter-Reformation." It needed the wealth, interest, and authority of the Church to give skepticism intellectual currency; apart from that, the manuscripts of Sextus might have moldered in the libraries of Florence and Venice. Instead, there was a sustained effort, from the recovery of Sextus in the 1560s well into the next century, to put Pyrrhonism to work in the service of the Church. If, as Sextus was supposed to prove, no assertion can resist the arguments that can be opposed to it, the only certainty lies in revelation and the only thing to bind us to this truth is the tradition and authority of the Church. "By adapting the pattern of argument of the skeptics to the issue at hand, the Counter-Reformers constructed 'a new machine of war' to reduce their opponents to a 'forlorn skepticism' in which they could be sure of nothing."[3]

According to Popkin, this new machine of war was well and widely deployed in the theological controversies of the Reformation; Jesuits in particular specialized in Pyrrhonist arguments against reformers. Yet by the end of the sixteenth century, Luther and Calvin were not the only revisionary contenders for the truth, and with Galileo the stakes were no longer narrowly theological. It becomes difficult to understand why, if skeptical dialectic had any value at all, its corrosive effects are limited to the claims of ecclesiastical reformers and do not impugn any claim whatever. Montaigne had already posed the question in its most general form, and for the next two centuries philosophy took skepticism seriously indeed.

This accounts for a different and historically modern philosophy of truth. I emphasized the classical assumption that the truth depends on something whose existence and identity is determined quite apart from conventional practice. This "something" is what *has to exist*—fully determined and identical to itself—if the occasional truth is "made true" because something else is what it is. Call this "something else"—what has to exist if there is truth—truth's *ontological a priori*. In classical philosophy, this office is filled by natural substances. It is because these are, and because they form a natural order independent of convention and practice, that there can be truth in what we think and say.

The chief difference between classical and modern philosophies of truth concerns truth's ontological a priori: a difference in the entity posited as determining, ontologically, the possible existence and content of truth. In modern philosophy, it is not nature or substance but the self-evident sameness of what is and what is affirmed when a subject is reflectively aware of itself as presently feeling, thinking, or apparently perceiving one thing and not another which demonstrates, against all skeptical doubt, the possibility in principle of a true-making sameness between thought and being. As Locke put it, "The Mind clearly and infallibly perceives each *Idea* to agree with itself, and to be what it is; and all distinct *Ideas* to disagree, *i.e.* the one not to be the other: And this it does without any pains, labour, or deduction; but at first view, by its natural power of Perception and Distinction."[4] Thus the significance, from Descartes to Kant, Husserl, and Moore, of subjectivity: a domain where thought and existence are unified; where what is judged and said cannot fail to coincide with what is. With this, the subject moves into the position formerly reserved for nature, and the way is open to Kant's thesis that nature is constituted by the spontaneous auto-affection of subjective reason.

A different understanding of truth's ontological a priori yields a different account of truth in signs. As ancient and modern philosophy agree that utterances owe their truth-value to something that is not itself linguistic or conventional, so they agree in the theme of the secondary sign, but as they differ in what supposedly has to exist if there is truth, so they differ about what to pair against the sign as the original in relation to which it is derived and secondary. Aristotle views speech as secondary in relation to affections of the soul, but this is not very different from regarding it as secondary in relation to the things themselves; for to his way of thinking those affections are not very different from the results of other natural processes. He moves from *phantasma* to *pragma* without a thought of the epistemological abyss. Yet where Aristotle is indifferent Kant is mystified. Referring to "inner determinations of our mind *(Gemüt),*" he asks with what right "we posit an object for these representations, and so, in addition to their subjective reality, as modifications, ascribe to them some mysterious kind of objective reality?"[5] Speech is certainly secondary in relation to experience, but the objectivity of experience is itself secondary in relation to the transcendental subjectivity that grounds the existence of truth. The subjective self-presence of experience acquires epistemological priority over the identity and existence of its object, and the sign becomes uniquely secondary in relation to this more originally determinate subjectivity.

Husserl's formulation is especially striking: "the sense-informed expression breaks up, on the one hand, into the physical phenomenon, forming the physical side of the expression, and, on the other, into the acts which give it meaning . . . In virtue of such acts, the expression is more than merely sounded word. It *means* something."[6] *More than merely sounded word:* Here is the secondary sign in theme and variation. *Theme:* Signs are secondary, deriving their being as signs from a more powerful and originally determinate nonsign. *Variation:* The original source of the difference between a sign and an insignificant thing is the subject's power to impose intentional identity or conditions of satisfaction upon its utterances. The sign would be less than a sign (mere sound, a mere thing) were it not for this original, intentional, subjective power.

More recently, John Searle's philosophy of original Intentionality (his capital letter) offers another variation on this theme. "Since sentences—the sounds one makes or the marks one makes on paper—are, considered in one way, just objects in the world like any other objects, their capacity to represent is not intrinsic but is derived from the Intentionality of the mind. The Intentionality of mental states, on the other hand, is not derived from some more prior form of Intentionality but is intrinsic to the states themselves."[7] The material of actual communication would be so much empty sound or unmotivated motion were it not for this relation to an originally intentional power—a power that "is not derived from some more prior form . . . but is intrinsic" (Searle); a power by which "the expression is more than merely sounded word. It *means*" (Husserl). Yet philosophers from Sellars and Quine to Rorty and Derrida are skeptical of this alleged power of the mind to make things that mean one thing more than another. When I discuss Wittgenstein's "private language argument," I shall add another reason for suspecting that "intrinsic intentionality" is a sheer mystification of historically contingent symbolizing practice.

Not every thinker whose name might appear on a syllabus of modern philosophy has something important to say about truth, but several do. A place to begin is with the equivocal position of Locke. His "new way of ideas" is exemplary modern revisionism, yet it obliges him to posit two kinds of truth, real and nominal. When words agree with ideas, speech is nominally true: a truthful representation of subjective impressions. But that does not mean the ideas that those words signify are, as ideas, agreeable to the actual real existence of things. So while Locke can say, "*Truth* then seems to me, in the proper import of the Word, to signifie nothing but *the joining or separating of Signs, as the Things signified by them, do agree or disagree one with another*," he must distinguish "*real Truth* from *chimerical*, or (if you please,) *barely nominal*," and bid one "consider, that though our Words signifie nothing but our *Ideas* . . . they contain *real Truth* . . . when our *Ideas* are such, as we know are capable of having an Existence in Nature."

One can only assume that Locke does not mean what he says—that an idea is true if it is *capable* of having (copying) an existence in nature, which would make every merely consistent idea true (hence the truth of the golden mountain, and so on). Presumably, an idea is true when it does in fact agree with actual real existence. It is more difficult to know how Locke understands this true-making relation of agreement. Elsewhere in the *Essay Concerning Human Understanding* he maintains that all agreement and disagreement of ideas reduce to four kinds: identity, relation, co-existence or necessary connection, and real existence. Locke does not connect what he says here of agreement to the agreement of ideas that defines truth, although his single example "of *actual real Existence* agreeing to any *Idea*" is the sentence "G O D *is*," which he regards as demonstrably true. This suggests that it is an agreement with actual real existence which makes an idea true, and elsewhere he says our ideas "may very fitly *be called right or wrong* ideas, according as they agree or disagree to those patterns to which they are referred."[8]

Berkeley thought that any philosopher who holds this view must be a skeptic, regardless of what he may think he knows. Locke, for his part, dismisses those who "question the Existence of all Things, or our Knowledge of any thing." He was content to observe that "the certainty of Things existing *in rerum Natura*, when we have *the testimony of our Senses* for it, is not only *as great* as our frame can attain to, but *as our Condition needs.*" This is Locke at his most pragmatic. "Such an assurance of the Existence of Things without us, is sufficient to direct us in the attaining of the Good and avoiding the Evil, which is caused by them, which is the important concernment we have of being made acquainted with them." Yet what distinguishes this evaluation of cognition from the pragmatism of William James or John Dewey is Locke's allegiance to the traditional interpretation of truth as a copy. If the excellence of the understanding is entirely utilitarian, one ought to say the same about the excellence (truth) of the ideas with which it is occupied when it is working well: Not that they agree "with the real being and existence of things," but that "they serve to our purpose well enough, if they will but give us certain notice of those Things, which are convenient or inconvenient to us."[9]

But that was not Locke's way. He abides by truth's classical interpretation as a copy, while taking up Boyle's corpuscular hypothesis as a scientific armature on which to build a philosophy of human understanding, unmoved by doubt about whether there are any corpuscles to copy. He says, "The *Ideas* in our Understandings *are* without the use of Words *put together, or separated* by the Mind, perceiving, or judging of their Agreement, or Disagreement"—as if one could *see* that ideas and nonideas are occasionally the same in a way that makes for truth. Yet his own definition of *idea* ("whatsoever the mind perceives *in itself,* or as the immediate object of perception, thought or understanding") rules out the perception of an agreement between an idea and what is not an idea. This makes Berkeley the more scrupulously empirical when he infers that there simply is no clear and distinct concept of true-making agreement between ideas and nonideas: "But say you, though the ideas themselves do not exist without the mind, yet there may be things like them whereof they are copies or resemblances, which things exist without the mind, in an unthinking substance. I answer, an idea can be *like* nothing but an idea."[10]

This is Berkeley's best argument. What is like or agrees is similar in some respect, as what is unlike or disagrees is different. But what is similar must be commensurable; where there is no commensuration there is neither sameness nor determinate difference. To be like an idea in a way that would make the idea true, therefore, nonideas have to be commensurable with ideas. But what is commensurable is comparable, so ideas and nonideas must admit of comparison. Yet if, as Locke says, an idea is whatever occupies the mind when it thinks, and if comparing and evaluating are mental acts, then an idea can only be compared with another idea. Berkeley was right. The notion of a true-making likeness between ideas and nonideas needs only to be clearly described and it is revealed as an obvious contradiction. I should point out, however, that this argument does not by itself lead to Berkeley's immaterialism, which requires a further assumption, namely, that the truth of ideas is their correspondence, assimilation, or full and final adequacy to *something*. Since for Berkeley this can only be the content of another mind, one apparently has to choose between theistic immaterialism or atheistic skepticism.[11]

There is another difficulty for realism that Berkeley did not formulate. Say that what is true or false in any case is a determination of the mind, a judgment, representation, or other mental act; say too that truth is an agreement or adequation to what is not a merely subjective determination of an individual mind, and one has to go a step further. The universal or a priori conditions of self-conscious subjectivity must also condition the existence and identity of its objects. This is Kant's highest principle of synthetic judgment again, which I mentioned in Chapter 1. At the uncritical level of empirical practice, we may say that a judgment is true and mean that it agrees with objective reality. But if we want to be critical, we must say that since every object of experience "stands under the necessary conditions of synthetic unity of the manifold of intuition in a possible experience," therefore "the conditions of the possibility of experience in general are likewise conditions of the possibility"—the being—"of the objects of experience."[12] With this Kant revises truth's ontological a priori in the direction of transcendental idealism. There is nothing determinate to know or be true to apart from the re-producibility or re-presentability which reason demands of its objects.

The philosophy of truth was modernized in a move from the classical idea of a broadly physical or natural order as truth's ontological *sine qua non* to the subjectivity of the subject as its ground or a priori condition of existence. The self-reflective subjectivity of the subject, which each one of us may confirm for ourselves, proves beyond doubt that truth's essential sameness can exist and can be known to exist, but it also makes idealism inevitable. When truth is adequacy to the object, and when the conditions of experience also condition the existence of truth a priori, consistency allows but one conclusion: The transcendental conditions of synthetic judgment also condition the existence and identity of whatever there is for these judgments to get right. Kant allows that "it seems at first strange, but is not the less certain, to say: the understanding does not derive its laws from, but prescribes them to, nature."[13] Combine the ancient idea that truth implies adequacy or fitness with the modern priority for self-reflective knowledge of representations, and one must conclude that what there is to "fit" has no form originally its own and no being (no identity or existence) apart from the actuality of a subject-centered Understanding, or Reason, or Will.

PART TWO

Nietzsche's Question

This unconditional will to truth—what is it?
Nietzsche

3 *Nietzsche, or A Scandal of the Truth*

There is a trinity against which the gates of hell will
never prevail: the true, which brings forth the good;
and from both of these the beautiful.

Diderot, *Mémoires pour Catherine II*

For a philosopher to say, "the good and the beautiful
are one," is infamy; if he goes on to add, "also the
true," one ought to thrash him.

Nietzsche, *The Will to Power* §822

What is historically modern in the philosophy of truth is a critical and
subject-centered sort of thinking: idealism from Berkeley to Hegel. The
classical reference from truth (in judgment) to nature ("out there") is
not renounced but reversed. Onto-logic is similarly revised. Possibilities of truth remain possibilities of being, not because the mind is a
mirror or truth mimetic but because the determination of being (of
identity and existence) is the work of the spirit.

Truth's superior value was destined to come under strain. Placing
emphasis on the subjective or transcendental constitution of truth encourages the assumption that it is not Nature but subjectivity or the
will which makes truths true. This disrupts the reassuring reference to
an order of things that is their own prior to perception or convention.
Truth's claim to unconditional value now depends entirely on the viability of theism. Yet in the meantime the high value of truth, the ideal
of science, the contempt for deception, and the fear of error characteristic of intellectual culture in the West had become an engine of secularization and a smasher of idols. The idea of a divine person designing

nature had become incredible, a mystification and error from which modern thought must free itself *in the name of the truth*. D'Holbach, the Enlightenment's boldest atheist, writes: "The human mind, confused by theological opinions, failed to recognize itself, doubted its own powers, mistrusted experience, feared the truth, scorned its reason, and passed it by in order blindly to follow authority . . . Let minds be filled in good time with true ideas, let men's reason be nurtured, let justice govern them, and there will be no need to oppose the helpless barrier of fear of the gods to the passions . . . It is only by being shown the truth that they will recognize their most cherished interests and the real motives that should lead them to the good."[1]

This is the "unconditional honest atheism" which Nietzsche describes as "the awe-inspiring catastrophe of two thousand years of training in truthfulness that finally forbids itself the *lie involved in belief in God*." It is "this rigor," he adds, "that makes us *good Europeans* and the heirs of Europe's longest and bravest self-overcoming" (*GM*3.27). When what was done in the name of truth (European Enlightenment) comes face to face with the "critical" implications of the modern philosophy of truth, the self-evident good of truth seems like . . . an error! With this one enters the ambit of Nietzsche's thinking, where atheism is *aufgehoben* and the value of truth "for once experimentally called into question."

What Good Is Truth?

Nietzsche addresses the first part of *Beyond Good and Evil* to "The Prejudices of the Philosophers"—above all, "that famous truthfulness of which all philosophers so far have spoken with respect." Philosophers have asked what truth is and whether we can possess it securely, but Nietzsche would pose "a still more basic question" concerning the value of truth. "Suppose we want truth: *why not rather* untruth? and uncertainty? even ignorance?" Curious questions. If one tries the experiment and takes them up as questions, Nietzsche thinks one will quickly see that "both the earliest and most recent philosophers" are of no avail: "They are all oblivious of how much the will to truth itself first requires justification; here there is a lacuna in every philosophy—

how did this come about?" Because "truth was posited as being, as God, as the highest court of appeal—because truth was not *permitted* to be a problem at all." Although it "scarcely seems credible," it appears as if the problem of truth's value has never even been put so far, "as if we were the first to see it, fix it with our eyes, and *risk* it. For it does involve a risk, and perhaps there is none greater."

> After Christian truthfulness has drawn one inference after another, it must end by drawing its *most striking inference*, its inference *against* itself; this will happen however, when it poses the question "*what is the meaning of all will to truth?*"
>
> And here again I touch on my problem, on our problem, my *unknown* friends (for as yet I *know* of no friend): What meaning would *our* whole being possess if it were not this, that in us the will to truth becomes conscious of itself as a *problem?*[2]

Having posed the problem of truth's value, Nietzsche worked on an answer. Much of this is in the notes and sketches toward a "revaluation of the highest values" from the late 1880s, posthumously edited and published as *The Will to Power*. This includes a revaluation of truth's value and of the metaphysical struts that prop it up. Like the pragmatism of James and Dewey, Nietzsche's work on truth is a revisionary effort to abolish the classical reference from truth to being and contemplation, and to bind truth instead to becoming and activity, elucidating its value by reference to life, or more exactly to the subjective experience of life, "the shooting of the gulf, the darting to a new aim," which, like Emerson, Nietzsche calls *power*.

Nietzsche famously or infamously said that "truth" is a word for "a will to overcome that has in itself no end . . . a word for the 'will to power'" (*WP*.552). Truth "is" power in the sense that what *passes* for true serves life somewhere. Experience fluctuates between activity or domination and reaction or affection. Ideas are good or bad depending on the activity or domination they facilitate, "and since one knows no way of honoring an idea other than by calling it true, the first predicate with which it is honored is the predicate 'true'" (*WP*.171). The will to truth "is" the will to power in that *that* (life, power), and not correctness, not adequacy *to things,* is the only value at stake in distinguishing truth from error. Fitting or failing to fit facts is beside the point. "The value for *life* is ultimately decisive" (*WP*.493).

This seems to be the result of Nietzsche's "experiment" with truth's value. Try approaching truth concretely, renouncing idealism and concerning oneself with what practically passes for the truth, and the most elementary consideration of human beings, born helpless, with drives and finite resources, makes it unlikely that anything is noninstrumentally or finally good, and certainly not truth. Whatever we fear when we fear errors or lies, it has nothing to do with a value attaching to truth *itself,* apart from everything else that may be at stake when something passes for the truth.

This is a point Nietzsche, Marx, James, and Dewey can agree on. I discuss James in the next chapter. For Marx, the dispute over the objectivity or truth of "thinking which is isolated from practice is a purely *scholastic* question." Dewey deplored what he called "the theory of 'ends-in-themselves'" because of "the simulation of final and complete rational authority" it confers "upon certain interests of certain persons or groups at the expense of all others." There is "no such thing as the single all-important end." In a passage Nietzsche might applaud, he says, "Ends are, in fact, literally endless, forever coming into existence as new activities occasion new consequences. 'Endless ends' is a way of saying that there are no ends—that is no fixed self-enclosed finalities." One does not have to be "Nietzschean" to see the implications of this for the value of truth. Dewey says: "If ideas, meanings, conceptions, notions, theories, systems are instrumental to an active reorganization of the given environment, to a removal of some specific trouble and perplexity, then the test of their validity and value lies in accomplishing this work. If they succeed in their office, they are reliable, sound, valid, good, true. If they fail to clear up confusion, to eliminate defects, if they increase confusion, uncertainty and evil when they are acted upon, then they are false."[3]

Nietzsche also mocks the idea of truth's inherent value, "as if there were an actual *drive for knowledge* that, without regard to questions of usefulness and harm, went blindly for the truth; and then, separate from this, the whole world of *practical* interests" (*WP*.423). Any of the thinkers I have mentioned might agree with this. Despite rife doctrine, it is unlikely that anybody cares much for truth "itself" apart from any anticipated good we more or less credulously associate with what passes for true. Yet more characteristic of Nietzsche is his provocative equivocation between "truth" as what passes for true and "truth" as the classical assimilation of being and thinking. For instance, "How is truth proved? By the feeling of enhanced power—by utility—by indispensability—in short, by advantages . . . But that is . . . a sign that truth is not involved at all" (*WP*.455). He can move back and forth like this in the same sentence: "There are many kinds of eyes. Even the sphinx has eyes—and consequently there are many kinds of 'truths,' and consequently there is no truth" (*WP*.540). What utility, advantages, "the feeling of enhanced power" evince is not the mimetic assimilation of thought to being. Cleave to the classical meaning of truth, and one must conclude that there is no truth at all. There is no truth *of beings*, nothing "according to itself" *(auto kath auto)* or "identical to itself." Nature does not exist. This, far more than mere atheism, is the meaning of Nietzsche's "God is dead."[4]

Change the Value of Currency!

"Revaluation of all values"—that, Nietzsche says, "is my formula for an act of supreme self-examination on the part of humanity, become flesh and genius in me" (*EH*.326). A revaluation of truth's value is part of this. Nietzsche systematically reverses the terms with which the classical philosophy of truth articulates its value.

Truth and being. For classical philosophy, being and truth are, as Thomas says, convertible terms. In Augustine's formula, "To be true is the same as to be." Nietzsche turns this on its head. What passes for true never discloses something as it is "according to itself," while what "is"—what appears to be stable and enduring—is false, a falsification. "Precisely insofar as the prejudice of reason forces us to posit unity, identity, permanence, substance, cause, thing, being, we see ourselves somehow caught in error, compelled into error" (*PN*.482). For Thomas, "each [thing] has so much of truth as it has of being." For Nietzsche, "the character of existence is not 'true,' is *false*" (*WP*.12);

"the *erroneousness* of the world in which we think we live is the surest and firmest fact that we can lay eyes on" (*B*.34). "This idea permeates my writings," he says in a note; "the world with which we are concerned is false, i.e., is not a fact but a fable and approximation . . . it is 'in flux,' as something in a state of becoming, as a falsehood always changing but never getting near the truth: for—there is no 'truth'" (*WP*.616).[5]

Truth and error. Like Plato, like the Stoics, Augustine opposes the disorder of error and the "perversion and corruption" of falsity to the superior value of truth: "Error in the soul is hideous and repulsive," but "where I found truth, there I found my God, who is the Truth itself."[6] With almost systematic rigor, Nietzsche reverses these evaluations too: "The falseness of a judgment is for us not necessarily an objection to a judgment; in this respect our new language may sound strangest" (*B*.4). Truth "does not necessarily denote the antithesis of error, but in the most fundamental cases only the posture of various errors in relation to one another" (*WP*.535).

Truth and logos. For classical philosophy, only an unchanging, fully present, self-identical being admits of being truly thought or spoken of, known, measured, or defined. Nietzsche entirely agrees: "Knowledge and becoming exclude one another." But where classical philosophy understands this to imply that knowledge properly concerns changeless being alone, condemning becoming as inferior and secondary, Nietzsche reverses values. An affirmation "of passing away *and destroying,*" of "*becoming,* along with a radical repudiation of the very concept of *being,*" are "the decisive feature[s] of a Dionysian philosophy" (*EH*.273). Having affirmed the priority of becoming and the deception of being, he draws the only possible conclusion for the classical (Platonic) interpretation of knowledge, referring to "the character of the world in a state of becoming as incapable of formulation, as 'false,' as 'self-contradictory.' Knowledge and becoming exclude one another. Consequently, 'knowledge' must be something else: there must first of all be a will to make knowable, a kind of becoming must create the deception of beings" (*WP*.517). We cannot speak the truth; words cannot mimic the way the world is; language imposes subjects and predicates on a world that does not have stable, enduring units corresponding to its terms. "Linguistic means of expression are useless for expressing 'becoming;' it accords with our inevitable need to preserve ourselves to posit a crude world of stability, of 'things', etc." (*WP.*715). Language, logic, *logos, ratio,* all measures and instruments falsify everything they touch precisely to the extent that they produce (what passes for) the truth. "The aberration of philosophy is that, instead of seeing in logic and the categories of reason means toward the adjustment of the world toward utilitarian ends (basically, toward an expedient *falsification*), one believed one possessed in them the criterion of truth and *reality*" (*WP.*584).

Truth and the good. The same story: "Truth is ugly" (*WP.*822); "everything man 'knows' does not merely fail to satisfy his desires, but rather contradicts them and produces a sense of horror" (*GM*3.25). "Everything which is good and beautiful depends upon illusion: truth kills—it even kills itself (insofar as it realizes that error is its foundation)."[7]

As if to reoccupy the position of the Good in this mock inversion of Platonism, Nietzsche offers his Dionysian thought of *Wille zur Macht:*

> And do you know what the "world" is to me? Shall I show it to you in my mirror? This world: a monster of energy, without beginning, without end; a firm, iron magnitude of force that does not grow bigger or smaller, that does not expend itself but only transforms itself . . . a play of forces and waves of forces, at the same time one and many . . . this, my *Dionysian* world of the eternally self-creating, the eternally self-destroying . . . beyond good and evil, without goal . . . do you want a *name* for this world? . . . *This world is the will to power—and nothing besides!* And you yourself are also this will to power—and nothing besides! (*WP.*1067)

Some may dismiss this as the metaphysics of an undergraduate, or as sublime perhaps, but not philosophy; for there is no argument. Heidegger, on the other hand, finds in Nietzsche a profound metaphysics, the last violent chapter in an epoch of Western thinking. He interprets the pronouncement "God is dead" to mean that "metaphysics, i.e., for Nietzsche Western philosophy understood as Platonism, is at an end.

Nietzsche understands his own philosophy as the countermovement to metaphysics, and that means for him a movement in opposition to Platonism."[8] But Heidegger claims that Nietzsche's reversal of Platonic-Christian values ensnares him in a metaphysical matrix he cannot control; a secret affinity with Platonic thinking condemns him to repeat the original, defining gesture of Western metaphysics.

Heidegger regards philosophy as governed throughout its history by indifference to the difference between being and what is. Instead of conserving this difference as a difference, metaphysical thinking assimilates being to what is, to what exists, as if being were itself something that there is. Precisely this is what happens when philosophers take a position on *what veritably is* (idea, substance, spirit, will, and so on). Such positions cannot fail to treat being as if it were *a* being, the highest or most necessary being, the ground of all the rest. For Heidegger, the entire history of metaphysics is a litany of these "names for being"—the thing-like predicates with which philosophers deny the difference of being "itself." I shall say more about this in Chapter 5. I mention it now because Heidegger thinks this "forgetfulness of being" is Nietzsche's fate too. "Nietzsche considers that which rules to be the fundamental characteristic of everything real, i.e., of everything that is, in the widest sense. He conceives as the 'will to power' that which thus determines in its *essentia* whatever is." Nietzsche's thought of *Wille zur Macht* "not only strikes down that which is as such, in its being-in-itself, but it does away utterly with being . . . the metaphysics of the will to power . . . precludes in advance that being itself will attain to a coming to presence in its truth." That is enough to convict Nietzsche of the same obliviousness, the same indifference to being (to its difference from what is), that has governed philosophy since its beginning. "Nietzsche remains in the unbroken line of the metaphysical tradition when he calls that which is established and made fast in the will to power . . . being, or what is in being, or truth." His work may reverse classical values, but "as a mere countermovement it necessarily remains, as does everything 'anti,' held fast in the essence of that over against which it moves. Nietzsche's countermovement against metaphysics is, as the mere turning upside down of metaphysics, an inextricable entanglement in metaphysics."[9]

I think Heidegger overlooks one thing. He seems to have no sense of the ironic, performative quality of affirmation in Nietzsche. He frames Nietzsche's sentences as so many "considerations" and "conceptions" about "the fundamental characteristic of everything real" and "the *essentia* of what is," and thereby simply rewrites them as unironical metaphysical assertions that are supposed to be as true as sentences of Plotinus. But this metaphysics of inverted Platonism is an artifact of Heidegger's reading, not the truth about Nietzsche. When he discovers nothing but more metaphysical seriousness about the *essentia* of what is, even Nietzsche might object to Heidegger's notorious philology.

> Forgive me as an old philologist who cannot desist from the malice of putting his finger on bad modes of interpretation; but "nature's conformity to law," of which you physicists talk so proudly, as though—why, it exists only owing to your interpretation and bad "philology" . . . somebody might come along who, with opposite intentions and modes of interpretation, could read out of the same "nature," and with regard to the same phenomena, rather the tyrannically inconsiderate enforcement of claims of power—an interpreter who would picture the unexceptional and unconditional aspects of all "will to power" so vividly that almost every word, even the word "tyranny" itself, would eventually seem unsuitable, or a weakening and attenuating metaphor . . . Supposing that this is also only an interpretation—and you will be eager enough to make this objection?—Well, so much the better. (*B.*22)

Why "so much the better"? These words are an exemplary gesture. Their inscription exemplifies freedom from that anxiety about error born of an extravagant evaluation of truth. The interest of this "so much the better," like that of the antinomic formulae Heidegger recasts as the metaphysical theses of an inverted Platonism, is not located in any propositional content but in a contextual potential for an exemplary performative effect. The effect is scandalous—the scandal of a so-called philosopher who is *indifferent* to the difference between truth and error. One cannot rely on Nietzsche's *logos* to survive the hard-hitting Parmenidean *elenchus*. But neither does it claim to be that Truth for which Parmenidean dialectic is supposed to be the Way. One should not overlook Nietzsche's explicitly personalizing qualifications, as when he writes of "what the 'world' is *to me,*" of the view from "*my* mirror," "*my* Dionysian world." The difference between *my "world"* and *the world* is one between artistic insouciance and theological anxiety of error; it is a difference between parody and seriousness, Aristophanes and Socrates, Plato and Nietzsche. Far from a contribution, however antithetical, to metaphysics, Nietzsche's writing exemplifies a scandalous indifference to the specious theoretic universality of metaphysical truth, impersonal and eternal or else entirely without value.

Before concluding this point, I shall make a brief digression. Discussing Socrates' claim that it is better to suffer wrong than to do wrong, Hannah Arendt remarks that although he never convincingly proved it, its impact on conduct as an ethical precept is undeniable: "this sentence has become the beginning of Western ethical thought." Plato's dialogues show us "time and again how paradoxical the Socratic statement, a proposition and not an imperative, sounded, how easily it stood refuted in the marketplace . . . how unpersuasive [it] remained for friend and foe alike whenever he [Socrates] tried to prove it." This raises the question of "how it could ever have obtained its high degree of validation. Obviously, this has to be due to a rather unusual kind of persuasion; Socrates decided to stake his life on this truth, to set an example . . . when he refused to escape the death sentence."[10] The Socratic proposition became true, was made true, or made to pass for the truth, when it came home to those who heard of it as an exemplary ethical performance. This style of ethical-rhetorical performance passed from Socrates to his contemporary Diogenes, and remained a staple of Cynic philosophy until Roman times. One may consider Socrates' refusal to escape the death sentence, saying that it is better to suffer wrong than to do wrong, as well as his last words ("I owe a cock to Asklepius"), as early contributions to a genre Diogenes would formally name and incorporate into Cynic teaching—the *chreia*. These were short, pointed statements, witty, neat, powerful—like aphorisms, but sometimes with an added performative component, as in Socrates' suicide or Diogenes' own most memorable *chreia*: lighting a lantern in broad daylight and walking with it through the streets of Athens "in search of a real man."[11]

Diogenes' motto was "Change the value of currency!" *(paracharatt-*

ein to nomisma). He might have said, *Revalue the highest values!* An ancient source reports that he taught men "to despise wealth, reputation, pleasure, life; and to be superior to their opposites, poverty, ill fame, hardship, death." It seems likely that he taught this as much by the audacity of his style as by any theoretical assertion he may have made or the rigor of his argumentation in the several writings attributed to him. Not until Nietzsche does this provocative technique figure again in philosophy. Of course Nietzsche's life is entirely free of the exhibitionism for which Cynics were notorious; however it is not in what one conventionally regards as the man's life but in his writing, his deployment of "the most multifarious art of style that has ever been at the disposal of one man" (*EH.265*), that one finds performative *chreiai:* texts that do not teach by asserting a content the disciple is expected to know and defend as true, but by deliberately performing an act (a writing) so ironic in its assertions, because so conspicuously indifferent to error, that it exemplifies—that is, actually possesses (as text) and also by that means signifies—freedom from the egregious Platonic-Christian overestimation of truth's value. Not any propositional content, not any thesis, doctrine, or metaphysical theory, but precisely this freedom is the summit of Nietzsche's teaching. He therefore evades the premise of Heidegger's interpretation. He remains true to his experimental suspension of the classical evaluation of truth, a value that still dominates Heidegger's wish to overcome the oblivion of metaphysics and retrieve the truth of being.[12]

Redeeming Truth

Ancient sources say that Diogenes taught an *askesis,* a discipline, or what Foucault calls a technology of the self, comprising four tenets: *apathia,* or indifference to hardship; *autarkeia,* or self-sufficiency, rejecting a share in public responsibility; *parrhesia,* or blunt freedom of speech on all topics; and *anaideia,* or scandalous indifference to what passes for virtue *(aretē)* in the city. Diogenes assembled these into an exemplary pattern for living, a *phronesis* or technique of the self, which continued to impress the ancient world as late as the sixth century. This was much more the effect of performance and reputation than dialectics. Diogenes' (lost) texts in praise of incest, cannibalism, and slavery (being a slave) taught as much by their mere existence and notoriety as by any argumentation they may have contained.[13]

One Cynic teaching enthusiastically taken up by later Stoics concerns the superior value of life according to nature *(phusis)* over the *nomos* or merely local order of the city. Nietzsche is admirably clear about what he thinks of this: "'According to nature' you want to *live?* O you noble Stoics, what deceptive words these are! Imagine a being like nature, wasteful beyond measure, indifferent beyond measure, without purpose and consideration, without mercy and justice, fertile and desolate and uncertain at the same time; imagine indifference itself as a power—how *could* you live according to this indifference?" (B.9).

Platonism is otherworldly when it condemns the value of sensuous experience as mere appearance. Neoplatonic Christian theology is otherworldly when it teaches the nullity of the body, the seductive nonbeing of the flesh. Nietzsche scoffs at the otherworldly Stoic, whose ideal of life according to nature is perfectly imaginary. Despite this, however, Nietzsche seems nostalgic for the equally imaginary self-sufficiency of the Stoic, for a life free of passion, *pathē*, reaction: "A strong nature manifests itself by waiting and postponing any reaction: it is . . . characterized by a certain *adiaphoria* [indifference]" (WP.45). But to deny the intersubjective, affective, and inescapably accidental aspects of human being, to think there might be life beyond some merely local *nomos,* is as otherworldly as anything from the history of religions.

Nietzsche stands in the Platonic-Stoic-Christian line of idealistic mendacity when he dismisses what is contingent or historically accidental about human beings as disorder, as "pathology."

I find man in ruins and scattered over a battlefield or a butcherfield. And when my eyes flee from the present to the past, they always find the same: fragments and limbs and dreadful *accidents*—but no human beings. Present and past on earth—alas, my friends, that is what I find most unendurable; and I should not know how to live if I were not also a seer of that which must come . . . I walk among men as among the fragments of the fu-

ture—that future which I envisage. And this is all my creating
and striving, that I create and carry together into One what is
fragment and riddle and *dreadful accident*. And how could I bear
to be a man if man were not also a creator and guesser of riddles
and *redeemer of accidents?* To redeem those who lived in the
past and to redeem all "it was" into a "thus I willed it"—that
alone I should call redemption. (*PN*.250–251; my emphasis)

Why not call it a preposterous ultimate hope? or a purely imaginary
fullness which merely evades the present and its contingency?

"Zarathustra once defined, quite strictly, his task—it is mine, too—
and there is no mistaking his meaning: he says Yes to the point of jus-
tifying, of redeeming even all the past" (*EH*.308). But the affirmation
is more equivocal than Nietzsche lets on. The past is "redeemed" at the
price of cultivated, Cynic indifference to conventional, historically accidental differences of practice or politics. With redemption in the balance, who cares what happens to the *polis?* This is Nietzsche's idea of
great politics:

the truth speaks out of me. But my truth is *terrible;* for so far one
has called *lies* truth . . . I know myself to stand in opposition to
the mendaciousness of millennia. I was the first to *discover* the
truth by being the first to experience lies as lies . . . [W]hen truth
enters into a fight with the lies of millennia, we shall have up-
heavals, a convulsion of earthquakes, a moving of mountains and
valleys, the like of which has never been dreamed of. The concept
of politics will have merged entirely with a war of spirits; all
power structures of the old society will have been exploded—all
of them are based on lies: there will be wars the like of which
have never yet been seen on earth. It is only beginning with me
that the earth knows *great politics*. (*EH*.326–327)

This is no more a politics than "truth is error" is a metaphysical
thesis. It is a profession of indifference to "the wretched ephemeral
babble of politics" (*PN*.568). Nietzsche even has the audacity to describe this indifference as a return to health, to nature:

Man has all too long had an "evil eye" for his natural inclinations, so that they have finally become inseparable from his "bad conscience." An attempt at the reverse would *in itself* be possible—but who is strong enough for it?—that is, to wed the bad conscience to all the *unnatural* inclinations, all those aspirations to the beyond, to that which runs counter to sense, instinct, nature, animal, in short all ideals hitherto, which are one and all hostile to life and ideals that slander the world . . . The attainment of this goal would require a *different* kind of spirit from that likely to appear in this present age . . . it would require, in brief and alas, precisely . . . *great health!* (GM2.24)

Evidently a Dionysian antithesis to classical Greek ontology is compatible with the traditional theme of the secondary sign. Nietzsche preserves the priority of nature over convention, *nomos,* the "accidental" differences of value that constitute the entire field of historical social practice. What else is "counter to sense, instinct, nature, animal" except everything that belongs to language-games, social practices, and historically stratified (fragmented, discontinuous) cultural formations? Apart from this, what is there to our human being? We have no experience not permeated by "unnatural" (conventional, historical) determinations, no experience that is not interpreted through tradition and social symbolizing practice, no meanings secure from fragmentation or discontinuity, nor will we ever. To describe these conditions as disordered, pathological, or unnatural is absurd.

Freud differs from Nietzsche on two points relevant to my argument. On the one hand, Freud was profoundly loyal to the Socratic-Stoic idea of truth's ethical and therapeutic value. Anyone "who has succeeded in educating himself to the truth about himself is permanently defended against the danger of immorality, even though his standard of morality may differ in some respects from that which is customary in society." Writing in 1925, he proposes that "there should be a reduction in the strictness with which the drives are repressed and that correspondingly more play should be given to truthfulness."[14] The experiment has been tried. If truthfulness about sexuality is supposed to make us less nervous, less needful of psychological medicine, the result of the experiment is negative. This would not have surprised Nietzsche, who questioned precisely this faith in the power of truth for happiness. Yet Freud was skeptical, to say the least, of a redeemer, and more ironic than either Greek or Enlightenment thinkers about *how* good truth might be. In the early *Studies on Hysteria* (1895) he defines his therapeutic "ideal"—to replace hysterical suffering with common unhappiness. There is no reason to suppose he would have revised this as his experience with analysis deepened. But Nietzsche would probably see no value in mere reconciliation with the past, merely learning to bear its gruesome contingency. That is a second difference from Freud, who does not indulge the wish for an imaginary fullness beyond the fragmenting reach of historical accident. "If one considers chance to be unworthy of determining our fate, it is simply a relapse into the pious view of the universe."[15]

Nietzsche's hope is for new philosophers, free spirits, with the courage (if that is what it is) to put "the will of millennia upon *new* tracks," to "teach man the future as his *will*," to "prepare great ventures," and put "an end to that gruesome domination of nonsense and accident that has so far been called 'history'" (B.203). But in vain would Zarathustra posit the act that redeems all *it was* into *thus I willed it*. The fragmentation, discontinuity, nonsense and accident of our condition cannot be recouped by a will for once unconditioned by convention, history, or intersubjective dependence. As long as human beings speak or think or have some consciousness or culture, the nonsense and accident that has so far been called history is our fate. No *Übermensch* will change this, unless it can somehow teach the species to dispense with birth and maturation, language, labor, and desire. Until then, things are quite otherwise.

4 *William James, or Pragmatism*

A kind of new dawn is breaking among us
philosophers.

William James

In 1906 William James delivered eight lectures to a public audience at
Boston's Lowell Institute. The following year these were published
under the title *Pragmatism: A New Name for Some Old Ways of
Thinking*. Before he died in 1910, James published a volume of elucidations, *The Meaning of Truth: A Sequel to "Pragmatism."* These
texts define pragmatism in the sense James gave to Charles Peirce's
word. On the relative importance and originality of Peirce and James
opinions differ. Those with one notion of philosophy invariably rank
Peirce above James, while others, more ironic, reverse the order of
rank. Richard Rorty goes so far as to say that Peirce's "contribution to
pragmatism was merely to have given it a name, and to have stimu-
lated James." Ralph Barton Perry has a happy compromise, which is
that to be correct and just to all parties, the modern movement known
as pragmatism is the result of James's misunderstanding of Peirce.[1]

James speaks of pragmatism as "a kind of new dawn . . . breaking
among us philosophers" (*P*.10), one of "those secular changes that
come upon public opinion overnight, as it were, borne upon tides 'too
deep for sound or foam'" (*M*.39). He foresees "an alteration in 'the
seat of authority' that reminds one almost of the protestant reformation."

And as, to papal minds, protestantism has often seemed a mere
mess of anarchy and confusion, such, no doubt, will pragmatism

often seem to ultrarationalistic minds in philosophy. It will seem so much sheer trash, philosophically. But life wags on, all the same, and compasses its ends, in protestant countries. I venture to think that philosophic protestantism will compass a not dissimilar prosperity. (*P*.62)

The Pragmatic Difference

Like many American authors, James imagines nature as a wilderness, rough and dangerous, but unburdened by history—a place where something new can begin, including a new philosophy. "We condemn all noble, clean-cut, fixed, eternal, rational, temple-like systems of philosophy," he says. "These contradict the *dramatic temperament* of nature . . . We turn from them to the great unpent and unstayed wilderness of truth as we feel it to be constituted" (*M*.49). There is an errand to be undertaken in this wilderness of truth. Now that we see Nature in the light of the New World, philosophy cannot remain as it was in the Old World. It too must be made new and truer.

"We can no longer say there is nothing new under the sun," Thomas Jefferson wrote to Joseph Priestly; "for this whole chapter in the history of man is new." This exemplary newness was the New England Puritans' most durable contribution to the American imagination. On Election Day, 1670, the Reverend Samuel Danforth exhorts the Massachusetts colonists to remember that "John began his ministry not in Jerusalem, nor in any famous city of Judea, but in the wilderness, i.e., in a woody, retired, and solitary place, thereby withdrawing himself from the envy and preposterous zeal of such as were addicted to their old traditions." More than a century and a half later, Emerson is still denouncing this "worship of the past." "The centuries are conspirators against the sanity and authority of the soul . . . history is an impertinence and an injury, if it be anything more than a cheerful apologue or parable of my being and becoming." Emerson's "is the country of the Future . . . a country of beginnings, of projects, of designs, and expectations." "We have listened too long to the courtly muses of Europe." He foresees "an American genius" as new and different as California. "Luckily for us, now that steam has narrowed the Atlantic to a strait, the nervous, rocky West is introducing a new and continental element into the national mind, and we shall yet have an American genius." In California half a century later (1911), Santayana declares the late William James the fulfiller of this prophecy. James "may be regarded as representing the genuine, the long silent American mind"; his "way of thinking and feeling represented the true America . . . a new philosophical vista . . . a conception never before presented."[2]

It is curious to see this critic of America's "genteel" (that is, Puritan) tradition eulogize James with the Puritan rhetoric of a New World destiny. Yet James offers little resistance to such a reading. He situates the advent of pragmatism in a series of exemplary newness: "the changes from aristocracy to democracy, from classic to romantic taste, from theistic to pantheistic feeling, from static to evolutionary ways of understanding life" (M.39). There were "forerunners of pragmatism," James's new name for some old ways of thinking; but "they were preluders only. Not until in our time has it generalized itself, become conscious of a universal mission, pretended to a conquering destiny. I believe in that destiny," he tells his Boston audience, "and I hope I may end by inspiring you with my belief" (P.30).

James thinks philosophy has a kind of significance for life that is ill served by academic professionalism. "Philosophy's results concern us all most vitally"; "no one of us can get along without the far-flashing beams of light it sends over the world's perspectives," and this "give[s] to what it says an interest that is much more than professional" (P.10–11). Yet the philosophical alternatives of the present are inadequate to our deepest needs. James regrets the plight of "the seriously inquiring amateur in philosophy to-day who turns to the philosophy-professors for the wherewithal to satisfy the fulness of his nature's needs" (P.22). He offers "this oddly-named thing pragmatism as a philosophy that can . . . remain religious like the rationalisms, but at the same time, like the empiricisms, it can preserve the richest intimacy with facts" (P.23). For James, textbook predicates such as "empiricism" and "rationalism" stand for living options to be struggled over with something like religious emotion. "Within religion, emotion is apt to be tyrannical; but philosophy must favor the emotion that allies itself best with the whole body and drift of all the truths in sight. I conceive this to be the more strenuous type of emotion" (M.125).

The pursuit of philosophy is strenuous because all of the Old World assumptions must be thoroughly reconstructed, the old and curious problems of philosophy recentered, brought into true with that "great . . . wilderness of truth as we feel it to be constituted." That is why pragmatism is first of all a method, "primarily a method of settling metaphysical disputes that might otherwise be interminable." Wherever dispute is serious, "we ought to be able to show some practical difference that must follow from one side or the other's being right."

> The pragmatic method in such cases is to try to interpret each notion by tracing its respective practical consequences. What difference would it practically make to anyone if this notion rather than that notion were true? If no practical difference whatever can be traced, then the alternatives mean practically the same thing, and all dispute is idle. (P.28)

This method promises to situate philosophy squarely in practical life. "There can be . . . no difference in abstract truth that doesn't express itself in a difference in concrete fact and in conduct consequent upon that fact, imposed on somebody, somehow, somewhere, and somewhen." This defines the office of philosophy: "The whole function of philosophy ought to be to find out what definite difference it will make to you and me, at definite instants of our life, if this world-formula or that world-formula be the true one" (P.30).

James dramatizes pragmatism's difference and newness by contrasting it to the "rationalism" of European metaphysics. "The essential contrast is that for rationalism reality is ready-made and complete from all eternity, while for pragmatism it is still in the making, and awaits part of its complexion from the future" (P.123). Almost proudly, he declares "the alternative between pragmatism and rationalism . . . concerns the structure of the universe itself" (P.124). "On the one side the universe is absolutely secure, on the other it is still pursuing its adventures . . . really malleable, waiting to receive its final touches at our hands" (P.123). Yet in philosophy, as in life, everything eventually reduces to a question of temperament, and what began as cosmic speculation resolves into moral psychology. Pragmatism's is "a tramp and vagrant world, adrift in space, with neither elephant nor tortoise to plant the sole of its foot upon" (P.125).

Now the idea of this loose universe affects your typical rational-
ists in much the same way as "freedom of the press" might affect
a veteran official in the russian bureau of censorship; or as
"simplified spelling" might affect an elderly schoolmistress. It affects him as the swarm of protestant sects affects a papist on-
looker. It appears as backboneless and devoid of principle as
"opportunism" in politics appears to an old-fashioned french le-
gitimist, or to a fanatical believer in the divine right of the people
(P.125) . . . [It] is impossible not to see a temperamental difference at work in the choice of sides. The rationalist mind . . . is of
a doctrinaire and authoritative complexion: the phrase "*must
be*" is ever on its lips. The belly-band of its universe must be
tight. A radical pragmatist on the other hand is a happy-go-lucky
anarchistic sort of creature. (P.124)[3]

The imaginative and rhetorical debt to Emerson is evident. "Men
resist the conclusion in the morning," the latter writes, "but adopt it as
the evening wears on, that temper prevails over everything of time,
place, and condition."[4] For James, "temperaments with their cravings
and refusals do determine men in their philosophies, and always will
. . . Not only Walt Whitman could write 'who touches this book
touches a man.' The books of all the great philosophers are like so
many men" (P.24). History disappears as a significant difference; differences of class, race, gender, or historical experience are reduced to
individual psychological phenomena. A "genuine pragmatist" is anyone who prefers a loose and chancy universe "from which the element
of 'seriousness' is not to be expelled" (P.142). Pragmatism "has to fall
back on a certain ultimate hardihood, a certain willingness to live
without assurances or guarantees" (M.124). It holds out no reassurance for the "sick souls" who are "simply afraid, afraid of more experience, afraid of life" (P.140).[5]

Truth in Consequences

Of all that is new in pragmatism, James singles out the new philosophy
of truth as "a momentous philosophical alternative" (P.104). The

"whole scene of the philosophic stage will change in some degree" if it prevails (M.70). Pragmatism gives rise to a philosophy of truth when its method is brought to bear upon the language with which European philosophy has endeavored to define truth's essence. "Truth, as any dictionary will tell you, is a property of certain of our ideas. It means their 'agreement,' as falsity means their disagreement, with 'reality.'" Pragmatists and antipragmatists "both accept this definition as a matter of course. They begin to quarrel only after the question is raised as to what may precisely be meant by the term 'agreement,' and what by the term 'reality,' when reality is taken as something for our ideas to agree with" (P.96).

Truth is agreement with reality, of course; in the language of the schools, *veritas est adaequatio intellectus ad rem.* But let us be pragmatic and ask what this formula comes to in practice. What practical difference does it make to us to have true rather than false ideas? "The moment pragmatism asks this question, it sees the answer: True ideas are those we can assimilate, validate, corroborate, and verify. False ideas are those we cannot" (P.97). What then is the pragmatic meaning of that "agreement with reality" which makes an idea true? "To 'agree' in the widest sense with a reality," James says, "can only mean to be guided either straight up to it or into its surroundings, or to be put into such working touch with it as to handle either it or something connected with it better than if we disagreed. Better either intellectually or practically! . . . Any idea that helps us to *deal,* whether practically or intellectually, with either the reality or its belongings, that doesn't entangle our progress in frustrations, that *fits,* in fact, and adapts our life to the reality's whole setting, will agree sufficiently to meet the requirement. It will hold true of that reality" (P.102).

Interpreted pragmatically, the agreement essential to truth is not a static, formal *adaequatio;* it is the agreeable consequences that attend action guided by some ideas but not others, which ideas we then call true. "This function of agreeable leading is what we mean by an idea's verification . . . just such consequences being what we have in mind whenever we say that our ideas 'agree' with reality" (P.97). So we should not think of the relation between ideas or beliefs and the reality with which they are concerned in anything like the way Greek and

Scholastic philosophers did, as the mimetic assimilation of intellect and being. But James's point is not merely to destroy this traditional interpretation. Not for a moment does he doubt that nature (pragmatically understood as the source of experience) is the source of truth, or that truth has a rightful claim to the highest value. If he dissents from the European tradition, it is not because he would displace truth from the center of the moral universe, but in order to recenter it among goods by elucidating its value in practical, pragmatic terms. The preference for true over false beliefs is "essentially bound up with the way in which one moment in our experience may lead us towards other moments which it will be worth while to have been led to" (*P*.98). *Truth* names the good we admire in any "process of conduction from a present idea to a future terminus, provided only it run prosperously" (*P*.103), "the connexions and transitions [coming] to us from point to point as being progressive, harmonious, satisfactory" (*P*.97). True ideas "lead to consistency, stability and flowing human intercourse. They lead away from excentricity and isolation, from foiled and barren thinking" (*P*.103). That "is the practical difference it makes to us to have true ideas" (*P*.97). That, therefore, is "the only intelligible practical *meaning* to that difference in our beliefs which our habit of calling them true or false comports" (*M*.147).

Philosophers would understand pragmatism better than it has sometimes been understood if they did not assume that it offers a logical, conceptual, or semantic "analysis" of the predicate "is true." For instance, it is unhelpful to assimilate the pragmatic method of interpretation to the verificationist principle of the logical positivists, for whom "analysis" was at a premium.[6] The pragmatic method implies that serious differences among candidates for belief have to entail serious differences for practice, but to say that two candidates for belief imply no difference for practice is not to say that the sentences which symbolize those beliefs have the same logical meaning. The point is one of ethics. The point is not that the disputants fail to make logical sense, but that the logical sense they make makes no difference to their practice.[7]

A common criticism of the pragmatic approach to truth is first to point out, correctly, that a sentence like *It is expedient for Socrates to believe that* S, *but* S *is not true* is not a logical contradiction. From this it is inferred, again correctly, that the predicate "is true" is not logically equivalent to "is expedient," "is useful," or any other pragmatic predicate. The only mistake is to think that this reasoning has some critical bearing on the pragmatic philosophy of truth. The practical value pragmatism attributes to true belief is not the result of logical "analysis." As James tried to explain to Bertrand Russell, "Good consequences are . . . proposed as the *causa existendi* of our beliefs, not as . . . their objective deliverance or content" (*M*.146–147).[8]

Yet I can understand why Russell and others are misled. James routinely uses such language as: "You cannot define what you mean by calling [beliefs] true without referring to their functional possibilities. These give its whole *logical content* to that relation to reality on a belief's part to which the name 'truth' is applied" (*M*.118); or "My account of truth is purely logical and relates to its definition only. I contend that you cannot tell what the *word* 'true' *means,* as applied to a statement, without invoking the *concept of the statement's workings*" (*M*.120). Nevertheless, as he also tried to explain to Russell, the point of a reference to practical values is not analysis (at least not in the sense then current at Cambridge). It is an account of "belief's power to maintain itself" (*M*.150). The "pragmatic theory of truth" is not the logical analysis of a concept but a revisionary reworking of the tradition. The reference to consequences, to efficacy and prosperity, concerns not the formal essence but the practical value of truth. Pragmatism is a revisionary ethical work on truth's value, an effort as much rhetorical as philosophical to resituate truth in the circle of goods.

James sometimes elucidates his pragmatism by drawing an imaginary contrast between a pragmatist and an antipragmatic alter-ego whom he variously describes as an intellectualist, a rationalist, an addict to abstraction whose "one great assumption" is that truth is "an inert static relation"—as if "when you've got your true idea of anything, there's an end of the matter. You're in possession; you *know*; you have fulfilled your thinking destiny. You are where you ought to be mentally; you have obeyed your categorical imperative; and nothing more need follow on that climax of your rational destiny. Epistemologically you are in stable equilibrium" (*P*.96). Nietzsche called this a

Buddhism for Europeans. For James, this "truth of passive copying, sought in the sole interests of copying as such, not because copying is *good for something,* but because copying ought *schlechthin* to be, seems, if you look at it coldly, to be an almost preposterous ideal" (*M.57*). It should be left behind with all those fixed, eternal, temple-like systems of Old World philosophy. If the *only* property a belief had to have to be true were a formal Scholastic *adaequatio,* beliefs might as well be false. James makes this point unforgettably: "When the Irishman's admirers ran him along to the place of banquet in a sedan chair with no bottom, he said, 'Faith, if it wasn't for the honor of the thing, I might as well have come on foot.' So here: but for the honor of the thing, [reality] might as well have remained uncopied" (*P.112*).

From Heraclitus to Hegel, the conviction runs that the adequation of intellect and being is no mere indifferent reduplication but a spiritual harmony with the all-reigning *Logos.* That this was good almost went without saying. But for James, as for Nietzsche, this tradition has lost its self-evidence. What James and Nietzsche make of this, however, is very different. Schematically, where Nietzsche *reverses* truth's value "experimentally" as part of a projected revaluation of the highest values, James *reserves* the word "true" as a name for the proper good of belief, which he then analyzes in pragmatic terms, as "essentially an affair of leading—leading that is useful because it is into quarters that contain objects that are important" (*P.103*). This is a key difference. A philosophy that reverses the highest values presupposes Nietzsche's aristocratic solitude; it cannot be the public philosophy of a democratically inclusive political community. Yet that is what James wants pragmatism to be, and in this Dewey will follow him. To both men, academic philosophy at the turn of the century seemed out of step with the modernization they associate with science and social democracy alike. If James raises a new and radical question concerning the value of truth, his aim is by no means skeptical or deconstructive. Unlike Nietzsche, he never seriously doubts truth's claim to superior value. The point is not to unsettle this conviction, but to revise its grounds in terms of that "great . . . wilderness of truth as we"—in America—"feel it to be constituted."[9]

Pragmatism in Practice

For pragmatism, the value of a difference between true and false belief is the difference of value between good and bad consequences. "The truer idea is the one that pushes farther" (*M*.89). That, and not mimetic fealty, is the pragmatist's reason to prefer the truth. But if we are consistent pragmatists, we cannot assume straightaway that we understand what "pushing farther" comes to practically. How is this distance measured? How is truth determined in practice?

James says it is unreasonable to press him for a closer definition of the pragmatic predicates with which he interprets truth's value. Situations vary; no rule he could state would allow one to determine what is or is not "satisfactory" or "expedient" regardless of context (*M*.60, 132). But if there is a valuable difference between truth and its opposite, this has to admit of determination in practice. Furthermore the difference between beliefs that "work" and those that do not cannot *always* (authoritatively, standardly) be determined by the subject's say-so or acquiescence in their consequences. In that case, there would be no difference between having a belief and having a true belief, yet the whole point of this philosophy of truth is that there *is* a difference, a valuable, practical difference, between true and false belief. There must then be some means of evaluating the truth of ideas independently of the subject's naive sense of what works.

Precisely this is what distinguishes pragmatism from the subjectivism or relativism of Protagoras, whose (lost) work *On Truth* was supposed to have begun with the words, "The human being is the measure of all things, of what is that it is, of what is not that it is not." James scoffs at the suggestion that pragmatism has something to learn from Plato's refutation of this in the *Theaetetus* (*M*.142–143).[10] This implies that in his view, the evaluation of truth does not rely entirely on what the subject says or would say about what works. For at least as presented in the *Theaetetus*, the Protagorean idea implies that there is no difference (*a fortiori* no valuable practical difference) between having a belief and having a true belief: Believing just is true believing; there is no value to be differentiated by the opposition true/false. To make truth radically subjective in this way nullifies the difference James is keen to preserve between true belief and belief *simpliciter*. He allows that "truth supposes a standard outside of the thinker to which he must conform."[11] Yet if so, there is at least potentially a difference between beliefs that meet the standard and are therefore not only expedient but true, and beliefs that do not meet the standard and are therefore not true, however satisfactory, expedient, or useful the believer may feel them to be. The question is how to understand this difference pragmatically. James proves to be curiously evasive about this, even though it is exactly the kind of question he teaches one to ask.

Some of James's contemporaries thought it regrettably obvious what pragmatism comes to in practice, namely, a license to believe what one wants to believe, and to believe it just so long as it is useful to do so, regardless of any objective features of the independently real. James's colleague and friend Josiah Royce was "shocked and pained" at what he regarded as the opportunism and light-mindedness of James's pragmatism. He imagined a pragmatist taking the witness stand: "I promise to tell whatever is expedient and nothing but what is expedient, so help me future experience."[12]

The objection is not without a point. Whether a belief works seems likely to depend on what the believer asks of the belief, or what she or he is willing to put up with or count as "working." This suggests that whether a belief has the pragmatic value James identifies with the good of truth depends perhaps entirely on the believer's individual subjective constitution. In any case, it is at least unclear why James does not just say that "objective features of the independently real" simply drop out of the account. But then why call it an account of truth?

James is baffled by this criticism. "How comes it . . . that our critics so uniformly accuse us of subjectivism, of denying the reality's existence?" (*M*.130). He declares, "I begin with the abstract notion of an objective reality. I postulate it."

Anticipating the results of the general truth-processes of mankind, I begin with the abstract notion of an objective reality. I postulate it, and ask on my own account, *I vouching for this re-*

ality, what would make anyone else's idea of it true for me as well as for him.

The answer is that

> If the other man's idea leads him, not only to believe that the reality is there, but to use it [the idea] as the reality's temporary substitute, by letting it evoke adaptive thoughts and acts similar to those which the reality itself would provoke, then it is true in the only intelligible sense, true through its particular consequences, and true for me [i.e., objective reality] as well as for the man. (*M.*133)

Here James glosses "objective" as "adaptive" and introduces the potential for a discrepancy between a person's actual thoughts and those whose congruence to ones "which the reality itself would provoke" renders them more adequate to that reality, this *adaequatio* measured in terms of a pseudo-Darwinian adaptivity. On pragmatic principles, the legitimacy of this move depends on the practical possibility of differentiating between what somebody thinks in some case and what would have been more adaptive or closer to what reality itself would have preferred somebody to think. James refers to the anticipated results "of the general truth-processes of mankind," as if at the "end of inquiry" the difference between good and bad mental habits would be perfectly obvious to anybody. Perhaps it would be. But in the meantime life goes on, conduct is evaluated, decisions reached, powers of intervention in the name of truth and knowledge exercised and expanded. Two questions remain: First, how is the "adaptivity" of a mental habit and thus the "objectivity" of belief evaluated in practice? by what criterion, procedure, or authority? Second, what guarantees the connection between such criteria (or the practice of their application) and the prosperity James anticipates from having the truth?

It is not impossible to answer the first question, though it is difficult to do so and remain sanguine about the answer to the second. In a large and expanding range of cases the difference between true and false is determined by professionals whose position in the economy of knowledge gives their judgments a certain truth-power in practice: a power to determine—not without qualification or finally, but in the first instance and with the balance of presumption—what from case to case *passes for the truth.* For instance, to take a case that is close to James's interests, the power to determine the difference between adaptive and maladaptive mental habits is invested in our physicians, psychiatrists, forensic psychologists, and others who work in the ensemble of professional knowledges that intersect at the hospital, the school, and the courts.[13]

It is James's blind spot to think there is some natural, simply given difference between adaptive and maladaptive mental habits, or that it is possible in principle ("anticipating the results of the general truth-processes of mankind") to judge this objectively. James should admit that his pragmatism cannot supply an interesting, practical difference between passing for true and really being so. But if we look at what passes for true in practice, we see that whether what in any case passes for the truth on some matter is useful or expedient all depends on who more particularly you are.

It may be tempting to think of James as one of the "unknown friends" to whom Nietzsche dedicated his statement of the problem of truth's value (*GM*3.27). Unfortunately, this is untenable. Nietzsche spoke of a lacuna in every philosophy, namely, that rather than being seriously questioned, the superior good of truth is instead a guaranteed result. For his part, James never doubts that the pragmatic method will confirm that it is always good to have the truth, the more truth the better. In private correspondence he is "in favor of the eternal forces of truth which always work in the individual and immediately unsuccessful way [*sic*], underdogs always, till history comes, after they are long dead, and puts them on top." In public oratory, for example in his "Address on the Philippine Question" (1903), he is in solidarity with "the long, long campaign for truth and fair dealing which must go on in all the countries of the world until the end of time . . . Everywhere it is the same struggle under different names,—light against darkness, right against might, love against hate. The Lord of life is with us, and we cannot permanently fail."[14]

Pragmatism was to alter "the centre of gravity of philosophy" (*P*.62), recentering philosophy in the circle of goods. James favored a kind of social or community idealism, which he called Humanism. "When we talk of a reality 'independent' of human thinking," he said, "it seems a very hard thing to find . . . We may glimpse it, but we never grasp it; what we grasp is always some substitute for it which previous human thinking has peptonized and cooked for our consumption . . . wherever we find it, it has been already *faked*" (P.119–120).

"The trail of the human serpent is thus over everything" (P.37). Yet James evades an implication of this which Nietzsche might insist on. This serpent's trail *divides* truth's value differentially among groups and individuals, because this serpent is itself riven by history and politics, by differences of power. James thinks of the production of knowledge as if it were happily situated in a community where what passes for true cannot fail to be empowering, or as if a more particular social identity (female, disabled, aboriginal, indigent, HIV-positive) is irrelevant to the good of the occasional truth. But there is no pragmatic difference between the truth and what passes for true, and there is no reason not to suspect that the good of the occasional truth depends on who more particularly you are. With this, as Nietzsche said, "the will to truth"—the demand, the desire or preference for it; the value, the good of it—"becomes conscious of itself as a problem."

PART THREE

From Nature to History, From Being to Politics

> the carnivorous
> Way of these lines is to devour their own nature, leaving
> Nothing but a bitter impression of absence, which as we know
> involves presence, but still.
>
> John Ashbery, "The Skaters"

5 Heidegger, or The Truth of Being

> Being, as the presencing of what is present, is already
> in itself truth, provided we think the essence of truth
> as the gathering that clears and shelters.
>
> Heidegger, *Der Spruch des Anixamder*

In what may have been the last thing he wrote, Heidegger refers to "that single question which I have persistently tried to ask in a more questioning manner. It is known as *die Seinsfrage,* 'the question of being.'" Elsewhere, in a remark directed to "the critics," he asks, "Has the question posed in *Sein und Zeit* regarding the 'meaning of being' (as being) been at all taken up as a question? . . . Have the critics ever asked whether the question posed is possible or impossible?"[1] About this question he at one place in *Being and Time* remarks: "if we are inquiring about the meaning of being, our investigation is not a 'deep' one, nor does it puzzle out what stands behind being. It asks about being itself . . . [not] the sustaining 'ground' of what is" (SZ.152). Later, he says that "truth rightfully has a primordial connection with being," and that "the phenomenon of truth falls within the problematic of fundamental ontology" (SZ.213). In Heidegger's personal copy this last sentence is underscored, and in the margin he writes: "not just [within], but at the center."

Two points stand out from these remarks. First, Heidegger's interest in *being (das Sein)* is not a deep-sounding metaphysical concern with how things stand in relation to the ground of their existence. The theme of what Heidegger called fundamental ontology is the being *of what is.* To confuse this with the "sustaining ground" of beings is the first mistake of metaphysics, which regards the *being* of beings as if it were "itself" an entity. Against this, Heidegger insists on the *ontological difference,* the unique difference between:

> *das Seiende:* what is, the beings that there are, values for variables in true sentences of the form $(\exists x)(\ldots x \ldots)$

and

> *das Sein:* being, the being or existing of what is, the presencing of what happens to be.

Second, Heidegger reaffirms the classical onto-logic of truth and being. "If a thing has less truth," Plato urges, "has it also not less being *(ousias)?*" For Heidegger too, being "is itself truth," provided, that is, that we understand "the essence of truth" as "the gathering that clears and shelters" (*EGT.*37). This "gathering" he identifies with the *logos* of Heraclitus, which recalls Hegel's claim that for Heraclitus *logos* is the essence of truth. Yet Heidegger elsewhere defines the essence of truth as *freedom* (*BW.*125). This makes free human being the "gathering that clears and shelters," and the essence of truth. Naturally this raises a number of questions, not least whether Heidegger is some kind of idealist. The necessary starting point, however, is his idea of ontological difference.[2]

Ontological Difference

Wittgenstein once remarked, "The aspects of things that are most important for us are hidden *(verborgen)* because of their simplicity and familiarity. (One is unable to notice something—because it is always before one's eyes.) The real foundations of his enquiry do not strike a man at all. Unless *that* fact has at some time struck him.—And this means: we fail to be struck by what, once seen, is most striking and powerful" (*PI.*129). Although it is unlikely that Wittgenstein had ontological difference in mind, his words are surprisingly apt. Heidegger says that this difference "is the thing most used, and thus most usual, in all our stating and ideas, in all we do." "We constantly reside in the difference between being and beings . . . we revolve in this difference between beings and being, rather as we find ourselves already within the difference between right and left." Yet we tend to overlook it constantly, "with an almost unimaginable obstinacy." Because being is not an entity and is therefore in no determinate way the same or different from anything that there is, the difference of being and beings is hidden, concealed by its very simplicity, "the simple nearness of an unobtrusive governance."[3]

We are accustomed to regard difference as a matter of entities that are not the same, that are distinct and discernible, in contrast to things that are the same, or indiscernible, or identical. Heidegger uses the term *ontic* to refer to these and all other relations among beings, and contrasts all of that to the properly *ontological* concern with being, which is *ontologically* different from what is as such. "Ontic" sameness and difference comprises:

1. Resemblance or similarity, where distinct things are variously the same or different in some respect, such as color, age, extension, or mass.
2. The formal identity of $A = A$; the difference of $A \neq B$.
3. The sameness of a copy or accurate representation; difference as discrepancy, deviation from an original or a standard.
4. The same as the analogous: The human being was said to be *like* God, yet different in every respect.
5. The sameness of explanations, reductions, and analyses: different *concepts, descriptions,* or *signs* referring to one and the same *entity.*

To model ontological difference after any of these is to fall into the oblivion of "metaphysics" in the precise sense Heidegger gives to that term: any thinking that regards being as if it were itself something that exists. Heidegger is well aware that the "difference" in "ontological difference" is far removed "from its usual and customary usage. What it now names is not a generic concept for various kinds of differences. It exists only as this single difference. It is unique." Ontological difference "no longer means a distinction established between objects . . . The difference *(Unter-Schied)* is neither distinction nor relation.

The difference is, at most, dimension for world and thing . . . [and] metes out the measure of their presence *(Wesen)*" *(PLT.202–203)*.

One can approach Heidegger's thought by comparing ontological difference to the difference between *what* happens and its happening, or to the difference between *what* a thing is and its happening to be there, when and where it is. These show the difference between a being and its place in a temporal order—a being and its temporal presence, its happening to be. The difference between being and beings now comes into view as that between time "itself" and what happens. What is (beings) is what happens to be temporally situated, somewhere sometime present. "Ever since the beginning of Western thinking with the Greeks," Heidegger claims, "all saying of 'to be' and 'is' commemorates the determination, binding for thought, of being as presence . . . From the dawn of Western European thinking until today, 'to be' means the same as 'to be present' *(Anwesen)*" *(TB.2)*. References to "presence" in Heidegger presuppose an onto-logical interpretation of verbal or linguistic tense as referring to tensed *being:* the tensed *temporality* of what is; a thing's prevailing or lasting, its durable identity, unity, and standing in a temporal order of presence and absence. Being is not "itself" a being, nor is time "itself" something that happens; yet these belong together, they are mutually appropriate to each other, in a sense they are even the same. There being what there is happens to be the same "event" (Heidegger calls it *the* Event, *das Ereignis*) as there being tensed temporal presence and absence.[4]

A comparison with Aristotle may clarify Heidegger's conception. In Chapter 1, I mentioned Aristotle's view that while there is no one meaning of "to be," the verb is not merely equivocal; there is a definite kind of order in the different ways that "to be" is said. "There are many senses in which a thing may be said to be, but all that is is related to one central point, one definite kind of thing, and is not said to be by a mere ambiguity . . . all refer to one starting point" (1003a–b), namely, substance *(ousia)*. "There are several senses in which a thing may be said to be . . . [but] that which is primarily is the what, which indicates the substance of the thing . . . it is in virtue of this category that each of the others also is" (1028a). Thus "some things are said to be because they are substances, others because they are affections of substances, others because they are a process towards substance, or destructions or privations or qualities of substance, or productive or generative of substance, or of things which are relative to substance, or negations of one of these things or of substance itself" (1003b).[5] However different Heidegger's conception of ontology may be, he does in one way model it after Aristotle. He does *not* look to any one entity (like *ousia, idea,* or *Geist*) or to a merely posited totality (physical universe, logical space) to provide the unifying focal meaning of "to be." In his terms, that would overlook the ontological difference and treat being as if it were something that is. Mindful of the difference, Heidegger looks instead to one *be-ing,* one manner of existing, as unifying all the rest, "gathering and sheltering" what is. He finds this in *time,* which is not itself a sometime present entity but the temporality or tensed ordering of what is (sometime present). Time is not a being but a way in which entities are, namely, temporally tensed and sometime present. Tensed temporality transcends what is and lets beings be, that is, come to presence and endure for a while as what is present.

But, to continue the interpretation, to be present is not originally or most fundamentally to be actual or fully present through an arbitrarily determinate interval. "With the word 'time' we no longer mean the succession of a sequence of nows . . . such as we have in mind when we note, for instance, that within a time span of fifty years this and that happened." The more original experience of time, from which Heidegger claims our conception of linear, infinite, arbitrarily determinable intervals derives, is of presence as the enduring abiding of things that concern human beings, the presence that solicits our care. This is not in the first instance a tenseless date or precise interval. "What do we think, when we say 'presence'?"

> Presence implies endurance. But we are too quickly content to conceive of endurance as mere duration, and to conceive of duration in terms of a habitual representation of time as a linear span from one now-point to another. To talk of presen*cing (Anwesen),* however, requires us to perceive the during of endurance as preserving. (*TB*.12)

> Presencing preserves *(wahrt)* in unconcealment what is present at the present time and not at the present time . . . But what is at the present time present is not a slice of something sandwiched be-

tween two absences . . . What is presently present in unconcealment lingers in unconcealment as in an open expanse. (*EGT*.36–
37)

"One day," he adds, "we shall learn to think our exhausted word
for truth *(Wahrheit)* in terms of . . . the preservation *(Wahrnis)* of
being; and to understand that, as presencing, being belongs to this
preservation . . . [and] preservation belongs to the herdsman . . . Both
are the Same" (*EGT*.36). The "herdsman" is Heidegger's rustic reference to the entity we ourselves are, the human being, or what he calls
Dasein. He is saying that we should think of truth in terms of the care
that conserves or as it were shepherds presencing. This concern, he
says, is the same as the presencing, the being, it preserves; yet not the
same entity, not entities at all. To look into this sameness further requires a word about Dasein.

One cannot define Heidegger's term more closely or explain more
precisely who or what Dasein is without recourse to indexical and self-
referential language: Dasein is that entity which "we ourselves" are.
Not only the social self-reference of the plural "we" but also the reflex-
ivity, the tensed element of the spoken demonstrative ("we ourselves
here now"), are essential and ineliminable. Heidegger begins *Being
and Time* with the words: "We ourselves are the beings to be analyzed.
The being of this entity is in each case *mine*" (*SZ*.41–42). He reserves
the term *Existenz* (existence) exclusively for the being of an entity
which is in each case "mine"—the being of Dasein. In his language it
is terminological stipulation that only Dasein exists. Frogs and hydro-
gen atoms, for example, do not exist. These *are,* they "have being,"
but Heidegger claims theirs is a different mode of being from that of
the Dasein. He marks this difference terminologically with the distinction between *Existenz* (reserved for Dasein) and *Vorhandenheit* (presence-at-hand, extantness), which is the kind of being peculiar to what
is not Dasein, to "mere things" (including animals).[6]

What sort of difference has he in mind? The ontological peculiarity
of Dasein's being is that unlike the extantness of the stone or the star,
our existence is never a matter of indifference to us. "Dasein is never
to be taken ontologically as an instance or special case of some genus
of entities that are present-at-hand. To entities such as these, their

being is a matter of indifference." For Dasein, by contrast, "*being* is that which is an issue for each one of these entities" (*SZ*.42). To be extant, to be a thing or a natural or purely physical entity, is to be somewhere sometime fully or self-identically present. But it is never like that for us. No God or Nature or Human Nature predetermines our essential possibilities once and for all. In the traditional sense of *essentia,* the essence of a being is *what* it most truly is, its "quiddity," nature, or defining formal principle. Heidegger claims that human beings lack essence in this sense. There is no *what* which is what a human being essentially is, nothing we are made to be by nature, nothing always and everywhere determinately the same. Lacking a formal *essentia,* our existence is characterized by a corresponding freedom from natural determination, which leaves that existence radically open to the possibilities peculiar to its local, historically contingent situation. The Dasein's existence is in each case a problem, an issue, a question, and a project radically up to us. Whatever constrains us is in a sense self-imposed; for it is only by freely taking up some possibility of existence that anything in nature or history is disclosed as a limitation or a resource. Our lack of formal essence is therefore not a deficiency. For Heidegger, it is the essence of freedom, and freedom is the essence of truth.

I used the idea of temporality to explicate the ontological difference of being and beings. It is useful again to interpret the difference between the being of Dasein (existence) and the being of extant things. Each moment of human existence is originally and indefinitely stretched out into temporal nonpresence (past and future). In Heidegger's language, the temporal character of Dasein's existence is originally "outside itself" or "ecstatic." "The term 'ecstatic' has nothing to do with ecstatic states of mind and the like. The common Greek expression *ekstatikon* means stepping-outside-self." Heidegger uses this idea of temporal ecstasy to interpret the Dasein's kind of being *(Existenz),* "which, viewed ontologically, is the original unity of being-outside-self . . . In its ecstatic character, temporality is the condition of the constitution of the Dasein's being" (*BP*.267). Dasein "is as such out beyond itself." For us, *to be* "always already means to step beyond or, better, having stepped beyond" (*BP*.300).

The ecstatic temporal character of the Dasein's existence entails a radical nonself-identity for the human being, who is not for so much as an instant fully present and self-identical, never a finally finished *what.* This nonself-identity fundamentally distinguishes human existence from the extantness or presence-at-hand of mere things, whose being (for Heidegger) *does* entail all of the traditional predicates which the Dasein's being ecstatically transcends: unity, self-identity, fully present actuality. One way to frame Heidegger's objection to Greek ontology is that it treats all beings as if they were things present-at-hand and is thus insensitive to the difference between the Dasein's kind of being and that of what is extant or self-identically present. He thinks it is not surprising that, after Greek ontology leveled off this difference, later tradition should regard being merely as the most abstract, general, or indeterminate predicate about which there is nothing more to say.

Time, temporality, the tensed order of temporal presence and absence, is not an entity *in* time, not something present or extant. But, Heidegger claims, if "there is" time at all, and therefore if "there is" presence and ontological difference, it is because the Dasein—the historically contingent entities we ourselves are—happen to exist. The idea is not, of course, that Dasein is the ground which determines the identity or existence of every (other) being. Rather, it is the *difference* of our being in contrast to the extant things it transcends as a whole (being wholly different ontologically) that opens and holds open (conserves, "shepherds") the ontological difference of being and beings. Apart from our contingent existence, and apart from the peculiar temporal character of that existence, there is no being, no presencing, and no truth. Whether in that case extant entities would still be what and as they are is a question I shall consider in a moment.

It is not difficult to see why Heidegger should think that temporal presence or tensed time is nothing for itself apart from human existence. He takes this to be established by Kant's analysis of time as the form of sensory intuition. There would be no ordering of events in terms of past, present, and future apart from the possibility of identifying a moment as *now,* as *the present.* That possibility is uniquely given by the peculiar temporal structure of consciousness, where, in Husserl's formula, "every experience generally (every really living one, so to speak) is an experience 'which is present.'" Interpreting Kant,

Heidegger writes, "time is not an efficacious affection working on a subject . . . [It] constitutes the essential structure of subjectivity . . . the self originally and in its innermost essence is time itself." He is saying that there is no difference between *there being tensed temporal order* and *there being the entities we ourselves are*. These are the same *being*, but not the same entities, not entities at all.[7]

If time or temporal presence is nothing for itself apart from our existence, what of being "itself"? What of ontological difference? Were there nothing of our Dasein, would there still be a difference between being and beings? No; for what is "being"? Heidegger writes: "Because being 'is' not [a being] and thus is never alongside other beings, there is no proper sense at all or legitimacy in asking, What manner of being-in-itself is being? However, one could ask, What in beings corresponds to their being, to the 'being' of their being there at all?" The answer is that "being, primordially and in itself, is there when beings are accessible *(zugänglich)*" (MF.153). Ontological difference, and therefore being itself, "is there" so long as there is something that needs or is concerned with beings, while this concern is for Heidegger the essential ontological structure of the being (the existing) of the entities we ourselves are.

In *Being and Time* Heidegger says that while "beings *are*, quite independently of the experience by which they are disclosed," nevertheless "only as long as Dasein *is* 'is there' being" (SZ.183, 212). In lectures from the same time, he says: "The distinction between being and beings *is there*, latent in the Dasein and its existence . . . The distinction *is there*; that is to say, it has the mode of being of the Dasein; it belongs to existence. Existence means, as it were, 'to be in performance of this distinction'" (BP.319). Two decades later, in the new language of the "Letter on Humanism" (1947), he writes that the human being "happens to be the 'there' *('Da')*, that is, the lighting appropriate to being. This 'being there,' and this alone, has the basic character of existing *(Ek-sistenz)*, that is, ecstatic standing within the truth of being" (BW.205). Elsewhere he says that "being in its essence *needs to use (braucht)* the essence of man . . . the essence of man consists in thinking the truth of being" (EGT.58). To an interlocutor he explains, "The ground thought of all my thinking is precisely that being, the disclosing of being, *needs* man, and that conversely man is only man when he stands within the disclosing of being."[8] Human being, tensed temporality, ontological difference, and being "itself" are mutually appropriating and appropriated. Presupposing each other, assimilated to each other, they happen to be the same, despite their ontic nonidentity.

With this, Heidegger thinks, we approach "the one single question which all traditional thinking must first be brought to face."

> Every philosophical—that is, thoughtful—doctrine of man's essential nature is *in itself alone* a doctrine of the being of beings. Every doctrine of being is *in itself alone* a doctrine of man's essential nature. But neither doctrine can be obtained by merely turning the other around. Why this is so, and generally the question of this relation existing between man's nature and the being of beings, . . . is in fact the one single question which all traditional thinking must first be brought to face . . . But it is a question of abysmal difficulty . . . To speak to the heart of the matter: there is no such thing here as members of the relation, nor the relation as such. Accordingly, the situation we have named between man's nature and the being of beings allows no dialectical maneuvers in which one member of the relation is played off against the other. (*WT*.79)

The more meticulously one endeavors to regard the being of what is from the perspective of ontological difference, the more a certain belonging-together of being (as presence) and the Dasein's existence (as concern, care, conserving presence) comes into view. The challenge for thinking, as Heidegger sees it, is to hold on to this idea of being and Dasein as mutually appropriate without representing them as entities that are the same, that is, as an ontic identity. This is his objection to idealism.

In a lecture entitled "The Principle of Identity," Heidegger extends an important credit to "the era of speculative idealism." He refers to "one thing we have to keep in mind: since the era of speculative idealism, it is no longer possible for thinking to represent the unity of identity as mere sameness, and to disregard the mediation that prevails in unity . . . Thinking has needed more than two thousand years really to understand such a simple relation as that of the mediation within identity."⁹ The kernel of truth in idealism is that the identity, unity, presence, or being of beings is not simply given, as it was for Greek ontology, but mediated, conditioned by the conditions of perception or thought. In Chapter 2 I showed how this idealist thesis emerges with the revisi truth in modern philosophy. Beings do not sp gether of their own accord into the unity of the s unity is synthetic, its identity constituted or mediconcerns us, it refers to our existence, which is like a at clears and shelters," and to our language or *logos*, rs all present beings into presencing and thereby lets them (*EGT*.76).

entiate Heidegger's position from modern metaphysical one must distinguish the thinking that would preserve the al difference from the speculative construction that makes the or subject-centered reason, or will the ground, principle, or use of what is. Heidegger reassures us that beings "are in them- what they are and as they are, even if, e.g., Dasein does not t" (*MF*.153); also that "the cosmos can be without humans inhab-ng the earth, and the cosmos was long before humans ever existed" (*MF*.169). Elsewhere, he contrasts himself to Hegel: "For Hegel, the matter of thinking is: being with respect to beings having been thought in absolute thinking . . . For us the matter of thinking is the Same, and thus is being—but being with respect to its difference from beings . . . the matter of thinking is the difference *as* difference." This, he says, is "something that has not been thought . . . what has always remained unasked throughout this history of thinking." What "gives *us* thought . . . is the *oblivion* of the difference." This entails a relationship to the historical discourse of philosophy fundamentally different from Hegel's own: "For Hegel, the conversation with the earlier history of philosophy has the character of *Aufhebung,* that is, of the mediating concept in the sense of an absolute foundation. For us, the character of the conversation with the history of thinking is no longer *Aufhebung* but *Schritt zurück,* the step back."¹⁰

This is a step back *to* the earliest thought that appropriates being and thinking, letting them belong together, as in Parmenides' dictum that "thinking and being are the same." But it is also a step behind or beyond this, to retrieve a difference that was not made thematic in Greek ontology. Although the ontological difference was "always a prior datum, for Parmenides as much as for Plato, Kant as much as Nietzsche," Heidegger says it is "given beforehand in such a way that this duality does not as such receive specific attention" (*WT*.227). "Wherever the thinking of the Greeks gives heed to the presence of what is present, traits of presence . . . find expression: unconcealedness, the rising from unconcealedness, the entry into unconcealedness, the coming and the going away, the duration . . . These are the traits of presence in whose terms the Greeks thought of what is present. But . . . presence did *not* become problematic, questionable to them as the presence *of* what is present," while for "subsequent European thinking" the "presence of what is present becomes . . . even less problematic" (*WT*.237–238). As I pointed out in Chapter 1, Greek ontology does not hear an impressive difference between *What is it?* and *Is it?* In Heidegger's terms, Greek ontology overlooks the ontological difference in favor of a theoretical account of what is. This fateful contingency, this early "forgetfulness" or "oblivion" of being (as different), became the destiny of being in Western metaphysics.

I have already mentioned this idea in connection with Heidegger's interpretation of Nietzsche. Its importance for Heidegger's thinking justifies citing at length from his essay "The Anaximander Fragment" (1946):

> From early on it seems as though presence *(Anwesen)* and what is present were each something for itself. Presence itself unnoticeably becomes something present. Represented in the manner of something present, it is elevated above whatever else is present and so becomes the highest being present. As soon as presence is named it is represented as some present being. Ultimately, presence as such is not distinguished from what is present: it is taken merely as the most universal or the highest of present beings, thereby becoming one among such beings. The essence of presencing, and with it the distinction between presence and what is present, remains forgotten. *The oblivion of*

being is oblivion of the distinction between being and beings
. . . Oblivion of being belongs to the self-veiling essence of being.
It belongs so essentially to the destiny of being that the dawn of
this destiny rises as the unveiling of what is present in its presencing. This means that the history of being begins with the oblivion
of being, since being—together with its essence, its difference
from what is—keeps to itself. The difference collapses. It remains
forgotten . . . The oblivion of the difference . . . is all the same
not a lack, but rather the richest and most prodigious event: in it
the history of the Western world comes to be borne out. It is the
event of metaphysics. What now *is* stands in the shadow of the
already foregone destiny of being's oblivion . . . the destiny of
being which unfolds in world history as Western metaphysics.
(*EGT*.50–54)

Heidegger envisions a step back from this, toward a position that
conserves the ontological difference and rethinks the relationship of
thinking (or human existence) to being. This is not any kind of ontic
identity (as in idealism). But there is a unique ontological sameness of
Dasein's existence and being, a mutual appropriation for and in the
event *(das Ereignis)* of presencing as such. This is first spoken of in
Parmenides. Speculative idealism makes an advance when it sees that
the identity and unity which make something some one determinate
thing are never unconditional, never simply given. But idealism misun-
derstands the mediation that prevails in identity as the act of an absolute subject, substituting God or *Geist* for *ousia* in a subject-centered
philosophy of nature. Heidegger's step back moves toward a position
prior (as unthought) to metaphysics, idealist or otherwise. I turn next
to its implications for Heidegger's work on truth.

The Essence of Truth

In lectures from 1925–26, Heidegger discusses Aristotle's formula: to
say of what is that it is, and of what is not that it is not, is true. "When
as a twentieth-century European one reads this determination of truth,
one thinks: That is entirely trivial. But one must realize that this defini-

tion is the result of the greatest exertions Plato and Aristotle have made." The essential thing to bear in mind, he says, is that Aristotle does not understand "saying what is" as a "judgment, but rather . . . as letting what is be seen." When in accordance with this stricture he translates Aristotle's Greek, the effect is something like this: "For speaking which lets what is be seen as not being, or what is not as being, is concealing, but letting what is be seen as being, and what is not as not being, is uncovering"—is truthful, *aletheia*. Yet this is not merely a philological claim about Greek *aletheia*. Heidegger thinks it is the truth, or almost the truth, about truth. What we must see and hold onto in the interpretation of truth is that "sentential truth is . . . rooted in [a] prepredicative manifestness of what is." The occasional truth presupposes a prelinguistic, preconventional, precognitive disclosure of beings, which Heidegger identifies with the advent of ontological difference and the ecstatic temporal being of Dasein.[11]

I emphasize Heidegger's determination to read a reference from the occasional truth to *a* being, the one it unveils, whose being makes the truth true. In *Being and Time* he gives this description of assertoric truth: "To say that an assertion 'is true' signifies that it uncovers a being as it is in itself. Such an assertion states, points out, lets a being be seen in its uncoveredness. The being-true (truth) of the assertion must be understood as *being-uncovering*" (*SZ*.218). In lectures a year later: "assertion lets that which is talked about in it be seen in the way of determinative predication . . . This predicative exhibition of a being has the general character of unveiling letting-be-encountered . . . This unveiling, which is the basic function of assertion, constitutes the character traditionally designated as being-true" (*BP*.215). Elsewhere he explains that "the basic achievement of speech lies in making visible—manifest—that *about which* one is speaking, that which is being spoken *of*. What is spoken of shows itself in this making-manifest."[12] Finally, listen to Heidegger's description of *what happens* when, supposing a round coin on a table, somebody states that the coin is round:

the statement regarding the coin refers to this thing in that it presents it . . . What is stated by the presentative statement is said of the presented thing in just such a manner *as* that thing, as presented, is . . . [T]o present here means to let the thing stand opposed as object. As thus placed, what stands opposed must traverse an open distance, and yet also maintain its stand as a thing, showing itself as something with some standing. This appearing of the thing across a distance comes to pass in an open region, the openness of which is not first created by the presentation but rather is only entered into and taken over as an entire domain of relation. (*BW*.123–124)

Truth is astonishing, or so it seems to Heidegger. He represents the occasional truth as an almost improbable accomplishment, as if it *did* something unique. (Wittgenstein: "a misunderstanding makes it look to us as if a proposition *did* something queer" (*PI*.93).) When true, our words are said to uncover *(entdecken)* beings, to unveil *(enthüllen)* what is, to remove concealments *(Unverborgenheit)* and let beings be seen just as they are. Heidegger makes no secret of the fact that his interest in these metaphors, variations on a figure of visual discovery, is to conserve the classical reference from truth to the beings truths are true to, conserving the onto-logic which determines being as true-making. He explains that he has "merely drawn upon *one* peculiar feature of seeing, that it permits uncovering access to beings in themselves."

Of course every "sense" does this . . . But from the beginning onwards the tradition of philosophy has been oriented primarily towards seeing as a way of access to what is *and to being.* To preserve the connection with this tradition, we formalize a wide sense of "sight" and "seeing" as technical terms for characterizing any access to beings and to being in the sense of accessibility in general. (*SZ*.147)

Heidegger never doubts that where there is truth there are beings which truth uncovers, beings whose being makes truths true. He remarks, "the definition of being-true as unveiling, making-manifest, is not an arbitrary invention of mine; it only gives expression to the understanding of the phenomenon of truth as the Greeks already understood it . . . For the Greeks truth means: to take out of concealment, uncovering, unveiling" (*BP*.215). Yet whatever phenomenon of truth the Greeks experienced was an artifact of their language, whose originally meaningless assimilation of *is* and *is true* the first philosophers spontaneously interpreted onto-logically. Two millennia of philosophical discourse on truth transformed this lexical accident into what Wittgenstein describes as a paradox with the form of a platitude: "When we say—*mean*—that such-and-such is the case, we—and our meaning—do not stop anywhere short of the fact, but mean: that *this and that—so and so—is*" (*PI*.95). What Heidegger proffers as a careful phenomenological description of the occasional truth (as showing, or unveiling, or uncovering beings) is not how truth gives itself to be. It is Heidegger's belated effort to make this platitude sound paradoxical, problematic, astonishing—something that cries out for onto-logical explanation.

Heidegger wants to ask *What is the essence of truth?* The question concerns what I called in Chapter 2 truth's ontological a priori. This is whatever onto-logicians say has to exist to make the occasional truth true. For classical philosophy, it is nature or natural phenomena, things with a principle of their own. For critical, modern, epistemological philosophy, it is the subjectivity of the subject. Uniting these positions beneath their opposition, making opposition possible, is the onto-logic of their common assumption, which is that the existence and content of truth is conditional on some extant entity whose being (identity and existence) is at some point given and evident and which makes truths true. Heidegger criticizes this assumption and wants to reframe the question of truth's essence in light of the ontological difference. With this shift of perspective nothing in the tradition is even a candidate for truth's essence. Previous ideas about this are all ontic ideas about the entity whose extantness makes truths true. What is required, however, is not an entity but being, not extant presence but ontological difference.

Yet this too cannot fail to be a version of what it corrects, and here another assumption of onto-logic comes into view. Heidegger's interpretation of truth as unveiling makes the *ontic* assumption that, of course, where there is truth there must be beings truths are true to. He questions this not as a skeptic might (as for example Derrida does), but with a view to reworking the historical discourse of philosophy from his *Schritt zurück*. He assumes truth is a unit or unity, something for itself, something always the same regardless of which truth you choose. "Snow is white," "The coin is round," and "Seventeen is prime" all disclose, or unveil, or uncover beings just as they are. The appropriate "relation to beings" supposedly indispensable for truth is what the tradition tries to name when it speaks of *rectitudo, adaequatio, Übereinstimmung,* or correspondence, and it is what Heidegger tries to name when he speaks of "unveiling letting-be-encountered."

The difference between Heidegger's account of truth's ontological a priori and the tradition (ancient and modern) is that he does not regard the truth of a statement as consisting in a formal or logical relation between extant entities (for example, a term in a proposition and the entity for which it supposits). Truth is a possibility of Dasein's comportment, a moment of ecstatic openness to beings which uncovers them and shows them as they are. The essence of truth, the ontological a priori of its existence, is not the extant presence of anything at all. Instead, it is the Dasein's temporal way of being ecstatically nonpresent which "bears the light in whose brightness a being can show itself" (*MF*.135). The true-making relation of statement and thing "is the accomplishment of that bearing *(Verhältnis)* which originally and always comes to prevail as comportment *(Verhalten),*" that is, the Dasein's action, activity, temporality, and ecstatic, intentional openness to beings. "The correctness (truth) of statements becomes possible only through [the] openness of comportment" (*BW*.124), and "'there is' truth only insofar and for so long as Dasein is" (*SZ*.226). Only when the Dasein exists, and when this existing is ontologically different from that of extant things, can we speak of a "correspondence" between a statement and reality. It is worth emphasizing that Heidegger does not think that the "correspondence theory of truth" is wrong but only superficial. If truth requires correspondence, correspondence requires presencing, and presencing requires ontological difference, which *is not* apart from the *Ek-sistenz* of Dasein.

It is not what we as entities supposedly are that makes truth possible, but what our existing, our being there at all, is *not,* namely, the extant presence of anything finished and durably identical to itself. The origin and essence of truth is in this difference, and not in beings of whatever sort. But how are we to understand "origin"? And what of Heidegger's claim that the essence of truth is freedom? To begin with the latter question, certainly freedom is not "what common sense is content to let pass under this name: the occasional inclination to choose one thing rather than another. Freedom is not absence of constraint with respect to what we can or cannot do" (*BW*.128). This too is not wrong but superficial. We must ask what makes something like free choice possible at all. The answer is the ontological difference between our existence and the extant beings of nature. Suspended beyond the present, dwelling with the past, anticipating a future, our existence is nothing that *could* be subject to an all-determining cause. Insofar as a "cause" is an event which is sometime present and determines the content of a later present moment, our existence transcends or is indifferent to natural causation as such. Ecstatic entities like us are not the sort of things whose careers might be totally determined by their situation in the causal plexus of nature.

How, then, is the essence of freedom to be understood? "[Freedom is] freedom for what is opened up in an open region . . . That which is opened up, that to which a presentative statement as correct corresponds, are beings opened up in an open comportment. Freedom for what is opened up in an open region lets beings be the beings they are. Freedom now reveals itself as letting beings be *(Seinlassen von Seiendem)*" (*BW*.127).

And why is this "freedom" the essence of truth? "To let be—that is, to let beings be as the beings that they are—means to engage oneself with the open region and its openness into which every being comes to stand, bringing that openness, as it were, along with it. Western thinking in its beginning conceived this open region as *ta alēthea,* the unconcealed" (*BW*.127).

Dasein's way of being ecstatically nonpresent entails an original nonself-identity, which is not only "the hitherto uncomprehended essence of freedom" (BW.125). It is also "nothing other than the existent possibility for beings to gain *entry to world*" (*MF*.193). Heidegger emphasizes that "world does not mean beings, neither individual objects nor the totality of objects" (*MF*.193). In *Being and Time* he explains that "the world itself is not a being within the world; and yet it is so determinative for such beings that only insofar as 'there is' a world can they be encountered and show themselves, in their being, as entities which have been discovered" (*SZ*.72). The *being* of beings, their presencing, or what Heidegger here calls entry into world, "is not a process of extant things . . . World-entry has the characteristic of happening, of history *(Geschichte)*. World-entry happens when transcendence happens, i.e., when historical Dasein exists . . . only Dasein, qua existing, provides the opportunity for world-entry" (*MF*.194). So, to speak in paradoxes, this Dasein and this world are themselves nothing, no *thing*, at all. "When Dasein exists, world-entry has simultaneously also already happened together with it, and it has happened in such a way that extant things entering there in principle undergo *nothing* . . . In fact the world is nothing—if 'nothing' means: not a being in the sense of something extant; also 'nothing' in the sense of no-thing, not one of the beings Dasein itself as such transcends . . . The world: a nothing, no being—and yet something; nothing of beings—but being" (*MF*.195).

"Being . . . is already truth." "The essence of truth is freedom." What grants the opening to beings, first securing the possibility of their disclosure in the occasional truth, is the free and open character of the Dasein's ecstatic nonpresence. This absence of *essentia,* this nothingness to which we are consigned, "the hitherto uncomprehended essence of freedom," is the ontological difference from what is present, which assimilates our existence to the advent or lighting of being. There happening to be this difference is the same "event" as the presencing or being of what there is (to be true to).

Heidegger writes of this Event *(das Ereignis)* in the dense, late essay "Time and Being" (1968). He speaks first of the appropriation, assimilation, or ontological sameness of being and time: "The destiny befalling being, time happening, shows the dedication, the deed which delivers over being (as presence) and time (as open region) themselves. The belonging together of time and being determine what we shall call: *das Ereignis* . . . What allows both to belong together, what not only brings them into their own but also secures them in their belonging together and holds them there . . . is *das Ereignis*" (*TB*.19).

But our being, too, appropriates us to being and time. This is because "in being (as presence) we encounter that which concerns us humans so essentially that in perceiving and submitting to it we have attained the distinction of being human."

> As the ones who, standing in their own time, perceive being, and since there is being and time only in the event of their appropriation, it belongs to this event to bring human beings into their own. Thus owned, human beings belong in the event of appropriation. This belonging comes to pass in the assimilation that distinguishes *das Ereignis*. This assimilation lets human beings into *das Ereignis*. (*TB*.23)

Here if anywhere is "the gathering that clears and shelters," and the essence of truth.

It is banal and uncontroversial to claim that if there were no speakers there would be no sentences, no assertions, and no truth. What more does Heidegger claim, assuming more is at stake than this? Earlier I cited his remark that beings "are in themselves what they are and as they are, even if, e.g., Dasein does not exist," and that "the cosmos can be without humans inhabiting the earth, and the cosmos was long before humans ever existed." These words are less reassuring than they may appear or may have been meant to appear. Dasein might not have existed, but suppose that were so. What then? What "would be" in the cosmos Heidegger says "can be" apart from the contingency of our existence? Would there be this or that one self-identical being? Would things have an identity and truth of their own, which *could* be unveiled or spoken of correctly—except that there happen to be no speakers to speak these sentences or to unveil what is? I think Heidegger has to say no. This seems to be an obvious implication of our appropriation to or for the "event" of being. As Heidegger said, "The ground thought of all my thinking is precisely that being, the disclosing of being, *needs* man, and that conversely man is only man when he stands within the disclosing of being." Were there no Dasein, there would be no tensed temporality, hence no presence and no presencing, nor the corresponding withdrawing of being in the event that lets what is be. Apart from us, then, there are no beings which "are there," present, durably identical to themselves. Indeed, Heidegger seems to describe an obstacle to the admission of precisely this point when, harkening back to the theme of inauthenticity in *Being and Time,* he says: "Dasein not only ex-ists but also at the same time *in-sists,* i.e., holds fast to what is offered by beings, as if they were open of and in themselves" (*BW*.135).

Is this idealism? Heidegger praised German idealism for the insight that identity is never original or simply given, that the unity of being is a mediation of differences. Where Heidegger does not follow the idealists, however, is in referring this mediation to the activity, actuality, or absolute self-presence of a spiritual being. From the perspective of the *Schritt zurück,* what "lets" beings presence, what "lets" beings be, is "freedom," that is, not the *presence* but the nonpresence, the nonself-identity, the ontological *difference* of the Dasein's being in relation to that of extant beings in nature. This is a significant departure from idealism, but clearly it does not make Heidegger more of a realist. What there is, the beings there are to get right or be true to, have no being—no existence and no identity—apart from the "usage" (*Brauch*) that "delivers to each present being the while into which it is released" (*EGT*.54).

I agree with what Heidegger seems to regard as the kernel of truth in idealism. There is nothing simply there, extant, determinately this or that, same or different, apart from the contingency we happen to be. But let me omit my reasons for believing this for now; they are not Heidegger's reasons, and I shall return to them in Chapter 7. Here I advance a critical observation instead. In Chapter 1, I took note of two features of the Greek "be" which proved decisive for the philosophical discourse on truth. First, the assimilation of *what is* to what distinguishes truth from falsehood. Classical ontology interprets this grammar onto-logically, making truth a fundamental character of being: To be is to be true-making; what is true or false acquires that value on account of what is and what is not. A second point was that classical Greek hears no impressive difference between *What is it?* and

Is it? In Heidegger's language, classical Greek is oblivious to the difference between being and beings. Metaphysics was born when this grammar was naively interpreted onto-logically, thereby assimilating *being* to being *this* or *that*.

Heidegger takes curiously different attitudes toward these two features of the premetaphysical "be" and the doctrines that were made of them. On the one hand, he regards the assimilation of being and beings as something it is important to step back from, something it is needful to think otherwise about. It was the destiny of Western thinking, or perhaps the destiny of being "itself," to obliterate the difference and deliver us over to an epoch of metaphysics from Plato to Nietzsche (supposedly). Heidegger cannot say that this is a mistake. It is not an error in the sense of a falsification or distortion affecting the accuracy with which a being is represented. Yet if not exactly a mistake, still it is something that might have been otherwise, or might one day be otherwise, and which for a reason Heidegger never adequately clarifies it is the outstanding task of philosophy to try to think otherwise. On the other hand, however, he regards the assimilation of truth and being as a kind of hint worth taking up and conserving. He says, justly, that "from time immemorial philosophy has associated truth and being," but he regards this as evidence that "being does indeed go together with truth" (*SZ*.213). He says, justly, that "in ontological problematics being and truth have from time immemorial been brought together if not entirely identified," but he thinks that "this documents *(dokumentiert)* a necessary connection between being and understanding" (*SZ*.183). He takes this originally meaningless feature of a historically contingent language-game for evidence that "being and truth are connected in principle" (*SZ*.349).

Why this different attitude toward equally fortuitous contingencies? Why view the assimilation of being and truth as an insight, while regarding the Greek and subsequently traditional indifference to ontological difference as a challenge to think otherwise? Why not treat like cases alike?

I suspect Greek ontology contains no profound hint to be recovered or conserved. It was conceived in a language whose copula verb also had the force of "is true" while subordinating existence to predication, and it is therefore no surprise that truth and being are assimilated, or that the distinction between what is and its existing is not thematic. The retrospective appearance of this coincidence as the fate of Western thinking, "the hidden source of its destiny" (*EGT.*76), is the effect Freud describes as *Nachträglichkeit*—deferred or belated significance. A Heideggerian formula like "oblivion of being belongs to the self-veiling essence of being" reifies a distinction that *did not exist* until it became possible (a sheer accident historically) for philosophical discourse in a language that allowed prominence to the distinction between being and beings. The Latin of St. Thomas Aquinas gives him a distinction between *essentia* and *esse,* while the Bible tells him that the name of God is "Who Is," that is, "Being." Of course Heidegger explicitly distinguishes his ontological difference from the Thomist teaching on essence and existence, but this is the anxiety of a revisionist and does not make his discourse any less belated in relation to Thomas, whom he tries to correct.[13]

Heidegger's determination to overcome, or at least evade, metaphysics by conserving the ontological difference leads him to let too many assumptions about extant or natural beings go without question. He does not doubt that there is a realm of extant Nature. He has no argument with classical onto-logic about what there is. This is important because were one to doubt that the fullness of the fully actual or durably self-identical has ever come to pass, as for instance Derrida does, Heidegger's *Seinsfrage,* the question concerning the presence of the present, would lose its point.

I elaborate on this suggestion in the next chapter. But it does not spell the end of truth, as Derrida allows. To understand the difference between true and false we do not need the idea of ontological difference; for this is not a difference that is *made* by the presence or absence of the beings an onto-logician like Heidegger supposes truth discloses. Why this is so, and how we may understand truth otherwise, are subjects for Chapters 7–8.

6 *Derrida, or Difference Unlimited*

> We are to perceive as "normal" . . . what Husserl believed he could isolate as a peculiar and accidental experience, something dependent and secondary—that is, the indefinite drift of signs, as errancy and change of scene, linking up representations one to another without beginning or end.
>
> Derrida, *Speech and Phenomena*

In Chapter 1, I introduced the theme of the secondary sign. To affirm the sign's secondary status is at the same time to affirm the existence of something else whose identity does not depend on reference to another, as does a sign's. An ontological asymmetry between signs and nonsigns in terms of prior and derived or original and secondary, and the ensemble of oppositions with which this has been articulated (nature/convention, intention/expression, object/representation, and so on), evince a tenacious determination to contain, limit, and finally efface the sign, pronouncing it to be nothing apart from what is originally not itself a sign.

Derrida proposes "to restore the original and nonderivative character of signs, in opposition to classical metaphysics." One effect of this is "to eliminate a concept of sign whose whole history and meaning belongs to the adventure of the metaphysics of presence" (*SP.*51). He finds in Saussure a theory of language and of the sign which he uses to overrule, as it were, the decision in favor of a secondary sign. As it happens, this also overrules Saussure, who is another in a long line of theorists of the secondary sign.

Semiological Difference

Linguistic signs have usually been understood to depend on a relation between a thing (or an idea) and the vocable that signifies it. It is understood that the thing can exist apart from that or any sign, while the identity of a given sign (*what* sign it is) is determined by the identity of the nonsign it stands for. Although some signs stand for other signs (what medieval logic called material supposition), and although so-called syncategorematic signs do not themselves stand for anything, these exceptions prove the rule; for their function is to facilitate a combination of signs which ultimately stand for nonsigns if they signify at all. In Western semiotic from the Stoics to Locke, the sign's essential function is to signify what is not itself a sign, while language is first of all an apparatus for naming and predication.[1]

In a gesture that has been compared to Wittgenstein's critique of "the Augustinian picture of language"—"individual words in language name objects, sentences are combinations of such names" (*PI*.1)— Saussure dismisses this traditional doctrine as a fallacious "nomenclaturism." The revisionary sign whose concept he advances remains a bipartite structure, but the duality of Saussure's sign does not involve reference to what is not itself a sign. The identity of a sign as language, or what Saussure calls its "linguistic value," is determined entirely by relations among other signs. Whether we consider these as verbal signals (Saussure's *signifiant*) or as significant units of verbal meaning (Saussure's *signifié*), there is no identity or determination for a linguistic sign which does not come from differential relations *to other signs*. "In a language, as in every other semiological system, what distinguishes a sign is what constitutes it, nothing more. Difference is what makes characteristics . . . In a language there are only differences *and no positive terms*." Whether we consider signal or sense, "what characterizes each most exactly is being whatever the others are not." This is Saussure's principle of semiological difference. He went so far as to call it "the absolutely final law of language."

The absolutely final law of language is, we dare say, that there is nothing that can ever reside in *one* term . . . *a* is powerless to

designate anything without the aid of *b,* and the same thing is
true of *b* without the aid of *a* . . . both have no value except
through their reciprocal difference . . . neither has any value
. . . other than through this same plexus of eternally negative differences.[2]

Languages now come into view as systems of elements whose identity or value is indifferent to anything which is not another, different
sign. The identity of the occasional sign is determined or constituted
(such as it is) entirely by negative differences, by relations of not being
some other, equally differential sign. With this principle of semiological difference Saussure claims a strong autonomy for languages in relation to nature or the physical, and for linguistics as a form of scientific
inquiry. At the same time, Saussure breaks sharply with the epistemological framework in which Locke situated the science of signs he
named *semeiotikē.* Saussure's linguistics promises nothing of interest
for epistemology concerning the relation between language and reality.
This is because for Saussure nothing strictly indispensable to verbal
meaning depends on anything that is supposed to "be what it is" regardless of whether or how language speaks of it. For example, he says
that differences of intra-linguistic contrast give "sheep" and "*mouton*"
distinct significations. Whether they "refer to the same thing" is a
question he does not ask, since he holds such extra-linguistic reference
to be of no consequence for the identity or linguistic value of signs. His
signifié or "signified" is a conceptual (rather than phonic) difference,
not a referent or nonlinguistic entity. Even the identity of the linguistic
signal is indifferent to physical features of the auditory stimulus as
such. Saussure's *signifiant* (a signifier or a sign's signifying, signaling
aspect) is not the real acoustic energy of enunciation but the perception
this causes (an *image acoustique*). "Linguistic signals are not in essence
phonetic. They are not physical in any way. They are constituted solely
by differences which distinguish each such sound pattern from another," distinctions that have no natural or purely physical existence
apart from an arbitrary ensemble of opposed values.[3]

This is unprecedented on more than one count.[4] First, there is the
ontological singularity of the principle of difference. For Plato,

"among things that exist, some are always spoken of as being what they are, just in themselves, others as being what they are with reference to other things . . . And what is different is always so called with reference to another thing."[5] Differences are secondary, derivative, relative to the more original "self-identical being" of a being. Yet for Saussure, language (indeed, the entire field of signs, of the semiological) is a domain where, contrary to the Platonic principle, difference is original and identity (the "being identical to itself" of one sign) secondary and derived.

Saussure's principle is singular too in contrast to earlier work on signs in logic and philosophy. His principle of difference implies that languages exist and function with all of their familiar effectiveness without requiring the existence of anything in relation to which their signs must, as signs, be judged secondary or derivative. One must wonder what becomes of truth, although Saussure nowhere considers this. He has a lot to say about language and its signs, but nothing of a philosopher's interest in truth. It fell to Derrida to take the measure of Saussure's principle here. Before I turn to this matter, however, I want to show how even for Saussure the occasional sign remains secondary in relation to a sovereign nonsign.

Any occasional, empirical, token sign has a determinate identity or value only if there is a momentarily changeless and formally closed total distribution of differences. In the case of the specifically linguistic sign, Saussure refers to this structure as a language *(une langue),* which he thinks of as a static, synchronic, formally closed total state of linguistic values or differences *(état de langue).* He says that "amid the disparate mass of facts involved in language *(langage)*" the synchronic system of *langue* "stands out like a well-defined entity. It can be localized." Unlike talking *(parole),* in which linguistic signs circulate and change their values, *la langue* is a "system of pure values, determined by nothing else apart from the temporary state of its constituent elements." He concedes that "in practice a linguistic state occupies not a point in time but a period of time of varying length during which the sum of changes occurring is minimal." In theory, however, it is a point, a temporary state "from which the passage of time is entirely excluded."[6]

Saussure defines a *langue* as "a system . . . in which the value of one element depends on the simultaneous co-existence of all the others." This system, he says, "is no less real than speech, and no less amenable to study. Linguistic signs, although essentially psychological, are not abstractions. The associations, ratified by collective agreement, which go to make up the language are realities localized in the brain." In light of the favor this perspective has found in later linguistics it is well to remember that it is not an established result but a stipulation and a directive for research. Why does the idea of a synchronic language-state come into the picture for Saussure? Because he wants the signs of language to have values determinate in themselves and objectively determinable by a synchronic science indifferent to history. Since the identity of the linguistic sign is conditioned entirely by differences, the units of *langue* have no identity apart from *all* the differences. "One element depends on the simultaneous co-existence of all the others"; once in circulation, any symbol "is absolutely incapable of defining at any given instant what its identity will be at any subsequent instant." A sign has no identity or value, nor verbal meaning any existence, therefore, apart from the synchronic temporal presence of a total language-state.[7]

Saussure implicitly agrees with classical onto-logic concerning the conditions of objective description and truth. If there is something for a science of languages to get right or be true to, there must be a synchronic self-identity to the systems of language. Saussure *posits* this "structure"; it is the ontological a priori of the linguistic science he envisions. With this venture into ontology he gains a sphere of objectivity for his new science of language, but he also reiterates, now in a "structuralist" variation, the theme of the secondary sign. For Saussure as much as for Aristotle, Augustine, or Locke, it is finally by reference to something that is not itself another sign that the occasional sign derives its identity and existence as a sign or as language—something "fully present" and "identical to itself"; in this case, *la langue*. This entity is certainly not itself a sign differing among signs, yet it *must* exist, Saussure thinks, if there are signs, or languages, or verbal meaning. Thus does the most innovative work since antiquity on language and its signs nonetheless confirm the "metaphysics of presence" which has always condemned the sign to a secondary status. *La langue* is Saussure's name for the self-identically present being over against which the identity and existence of the occasional sign is newly determined as secondary.[8]

It is possible to detach Saussure's principle of difference from his dream of a synchronic science of language. It seems necessary to supplement the sign's differential determination by positing the synchronic totality of a *langue* because Saussure assumes that *to be* is to be "fully" determinate or "self-identical." The cash-value of the postulated totality is precisely to guarantee this identity and objectivity for the signs of language. Only then is there a truth and thus potentially a science of language. Saussure's philosophy of science is implicitly Aristotelian. The first element of any science is "that which it posits, the subject whose essential attributes it examines," and "the existence as well as the meaning of which it assumes" (76b). But one might equally well regard the principle of difference as implying that the identity and existence of signs have nothing to do with any supposed self-identity, unity, endurance, static presence, pure form, or any of the other predicates philosophy habitually associates with being. To the extent that it is plausible to view signs as essentially contrastive or differentiating, so far is it evident that a sign does not *need* to be "identical to itself" in order to admit of interpretation, to bear linguistic value, or to function in communication. But with this I come to Derrida.

Difference Unlimited

Derrida agrees with Saussure that in a language (or any sign system) there are only differences; he says, "the system of signs is constituted solely by the differences in terms, and not by their plenitude. The elements of signification function due not to the compact force of their nuclei but rather to the network of oppositions that distinguishes them, and then relates them to one another" (*M*.10). But Derrida refrains from positing a totality whose synchronic presence would finally put a stop to the reference from sign to sign. Instead, he seizes the most obvious implication of Saussure's principle of difference and concludes that differing among signs—and not a "purely synchronic" differing but one open to time, at no point nonarbitrarily limited—determines whatever value or identity there is for the occasional sign. I summarize the results in three points.

1. A sign attains its identity as the one that it is by differing from other signs. These differences, which elude totalization, which are open to history, give a sign what value it has as a signifier or as a signification. This introduces the need for a far-ranging reconsideration of reference. All signs, whether linguistic or nonlinguistic, spoken or written, are now, so far as concerns their reference-value, in the position traditionally reserved for the special, limiting case of writing.

Western thought about language traditionally maintains that writing is not itself language but is instead a historical supplement or extension, a convenient instrument for the representation of what is not just accidentally but by nature an originally spoken language. Bloomfield says that "the important thing about writing is precisely this, that the characters represent not features of the practical world ('ideas'), but features of the writers' language." For Saussure, "the object of study in linguistics is . . . not a combination of the written word and the spoken word. The spoken word alone constitutes that object." These remarks illustrate what Derrida describes as "the historico-metaphysical reduction of writing to the rank of an instrument enslaved to a full and originally spoken language" (G.29). The written sign is doubly secondary, a sign of a sign, deferring its identity as language to a pronunciation it anticipates and presupposes. If, however, the differences that condition the identity of a sign are unlimited and nontotalizable, then the prescribed distinction according to which some are signs "of signs" (writing) while others break out of the circle and refer to what is not itself another sign is untenable. "Writing is not the sign of a sign, except if one says it of all signs, which would be more profoundly true" (G.7). What was supposed to be peculiar to the written sign (remainder, trace, supplement) becomes the plight of signs without limitation. "The secondarity that it seemed possible to ascribe to writing alone affects all signifieds in general, affects them always already, the moment they *enter the game*" (G.43). A sign is at most a sign "of" other signs, a trace of the differing which constitutes it, and this "divides, from the start, every reference." Each occasional sign "begins by referring back, that is to say, does not begin . . . there is not a single reference but from then on, always, a multiplicity of references, so many different traces referring back to other traces and to traces of others."[9]

We have therefore to contemplate a sign adrift in time, one whose on-going differing and thus whose identity as a sign is at no point delimited by something whose signification is more originally determinate than a piece of writing.

2. There is nothing *to* a sign "itself" (or a language "itself")—no identity or determination at any level bearing on signaling or signifying values—that is indifferent to a change of time or context.

Saussure posited a limit to the differences of signs, a totality in which the constitutive differences would be contained and synchronically completed, thus determining a unique identity for each element of a language. But the demand for such an identity is not a *result* of inquiry; it is the a priori presupposition of a certain preconceived idea of "linguistic" science. On an unlimited interpretation of the principle of difference, that is, an interpretation which does not anticipate the non-arbitrary termination of references from sign to sign, the sign is radically open to time, historical through and through. The differences that give the occasional sign what value it has "are themselves *effects*. They have not fallen from the sky fully formed and are no more inscribed in a *topos noētos* than they are prescribed in the gray matter of the brain . . . differences [are] 'historical' from the outset and in each of their aspects" (*M*.11). To describe the differences to which a sign owes its identity as "historical" is in effect to say that the value or identity of a sign is never properly settled but constantly changing as history introduces new and different possibilities of contextualization.

It often seems to go without saying that of course there is *something* to signs that is the same regardless of their temporal or spatial (contextual) difference. For instance, it is a commonplace to describe the occasional sign as a "token" of an infinitely repeatable type. Besides a type-identity, signs (especially linguistic signs) are supposed to have something like intentional content, truth-conditions, or logical form, and this is supposed to be the same, at least sometimes, despite differences of time and place among signs. But since the differing that determines the value of the occasional sign is unlimited; since nothing *present* (from which the passing of time is excluded) limits this differing, securing totality, imposing nonarbitrary closure; since differing and therefore identity are wide open to historical contingency, there is nothing *to* the occasional sign that functions symbolically and that might simply repeat. Each occasional sign has a historically conditioned, circumstantial *effect,* but not a durable, self-identical content.

Here is a place for two observations on the popular distinction between tokens and types. The idea is familiar enough. A type is the infinitely repeatable form which the occasional token instantiates. The sequence "The cat is on the mat" contains six graphic word-tokens but only five types, the two occurrences of "the" being tokens of the same type. The first point is that linguistic practice, not physics, determines this count. It is impossible for physical similarity and difference (acoustic, spatial, and so on) to settle the count of tokens and types. One is counting signs, and sameness of sign has nothing to do with resemblance in respects that exist independently of the signs or their use. Furthermore, it should not be assumed that repetition in signs is the reinstantiation of a form whose identity is independent of historical differing among contingent tokens. That would subordinate the occasional sign to a durable, present being (a type) which is not itself a sign (not an occasional sign or token), but whose transcendent self-identity supposedly conditions the identity of the occasional sign. On an unlimited interpretation of the principle of semiological difference, nothing "constitutes" that identity except a contingent history of iteration, so there is in a sense nothing strictly or finally *constituted* about a sign: no durable self-identity indifferent to time; no self-same signifying form; no type-identity which must remain the same if that very sign is to repeat. The temporal movement from one occasional sign to another, or what Derrida calls *iteration,* "is not simply repetition . . . Iteration alters, something new takes place" (*L*.40, 53).[10]

One may object, "But if I say *cat cat cat,* am I not obviously doing the same, saying the same, repeating the self-same sign?" Compare saying *cat cat cat* with spending $5 in three consecutive transactions.

How "same" is a $5 note from one transaction to the next? Within certain parameters of person, place, and time, there may be indifference to its differences, but this is entirely circumstantial and not grounded in anything about the $5 note "itself." The exchange-value of a note is not "fully determinate" in a way that anticipates all its possibilities of transaction, and that iterating series of transactions ($5 $5 $5) is far from the simple repetition of a fixed and self-identical form or content. Likewise the iteration of signs, which is not a self-identical form contingently reinstantiated but a habitual, normative, lawful, contextually relative indifference to differences. The idea of the "type," like that of "content" or "proposition," merely reifies this indifference, positing something to be the same in each case and construing linguistic competence as the capacity to recognize and redeploy it. But there is nothing *to* the occasional sign which remains indifferent to place and time and simply repeats, contributing a self-same content to a new and different speech act.[11]

3. To abolish the secondariness of signs, to view their identity as historically and intertextually conditioned by differing, does not merely challenge a prevailing conception of signs. Saussure's limitation of "originary" difference to the sphere of signs, which he separates from a supposedly more primordial order of natural nonsigns, is not motivated by any consideration concerning verbal meaning as such. It derives from his idea of a synchronic science of language and his Aristotelian assumption about the conditions of scientific truth. Derrida exposes the independence of Saussure's principle, relieving it of a limitation to the specifically semiological, to languages or systems of signs in deference to physical nature.[12] The differing Saussure saw as the essence of the sign but also tried to limit to the specifically semiological and to totalize in a synchronic state is unlimited and nontotalizable. It is not just conventional signs (as opposed to natural nonsigns), not just linguistic (as opposed to physical) differences, not just symbols (as opposed to states of affairs) that are "constituted" (to the extent that they are constituted at all) uniquely by unlimited, relational differing. There is no limit to what receives its character (poor thing that it is) from difference, and differences do not formally terminate; they do not

admit of totality or nonarbitrary closure. The negative, contrastive, *original* difference that was supposed to be limited to signs is all the difference there is. A thing is therefore as much a trace, its identity as differential and as deferred, as the identity of a text.

"The enjoyment of the *thing itself* is thus undermined . . . There is nothing outside of the text" (G.154,159). In *Of Grammatology* (1967), Derrida described this as his "axial proposition." More than twenty years later, in the "Afterword" (1988) to *Limited Inc,* he offers these elucidations:

> the concept of text or context which guides me embraces and does not exclude the world, reality, history . . . the text is not the book, it is not confined in a volume itself confined to the library. It does not suspend reference—to history, to the world, to reality, to being, and especially not to the other, since they always appear in an experience, hence in a movement of interpretation which contextualizes them according to a network of differences. (*L.*137)

> the concept of text I propose is limited neither to the graphic, nor to the book, nor even to discourse, and even less to the semantic, representational, symbolic, ideal, or ideological sphere. What I call "text" implies all the structures called "real," "economic," "historical," socio-institutional, in short: all possible referents . . . every referent, all reality has the structure of a differential trace. (*L.*148)

"Nothing outside the text" does not mean "prison house of language." Neither does it mean that everything is a sign. But there is no basis for the subordination of signs to something that is emphatically not a sign, something whose identity and existence would be unconditioned by the contrivances of nomenclature. This introduces an unconventional element of temporal deferral into ontology. Contrary to a Greek and Scholastic assumption which passed uncritically into modern thought, what we call a "being," something that "is," is invariably less than identical to itself. The actuality or durable self-sameness which classical ontology demands of its beings never comes to pass, not fully, not finally. Difference is prior to identity, while the fully determinate self-identity which classical metaphysics regards as definitive of an entity's being is deferred *ad infinitum.*

Différance is what becomes of semiological difference once it has been radically unlimited, leaving identity and sameness nowhere primitive or given. Derrida's neologism fuses the ideas of irreducible, original difference with the interminable deferral of identity which this implies. What passes for actual or extant or for the same is always less, simulacra whose apparently determinate identity is a "special effect" (as cinematic motion is a special effect) of the "displaced and equivocal passage from one different thing to another" (*M.*17).

The Effect of *Différance*

Heidegger and Saussure have something in common. Both introduce an idea of original difference, that is, a difference which does not depend on identity but reverses the traditional priority, preceding and conditioning the identity of beings, and both limit this difference in a way that respects the traditional interpretation of being as *presence.* Saussure limits original difference to the sphere of the semiological, and it is in the name of the presence or self-identical being of signs that he posits the synchronic totality of *la langue,* while if Heidegger insists on the originality of ontological difference, on its irreducibility to differences of kind or respect among beings, it is for the sake of thinking more penetratingly about the presence (being) of what there is. Not only do ontic differences among beings remain as secondary and derived as they were for Plato; neither Aristotle nor Thomas would object to Heidegger's conception of science as "a kind of cognizing for the sake of cognizing as such . . . What is to be unveiled should become manifest, solely in view of its own self, in whatever its pure essential character and specific mode of being may be. What is to be unveiled is the sole court of appeal of its determinability, of the concepts that are suitable for interpreting it" (*BP.*320). Heidegger even produces a variation on the theme of the secondary sign: "The essential being of language is saying as showing. Its showing character is not based on signs of any kind; rather, all signs arise from a showing within whose realm and for whose purposes they can be signs."[13]

Derrida has observed "the ambiguity of the Heideggerian situation with respect to the metaphysics of presence and logocentrism. It is at once contained within and transgresses it. But it is impossible to separate the two" (*G*.22). Elsewhere he expands on Heidegger's dilemma:

> It remains that being, which is nothing, is not a being, cannot be said, cannot say itself, except in the ontic metaphor. And the choice of one or the other group of metaphors is necessarily significant. It is within a metaphorical insistence, then, that the interpretation of the meaning of being is produced. And *if Heidegger has radically deconstructed the domination of metaphysics by the present, he has done so in order to lead us to think the presence of the present.* But the thinking of this presence can only metaphorize, by means of a profound necessity from which one cannot simply decide to escape, the language that it deconstructs. (*M*.131, my emphasis)[14]

Despite his wish to think differently from the metaphysics which has prevailed since the Greeks, Heidegger abides by the Greek determination of being as presence, with its interpretation of *a* being as a unity, self-identically this or that, somewhere sometime present. Even if this presence (being) has presuppositions which ancient and modern philosophy alike are in no position to accommodate, Heidegger nevertheless assumes that (with the unique exception of the Dasein), "what is" is in each case fully present and identical to itself.

Yet if self-identity defers to *différance* and presence to differential iteration, the idea of an "ontological difference" between self-identical, fully present beings and their presence or being as such must seem dubious. Although Derrida says he would not "dispense with the passage through the truth of being" or "criticize, contest, or misconstrue its incessant necessity" (*M*.22), elsewhere he suggests a more confrontational position: "No doubt Nietzsche called for an active forgetting of being: it would not have the metaphysical form imputed to it by Heidegger" (*M*.136).

The thought of unlimited, original, nontotalizable differences undermines *ontic* presuppositions of Greek metaphysics which Heidegger never questions. Unlimited and irreducible difference, and the deferral or *différance* this introduces into ontology, destroys the interpretation of *a* being as what is sometime present, with all of the traits classical ontology ascribes to such a presence: unity, enduring self-identity, truth. Being, as the presencing of what is present, is deferred *ad infinitum*. The ontological difference between *what* is present and this presence *itself* has never come to pass. Heidegger's question concerning the presence of the present is relieved of its reason, *aufgehoben*, deconstructed.[15]

How do things stand with truth? To approach this question I shall summarize what I have made of Derrida's argumentation in three points.

1. A secondary sign is untenable. The armature of Derrida's argumentation is Saussure's principle of semiological difference and its radical unlimitation by the oppositions that have traditionally hemmed in the sign, condemning it to a secondary, derivative sort of being.[16]

One might compare Saussure's principle to Tarski's work on truth. After Tarski it is difficult to assume that the inferential patterns in which truth-value is conserved in linguistic behavior, patterns which constitute the subject matter of logic, depend on or imply anything more than the patterns found in the metalanguage in which a truth-predicate is defined. What Davidson finds striking about Tarski's procedure for defining such a predicate is "not that the phrase 'is true' can be replaced, for that can be the point of definition; what is striking is that it is not replaced by anything else, semantic or otherwise." This is striking because it implies that semantically distinct truths (for example, "Snow is white" and "Grass is green") are not differentiated *ontologically* by differences in the beings that make them true. If "Snow is white" and "Grass is green" are different truths, it is because of *intralinguistic* differences of inferential relationship; it is not because different *beings* "make" these sentences true. "Nothing," Davidson says, "no *thing*, makes sentences and theories true."[17]

In a certain respect, Saussure's principle of difference has a comparable implication, namely, that contrary to a long tradition in Western reflection on language, verbal meaning and all its associated values (including reference and truth) are *indifferent* to the existence of anything that is not itself more verbal meaning. The effects of verbal meaning are effects of difference and do not evince the presence of anything that is emphatically not more of the same. Language is the transformation of language, language practice the transformation of its past. It does not exist except where it has already existed; it "begins" with repetition, which is to say that it does not begin, that it is historical through and through, at no point made to be as it is by nature. If Saussure draws nothing remotely like these implications from his principle of difference, it is because of his *other* idea, which was to found a synchronic science of language. To unlimit the principle of difference is also to eliminate, as empty baggage, Saussure's assumptions about truth and scientific objectivity.

2. Difference is irreducible and "older" than identity, sameness, unity, or being (presence). To describe differences as irreducible means that their existence is not a mere contingency which befalls what is. A thing is not first "identical to itself" and then accidentally distinct from whatever other self-identical beings happen to exist. Multiplicity, nonidentity, negativity are there from the start, but so is historical time, which is time without origin or closure, in which singularities (contingencies) are the rule.[18] Differences are interminable. Instead of what Thomas Aquinas called the "act of being" there is an original deferral of being, of unity, of self-identity, and so, by all onto-logic, of truth.

3. A rude paraphrase of "nothing outside the text" would be that there is nothing that is just there, present, durably identical to itself, indifferent to the speech or mind that would know it. Yet while this must disappoint those who anticipate the disclosure of being, it obviously does not mean that truth does not exist. Derrida writes: "the value of truth (and all those values associated with it) is never contested or destroyed in my writings, but only reinscribed in more powerful, larger, more stratified contexts . . . interpretative contexts (that is, within relations of force that are always differential—for example, socio-political-institutional—but even beyond these determinations) that are relatively stable, sometimes apparently almost unshakable" (*L*.146).[19]

I take the point to be that for truth-value (and associated values like reference, translation, relevance, implication, identity, and objectivity) to "be determinate" in any case depends on the effectiveness of histor-ically contingent practices of evaluation, and on nothing else. This de-pendence may be why Derrida also says that "there is something polit-ical in the very project of attempting to fix the content of utterances."

> This is inevitable; one cannot do anything, least of all speak, without determining (in a manner that is not only theoretical but practical and performative) a context. Such experience is always political because it implies, insofar as it involves determination, a certain type of non-"natural" relationship to others . . . non-nat-ural relations of power that by essence are mobile and founded upon complex conventional structures.

"Once this generality and this a priori structure have been recog-nized," he adds,

> the question can be raised, not whether a politics is implied (it always is), but which politics is implied in . . . a [given] practice of contextualization. This you can then go on to analyze, but you cannot suspect it, much less denounce it, except on the basis of another contextual determination every bit as political. In short, I do not believe that any neutrality is possible here. (L.136, 147)

Derrida's work may in a sense not contest or destroy truth's value. But if the relative stability of contextualizing practice is all there is to make the occasional truth true, and if this "making" is not a transcen-dental constitution but a historically conditioned effect of social power, a *making-pass* (for true, probable, relevant, known, and so on), then a different perspective opens on truth. With being, presence, and self-identical unity deferred *ad infinitum,* the value of truth can and must be "reinscribed" where it belongs: "in more powerful, larger, more stratified . . . interpretative contexts"—in other words, in the in-stitutional-social practice where truth always was anyway, even when philosophers preferred to avert their eyes from time, history, and con-tingency and dream of True Being.

Différance dispels the assimilating, mimetic sameness of thought and being. But one cannot say (except as a joke) that this is a theoretical result, a theorem now established. The discourse of *différance* is a cross-reading of Saussure and Heidegger, a doubly revisionary *tour de force,* but one so bound to the discourse it deconstructs that it cannot be said to prove anything except the possibility of their deconstruction. However interesting the proof may be, it is of limited value for philosophy. Suppose, for instance, that one were inclined to deny that semiological difference has anything like the importance Saussure ascribed to it. Then the argument for unlimiting this principle from the specifically semiological would be of little interest, and claims made on behalf of *différance* would remain exaggerated and unpersuasive. Or suppose one believed "that the word 'Being' is more trouble than it is worth," or that the *Seinsfrage* is merely a hook by which Heidegger gets "out from under theology while still keeping in touch with what theology (and the central books of the *Metaphysics* and the *Science of Logic*) had been about."[20] From this point of view, Heidegger's lugubrious revisionism and Derrida's tortuous deconstructions may seem worse than useless for discussing what is wrong with "truth-as-correspondence."

In the next chapter I argue that the correspondence that classical truth requires does not and cannot exist. Like truth in speech, the identity and existence of what there is stands or falls with the contingent, historical language-games by which identity and existence acquire practical determin*ability* and, with that, all the "determination" they have.

7 *Wittgenstein, or The* Aufhebung *of Logic*

> I've written a book called "Logisch-Philosophische Abhandlung" containing all my work of the last six years. I believe I've solved our problems finally. This may sound arrogant but I can't help believing it . . . it's all as clear as crystal. But it upsets our theory of truth.
>
> Wittgenstein, to Russell (1919)

> How can I be a logician before I'm a human being! *Far* the most important thing is to settle accounts with myself.
>
> Wittgenstein, to Russell (1914)

When he was a logician, Wittgenstein dreamed of a sign so pure you could see right through it. The "logic" that would make this possible is "a mirror-image of the world." Its crystalline forms *have* to exist, given that there is truth, reference, thought, or language at all. And yet, "the more closely we examine actual language," he later wrote, "the sharper becomes the conflict between it and our demand. (For the crystalline purity of logic was certainly not the *result* of an investigation; it was a demand.) The conflict becomes unbearable; the demand is now in danger of becoming empty.—We have got on to slippery ice where there is no friction and so in a certain sense the conditions are ideal, but also just because of that we are unable to walk. We want to walk, so we need *friction*. Back to the rough ground!" (*PI*.107).

Wittgenstein's *Tractatus Logico-Philosophicus* (1921) is engaged with a basic problem of onto-logic: the problem of how truth in signs has its cause in beings. After finding an answer, and finding out how little it did to settle accounts with himself, Wittgenstein worked on other things. He returned to Cambridge to write and teach philosophy in 1929. From 1933 *(Philosophical Grammar)* one begins to see a difference in his work. Before he returned to the rough ground, however, Wittgenstein composed perhaps the purest onto-logic ever in work on truth in philosophy.

An Old Problem

At one place in the manuscripts posthumously published as *Philosophical Grammar* Wittgenstein writes: "Here we have the old problem, which we would like to express in the following way: 'the thought that p is the case does not presuppose that it is the case, yet on the other hand there must be something in the fact that is a presupposition of the thought itself.' (I cannot think that something is red, if the color red does not exist.) It is the problem of the harmony between world and thought" *(PG.142)*.

This problem is an old one both for Wittgenstein, whose *Tractatus* is fundamentally concerned with it, and for onto-logic. In the *Cratylus*, Plato has Socrates demand "how anyone could ever compose a picture which would be *like* anything at all if there were not pigments in nature which resembled the things imitated, and out of which the picture is composed?"[1] How can a picture be *like* what is, or be true *to* a being, unless it admits of comparison, unless it is commensurable with reality? But how can a picture, or anything else, be commensurable with reality—determinately like or unlike, same or different—unless there is *something* in both that is the same?

Old problems indeed. Before there can be likeness, adequacy, or true-making sameness between something like a picture and what is, there has to be some comparability, some dimension of same/different commonly determined in symbol and reality alike. If, then, truth is some sameness, some adequation or assimilation between something said (something of signs) and the world of which we speak, the question must arise as to what kind of commensurability for symbols and situations translates into truth-value for a sign.

It was this which, looking back after more than a decade at the *Tractatus,* Wittgenstein remembers as "the old problem . . . of the harmony between world and thought."

> Here instead of harmony or agreement of thought and reality one might say: the pictorial character of thought. But is this pictorial character an agreement *(Übereinstimmung)?* In the *Tractatus* I had said something like: It is an agreement of form. (*PG*.163)

This idea was prominent in Wittgenstein's thinking from an early stage. In a notebook entry from October 1914, he writes:

> The form of a picture might be called that in which the picture MUST agree with reality (in order to be capable of depicting it at all).
> The first thing that the theory of logical depiction by means of language gives us is insight into the essence of the truth-relation.
> The theory of logical depiction by means of language says— quite generally: In order for it to be possible that a sentence should be true or false—agree with reality or not—for this to be possible something in the sentence must be *identical* with reality. (*NB*.14)

This insight into the onto-logic of truth later finds its way into the *Tractatus* when Wittgenstein writes:

> There must be something identical in a picture and what it depicts to enable the one to be a picture of the other at all. (*TLP*.2.161)
> What any picture . . . must have in common with reality in order to be able to depict it—correctly or incorrectly—in any way at all is logical form, *which is the form of reality.* (*TLP*.2.18, my emphasis)

The *Tractatus* postulates an absolute logical form, *the* logical form, which is not only not relative to a choice among formal languages and logical theories, but is not even peculiar to sentences. Reality, too, has logical form. One may think of this logical form as the respect in which arbitrary symbols and actual situations can be the same, a sameness that makes the sign true. It would be more accurate, however, not to speak of logical form as a respect of sameness, as one among many. More accurately, the many respects of real, potentially true-making sameness and difference are modifications or determinations of the one purely logical form. This logical form is a second-order determinable. A first-order determinable would be like spatial extension, duration, color, or pitch, and its determinations are simple in the sense of being not further determinable in that respect. A second-order determinable is one whose determinations are all first-order determinables, and are therefore themselves further determinable. Diagrammatically:

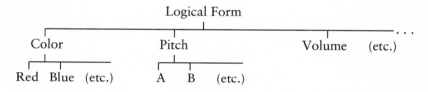

My interpretation suggests a comparison with Spinoza. Logical form is one, infinite, and eternal. Its attributes include *what is* ("body") and *what is said* ("mind"). What is, the facts in logical space, are configurations or finite modifications of the infinite modes of logical form: the colors, the pitches, spatial and temporal extension—in sum, all respects in which beings can be same or different. What Wittgenstein calls an "object" is not an ordinary thing. It is one simple (that is, not further determinable) determination of a logical form. He identifies these simple objects with the meaning *(Bedeutung)* of the logically simple signs that name them. An object, in this sense, might be a color, say, or a location, duration, or mass, while the situation of a color and a mass at a location for an interval would be a complex of objects, or what Wittgenstein calls a "state of affairs" *(Sachverhalt)*. What is said is the same; that is, propositions *(Sätze)* too are configurations of elements—not, however, of objects but of their names. One name stands for one object, another for another, and when combined with one another in a proposition "the whole group—like a *tableau vivant*—presents a state of affairs" *(TLP.4.0311).*[2]

Neither the number nor the precise identity of the logical forms can be decided a priori. (Wittgenstein has no "deduction of the categories.") Both their number and identity depend on the research Wittgenstein calls the "application" of logic, that is, the analysis of actual language, using a notation designed to display its logical forms perspicuously. "The *application* of logic decides what elementary propositions there are. What belongs to its application logic cannot anticipate . . . [Logic] cannot say a priori what elementary propositions there are" (*TLP*.5.557–5.5571). Nor, therefore, what forms of object make them true. "Logical forms are *without* number. Hence there are no preeminent numbers in logic, and hence no philosophical monism or dualism, etc." (*TLP*.4.128).

Wittgenstein emphasizes the systematic aspect of names or simple signs, ascribing a similar systematicity to the objects of their reference. Of signs he says, "where one can construct symbols according to a system, logical importance attaches to the system and not the individual symbols" (*TLP*.5.555). Of things, "Each thing is, as it were, in a space of possible states of affairs. This space I can imagine empty"—for example, nothing actually colored—"but I cannot imagine the thing [the color] without the space" (*TLP*.2.013). These observations hint at a fundamental principle for Wittgenstein's theory in the *Tractatus,* one that is already familiar, however unexpected in this context; for it is Saussure's principle that difference is original and constitutive of identity. Everything in Wittgenstein's ontology is either an object or a configuration or sign of objects, and the identity of objects, as of their signs or names, is conditioned entirely (originally) by differences.

Wittgenstein says, "If two objects have the same logical form, the only distinction between them, apart from their external properties, is that they are different" (*TLP*.2.1233). I take this to mean that when, considering any situation with many objects of the same form, we abstract from their contingent relationships in that situation (for instance, some red being beside some blue), the only thing that makes them *two* are their differences in relation to each and every other object of that form. In other words, tractarian objects are not atoms. They are not first of all identical to themselves and then contingently different from each another. There is nothing *to* a tractarian object apart from systematic difference in an ensemble, and this difference is original, not the result but the ground of an object's identity. Yet like Saussure and unlike Derrida, Wittgenstein limits this original difference with an a priori assumption of nonarbitrary totality for the differences original and proper to one logical form (all the color-differences, all the volumes, pitches, and so on). All of this is supposed to be determined once and for all, making up the timeless totality Wittgenstein calls "logical space."

The holistic priority of difference over identity is essential to the solution of thought's puzzling relation to reality. To see how, consider first Wittgenstein's concept of name. He introduces it with these remarks:

> In a proposition a thought can be expressed in such a way that elements of the propositional sign correspond to *(entsprechen)* the objects of the thought. I call such elements "simple signs," and such a proposition "completely analyzed."
>
> The simple signs employed in propositions are called names. A name means *(bedeutet)* an object. The object is its meaning *(Bedeutung)*.
>
> In propositions names stand for *(vertritt)* objects. (*TLP.*3.2–3.22)

Here Wittgenstein gives three names to the relation of simple sign and object: correspond, mean, stand for. Certainly the relation involves reference, but it would be a mistake to assume that the unity of this group is denotation. Although Wittgenstein describes the proposition as a picture *(Bild)*, he thinks of it less as a representation *(Vorstellung)* than as a copy, model, projection, or reproduction—something whose own presence is already a mimesis of being. The difference between a copy or model and a representation lies in the means by which the symbolizing parts of the sign refer. Representations refer to things with signs that denote them, and it is characteristic of denotation that the relation between sign and referent is arbitrary. This is not so for copies, reproductions, or models, and the difference turns out to be crucial for Wittgenstein's philosophy of truth.

To explain why I must digress. Nelson Goodman distinguishes two modes of symbolic reference: denotation and exemplification. He defines denotation as "the application of a word or . . . label to one or many things." Any predicate is an example: say, "is red." An example of the exemplificational sign would be a tailor's swatch, which exemplifies (and thereby refers to) properties of color and weave in the stock. The secret of exemplificational reference is that the sign both has and refers to the same property: It refers to a property in part by itself actually possessing that property. (In part; for the whole thing obviously presupposes the symbolizing practice that uses certain items as exemplifications.)[3]

These two modes of reference correlate with a difference in the arbitrariness of signs. Any occasional sign is a bundle of properties, some of which function symbolically and some of which do not. Under standard conventions, for example, the color of a printed predicate, unlike its spelling, does not function symbolically. A characteristic of the denotative sign is that every property functioning symbolically in the symbolizing material is also arbitrary in relation to the referent. All the symbolizing properties of the predicate "wet," for instance, are quite arbitrary in relation to the referent, and while "polysyllabic" is polysyllabic and is therefore in this respect nonarbitrarily related to its referent, this property does not function symbolically in the sign. It is not part of the means by which "polysyllabic" refers that it should have a polysyllabic part, but it *is* part of the means by which a sample of color refers that the material of the sign *be the same color*. Here is a property functioning symbolically in a sign yet by no means arbitrarily related to its referent, since it is in fact the same as that referent, this sameness functioning symbolically in the sign.

Simple signs name objects, but contrary perhaps to all expectation Wittgenstein does not think of naming as denotation. In the context of the well-formed propositional sign, a logically simple name does not denote but *exemplifies* one determination of one logical form. The idea is subtle, for to name a color a sign need not look colored. But what *does* a sign like "red" refer to? Not to a *look*. On the contrary, what "red" and a certain family of sensations or phenomenal states of consciousness have in common is that they are all signs referring to the same point on the logical space of color. A *look* is as much a sign as anything printed on a page. Like any determination of any logical form, a color is not a phenomenal or qualitative atom. There is no color apart from differences of color, and these differences are original; they are not consequences but conditions of the identity of the instances. I take this to be the reason Wittgenstein says, "If objects are given, then at the same time we are given *all* objects" (*TLP*.5.524). An object has no being, no identity or existence, apart from a texture of differences among other differentially constituted units; so if one is, all must be. This posited totality plays the same role in Wittgenstein's theory as the posited totality of *la langue* in Saussure's: the role of ensuring that each in an ensemble of originally different units has one determinate identity.

Differential determination in an ensemble (a logical form) is crucial to the solution of that old problem of harmony between thought and reality. Precisely because its identity is constructed of original differences, a propositional configuration of logically simple signs can exemplify a color-*difference* or a shape-*difference* even though the material of the sign (voice, for instance) *looks* neither colored nor spatial.

Any logically simple sign would have some qualities which are arbitrary in relation to the object it means, but these would not function symbolically in the sign, and properties that *do* function symbolically are not arbitrary in relation to the object. Wittgenstein says, "In order to recognize a symbol by its sign we must observe how it is used with a sense. A sign does not determine a logical form unless it is taken together with its logico-syntactical employment" (*TLP*.3.326–3.327). Thus the only symbolizing properties of a simple sign derive from syntactic constraint, and *these* properties are not arbitrary in relation to the referent: They are the same; they mimic the originally differential texture of its identity. So "although there is something arbitrary in our notations, *this* much is not arbitrary—that *when* we have determined one thing arbitrarily, something else is necessarily the case." The systematic differentiation that determines the identity of objects *is the same logical form* manifest—exemplified—in the syntactic differentiation that defines their logical names. This ultimate nonarbitrariness "derives from the *essence* of notation" (*TLP*.3.342).

In the context of a propositional sign constructed according to an ideally perspicuous logical syntax (a system for constructing "completely analyzed propositions"), a simple sign exemplifies one formal (real, potentially true-making) difference. Such a sign *imitates* syntactically the very texture of formal differences that originally constitute the identity of the object it means. To say that the proposition "shows" *(zeigt)* its sense is therefore not a metaphor. To one acquainted with the notation, a symbol syntactically suited for truth-value shows one or more differences as literally as a sample shows a difference of color or weave: "One name stands for one thing, another for another, and they are combined with one another. In this way the whole group—like a *tableau vivant*—presents a state of affairs" (*TLP*.4.0311).

Here is a solution to that old problem of harmony between symbol and situation. A proposition would be comparable to a situation precisely as is a copy to an original, a sample to a suit, or (to mention Wittgenstein's standard example) as a yardstick to the extension it measures. "A proposition has the same kind of relation to reality that a measuring rod has to an object. This is not a simile; the measuring rod is an example of the relation." A logical configuration of names is determinately true or false when it exemplifies one or more simple determinations of logical form, because this is also the form of reality. "*That* is how a picture is connected to reality; it reaches right out to it. It is laid against reality like a yardstick" (*TLP*.2.1511–2.1512).[4]

What Looks as if It *Had* to Exist

Not just this solution but the entire fabric of assumptions that create the problem it addresses receive far-reaching criticism in Wittgenstein's later work. I begin my look at the later work with an interpretation of one (almost) complete numbered section from near the beginning of the *Philosophical Investigations*. Without mentioning it by name, the passage obviously refers to the *Tractatus,* which it criticizes with characteristically understated indirection. Finally, recall that in the *Tractatus* he described objects as "the substance of the world," saying that "they cannot be composite . . . Objects are what is unalterable *(Feste)* and subsistent *(Bestehende);* their configuration is what is changing and unstable" (*TLP*.2.021–2.271).

"What," he now asks, "does it mean to say that we can attribute neither being *(Sein)* nor nonbeing to elements?"

One might say: if everything that we call "being" and "nonbeing" consists in the existence *(Bestehen)* and the nonexistence of connections among elements, it makes no sense to speak of an element's being (nonbeing); just as when everything that we call "destruction" lies in the separation of elements, it makes no sense to speak of the destruction of an element.

One would however like to say: Being cannot be attributed to an element; for if it did not exist, one could not name it and so one could say nothing of it at all.—But let us consider an analogous case. There is *one* thing of which we can say neither that it is one metre long, nor that it is not one metre long, and that is the standard metre in Paris.—But this is, of course, not to ascribe any extraordinary property to it, but only to mark its singular role in the game of measuring with a metre-rule.—Let us imagine samples of colour being preserved in Paris like the standard metre. We define: "sepia" means the colour of the standard sepia which is there kept hermetically sealed. Then it will make no sense to say of this sample either that it is of this colour or that it is not.

We can put it like this: That sample is an instrument in the language used in ascriptions of colour. In this language-game it is not something that is represented, but is a means of representation . . . And to say "If it did not exist it could have no name" is to say as much and as little as: if it did not exist we could not use it in our game.—What looks as if it *had* to exist belongs to the language. It is a paradigm in our language-game; something with which comparison is made. And this may be an important observation; but it is nonetheless an observation about our language-game—our method of representation. *(PI.50)*

There is perhaps a danger of taking an overly juridical view of standards, forgetting that in practice they can be modified *ad hoc,* abandoned, or ignored, or forgetting that official standards like the metre-bar sealed away in Paris co-exist with lots of unofficial standards actually applied in practice. Were they to begin to issue divergent results there is no telling what we should say. Still, there is something to learn from the curious logic of the standard. Suppose, then, we define: "sepia" means the color of the standard sepia which is kept hermetically sealed. Now consider something (anything) incommensurable with this standard object, something with which it strictly cannot be compared for sameness or difference of color. This might be atmospheric nitrogen, or Nova Scotia, or the Dow-Jones average. There can be just one reason why a thing would be incommensurable with the standard sepia, and that is because it is not colored. As I have already suggested, being colored entails and presupposes commensurability (same/different); what cannot be compared with a color cannot be colored. So by all onto-logic, no predication whose subject term refers to something incommensurable with the standard sepia is true or false to the color of anything.

Wittgenstein's hypothetical standard sepia is just such a thing. Since nothing can be compared with itself, since nothing is like or unlike itself, the standard sepia would be incommensurable with the standard sepia. So were a speaker to say of the standard "It is sepia," this statement would not seriously admit of evaluation in terms of true or false. It has no determinate truth-value. Certainly it is not true. The referent of "It is sepia" (ostensibly referring to the standard) cannot be colored sepia; for it is incommensurable with and therefore not the same as the standard sepia. Nor is the utterance *determinately* false, which would presuppose a differently colored referent. Neither would "It is sepia" said of the standard be true by definition. The sentence may figure in the establishment or explanation of a definition, but that does not mean it truly describes the standard object. The standard cannot be compared with itself, and the statement predicating sepia of the standard cannot seriously be evaluated for truth, and is neither true nor false.

But let me consider a plausible objection. Suppose that a thing X is compared with the standard and judged to be the same color. So X is sepia. But if X is sepia, and if it is the same color as the standard, then the standard is sepia.

The mistake in this argument is the assumption that when one compares a thing with a standard one is judging the sameness of two things in the respect determined by the standard. This is not so. One is evaluating one thing (the candidate) *by* the standard, which is not a term in a judgment of similarity but an instrument for estimating a respect of difference. The result of applying the standard to X is not that X and the standard are the same color, but that X is sepia.

Unlike ordinary incommensurabilities (for instance, thumbtacks and thunderstorms, incommensurable in respect of specific gravity), a standard sepia is incommensurable with the standard sepia because nothing can be compared with itself. Yet because it is incommensurable, no color may be predicated of it; it can only be used (not described) in a system of color-predication. I labor this point because Wittgenstein's hypothetical standard is an analogue of what in the *Tractatus* he called an object. Most of the formal features reappear: One cannot describe the standard sepia (with color predicates), but can only give it a name (*TLP*.3.221), that is, a logico-syntactical employment (3.327); it is what has to exist if predication of "sepia" is to have determinate sense (3.23); it is simple, that is, one determination of one logical form (2.02); and since the language-game that uses it can only take it for granted, as far as that practice is concerned the standard is unalterable and subsistent (2.027).

Yet there is one difference between the standard sepia and a tractarian object: What *has* to exist if there is a determinate difference between true and false predications of "sepia" is *the language-game* that credits the exemplary object with the value of standardly determining a respect of similarity and difference. "We can put it like this: This sample is an instrument in the language used in ascriptions of color. In this language-game it is not something that is represented, but is a means of representation." This possibility of true or false description therefore depends on the existence of a perfectly contingent practice *and nothing else besides.* "What looks as if it *had* to exist belongs to the language. It is a paradigm in our language-game; something with which comparison is made." If the language-game with the standard sepia did not exist, there would be no residual determination *in reality* that would be inaccessible to extant symbolizing practice.

Consider in this light something that Wittgenstein once said "forces itself upon us *over and over again*"—the necessity of positing "something Simple, Indivisible, an element of being, in brief a thing."

we feel that the WORLD must consist of elements . . . that the world must be what it is, it must be determinate . . . It seems as if to deny things were as much as to say: The world can be as it were indeterminate, in something like the sense in which our knowledge is uncertain and indeterminate. The world has a fixed *(feste)* structure. *(NB.*62)

Wittgenstein's later work leaves this intuition shaken. A text from *Philosophical Grammar* parallels the argument of *Philosophical Investigations* §50: "The proposition 'I could not think that something is red if red did not exist' actually refers to the image of something red, or the existence of a red sample, *as part of our language*. But of course one cannot say that our language *has to* contain such a sample. If it did not contain it, it would just be different" (*PG.*143). That counterfactual situation would be one in which language and practice differ from the way they are now, but not one lacking in the means to express a way the world is anyway, in its own right, apart from all language and practice.

Wittgenstein thought that "to understand a sentence means to understand a language," while "to understand a language means to be master of a technique" (*PI.*199). He says his term *language-game* "is meant to bring into prominence the fact that speaking a language is part of an activity, or of a form of life" (*PI.*23). I take the point that what is said—the "meaning" or "content" of the occasional use of language—has an identity no more determinate than what it derives from the habits and practice that sustain a language-game, whose thoroughgoing contingency Wittgenstein underlined.[5] I draw the same conclusion about the identity—the being determinately *this* or *that,* same or different—of what there is. The identity, similarity, and difference of things is as thoroughly conditioned by the contingencies of symbolizing practice as anything one might call a sign. What Wittgenstein called logical form, therefore, and regarded as the unalterable structure of reality, the substance of this or any possible world, does not exist. The forms of sameness and difference do not preexist the practice that refers to them; instead, these stand or fall together. What *has* to exist if there is truth in signs or identity and difference in things is the language-game, which is contingent, and nothing else besides.

Later I shall say something about the destruction this wreaks upon the *Tractatus* and its ingenious onto-logic. First, however, I need to elaborate on the argumentation I have introduced; for it is on the basis of these considerations regarding sameness and difference that I propose to answer the first of two questions posed in the Prologue: What is the objection to a correspondence theory of truth?

The Same Is Not the Same

A passage of the *Philosophical Investigations* reads: "Perhaps a logician will think: Same is same—how somebody satisfies himself of the sameness is a question for psychology. (High is high—it belongs to psychology that one sometimes *sees* and sometimes *hears* it)" (*PI*.377). The point at issue is whether being same and different have anything to do with the signs of sameness and difference, which this logician dismisses as secondary. What satisfies somebody that something is the same is "a matter for psychology," that is, something contingent, accidental, external to the sameness of what is same. Same is same—it is a matter of indifference how or even whether sameness is evaluated, measured, determined in practice.

And what is wrong with that? Where *a* and *b* name individuals and *R* some respect of similarity, there is nothing logically inconsistent about assigning the value *T* (for *true*) to sentences:

(1) *a* and *b* are same in respect *R*.
(2) Nothing is (ever) compared in respect *R*.

Logically speaking, these can both be true. Does that not imply that things can *be* same or different regardless of their evaluation (or its practical possibility)? What is wrong with that?

To criticize this onto-logic one might question the self-identity it would take to make a sentence like (1) true to beings that were simply there, being as they are according to themselves. Derrida suggests an argument along these lines. Or one might take an entirely different approach, as Davidson does. Closed sentences (no unbound variables) like "Snow is white" or like (1) and (2) are either satisfied by every sequence of "objects" (that is, names in a metalanguage) or by none.

In the first case, one may use the metalanguage to predicate "is true" of the object-language sentence, in the second case, "is false." But this does not secure the *ontological* differentiation of semantically different truths on the basis of differences in the objects that make them true. The truth of (1) would therefore neither entail nor presuppose beings whose own identity makes it true, and the logical consistency of (1) and (2) does not prove the ontological autonomy of sameness from the contingency of its signs.

Another approach focuses on the co-dependence or compossibility I have noticed between sameness and commensurability. Two things are same or different in respect of color, for instance, just in case both are colored and thus (so far as color goes) like points on one space; two things are same or different in length only when both are extended and thus spatially commensurable, and so on. Certainly things can be the same yet never actually compared, but it is difficult to see how similar things might not so much as admit of comparison, and not for accidental reasons like distance or expense but because they are incommensurable. How could things the same (or *determinately* different) be incommensurable?

So wherever there is what I shall perhaps incautiously call a fact of the matter about sameness or difference, there must also be commensurability, a possibility of comparison. Consider now the circumstances under which things are commensurable although not actually compared. First I should secure the point that commensurability is not a disposition or potency naturally present in things. This is because what "can be" measured or what "admits" of evaluation in a respect of possible difference has no determination save what it derives from mensural practice. It is only there—with the interpretations or applications practice produces, the signs this sets into circulation, and the normativity their currency reproduces—that "correct measurement" has its first determination.

Commensurability, therefore, presupposes historically contingent practice. In this it resembles nothing so much as the exchangeability of commodities. Two unexchanged commodities may differ in price, yet their existence presupposes that some commodities are in fact exchanged, or in other words that there is a historically established circulation of exchange-values. Sameness and difference in price have no determination, no cause or ground, in anything whose existence is indifferent to the history and system of monetary (symbolic) exchanges. Similarly, the commensurability of things uncompared though variously same or different stands or falls with the actual circulation, in a larger practice, of signs credited with determining, that is, evaluating, this value authoritatively, standardly, paradigmatically, correctly.

In Chapter 1, I pointed out how onto-logic discovers the most intimate relationship among being, identity, and difference. If a thing is, it has identity; it is a so-and-so. Although it may happen that there are no other so-and-sos or nothing else the same or different, the ontological possibility of a thing's being at all *is* the ontological possibility of that sameness and difference. Yet in light of the connection between sameness and commensurability, this means that possibilities of being, identity, and difference are themselves *historical* possibilities of practice. Being this or that, same or different, stands or falls with the circumstances of historically contingent practice. Heidegger spoke well, then, when he referred to the mediation which prevails in identity. Identity, sameness, and difference are mediated by everything that mediates their estimation in practice and their circulation as knowledge. Though a ruler may be misapplied, though differences may go unremarked, being same or different has no determination more original than the determin*ability* that first comes with the practice in which there is a circulation of signs of sameness.[6]

The same is not the same then, not if that means similarity is indifferent to these signs or their practice. The conclusion to which this points is that something like "purely physical order" does not exist, or that Nature does not exist, or at least that Nature no more determines what is same and what is different than what is cheap and what is dear. There is no identity and difference among beings "according to themselves" or "by nature," indifferent to the contingent practice that sustains their commensurability. Yet there was a time before human beings. We have solid evidence of things then in existence, of their properties, their similarities and differences. One might therefore wonder how seriously to take my suggestion that all of this presupposes what only came later and might not have come at all.

Consider a sentence about something in the prehistoric past: "*Australopithecus* is shorter than *Homo sapiens.*" As I pointed out in Chapter 1, to say that this is true has the effect of canceling the quotation marks one needs to refer to the sentence, leaving the sentence.[7] To assert its truth has a similar effect, immediately reducing to the assertion that *Australopithecus* is shorter than *Homo sapiens.* The sentence is true (let's say), and the assertion justified. Must one posit something for all of this to be adequate to? Something whose prehistoric identity and existence would be indifferent to the later circumstances of historical discursive practice? To what exigency or intuition would this respond? "It is certainly part of the meaning of the word 'true,'" writes Michael Dummett, "that if a statement is true, there must be something in virtue of which it is true."[8] Why is this certain? How is it known? What *kind* of knowledge is it to know what is certainly part of the meaning of a word? Moreover, as I also pointed out in Chapter 1, after Tarski it is difficult to claim that the very logic of "is true" presupposes or posits this "truth-maker."

Instead of a time prior to practice, consider the counterfactual possibility that it never existed. Would there not still be things variously similar and different anyway? And were culture with its conventions to vanish, wouldn't some natural order persist unperturbed? If the intuitive answer is "Yes!" this is an intuition before which I counsel skepticism rather than credulity. The relationship linking commensurability, contingent practice, and being same or different precludes any determinate "would-be's" about what would be were there nothing of our evolution and history on the earth. These "would-be's" have no autonomous, original, purely natural or physical determination, no more than what would be expensive or cheap were there no markets.

Somebody might object that while the *-ability* in "commensurability" may not indicate a disposition naturally present in commensurable things, this point falls short of my claim that were measures for sameness not extant and actually in use, nothing would be the same or different. Even granting that the sameness of two things, or the identity of one (as of a kind or having some property), demands the commensurability of things in the respect in question, there is room for doubt that whether or not such things exist or are the same or different depends on a contingent practice of evaluation. Of course any measure is conventional, and only by appealing to our actual practice can we specify what those conventions are or what property they evaluate. But the contingent existence of the practice may seem to be enough to establish the proposition that *were* our measure applied, a thing *would be* revealed as of a kind or as similar or different. The counterfactuality of this proposition's antecedent clause covers not only the circumstance that we are not around to apply the measure but also the possibility that we were never there to practice it at all. This suggests that while actual practice may fix the measure, whether or not a thing measures up to it is independent not only of whether anyone measures a thing in that respect but of whether anyone measures anything at all.

No doubt it is true that were a measure of R-ness *correctly* applied under these counterfactual conditions, or were someone to *do the same* as in some actual case where its application is not disputed, then a thing whose R-ness were to be determined would be revealed as determinate in respect of R. The question is whether it makes good sense to speak of correctness or of doing the same under these counterfactual circumstances. *Does* the actual existence of a practice determine what *would be* the result *were* its measure applied under circumstances counterfactually excluding that practice? I think not. Under conditions which by hypothesis exclude the existence of its practice, this correctness and this doing the same have no determination. A subjunctive proposition like *Were the* R-*measure applied, a thing's determination in respect* R *would be revealed* does not have a truth-value for the possible circumstance of the nonexistence of the measure's historical practice. It would be no more true or false under those conditions than would the statement "This is sepia" said of the standard.

Perhaps the rules or conventions of practice seem to fly ahead, as it were, and determine what would result from their application even under counterfactual circumstances which include the historical nonexistence of the practice. This would be like the impression that by meaning an order (for example, "Add 2!") in a certain way, the mind "as it were flew ahead and took all the steps before you physically arrived at this or that one," so that one becomes "inclined to use such expressions as: 'The steps are *really* already taken, even before I take them in writing or orally or in thought'" (*PI*.188). Wittgenstein's remarks concerning the following of a rule have attracted a lot of attention.[9] There is no consensus on their precise meaning or furthest implications, but one point it should be agreed he makes, and makes correctly, is that rules, normatively enforced and reproduced, have no power to "determine" anything except habits, dispositions, leanings— a power that is exhausted in predispositions, presumptions, and unreflective customary reactions.

> What has the expression of a rule—say a signpost—got to do with my action? What sort of connection is there here?—Well, perhaps this one: I have been trained to react to this sign in a particular way, and now I do so react to it.
>
> "But that is only to give a causal connection; to tell how it has come about that we now go by the signpost; not what this going-by-the-sign really consists in." On the contrary; I have further indicated that a person goes by a signpost only insofar as there exists a regular use of sign-posts, a custom. (*PI*.198)

The demands of life and especially of others make this solid enough. But conjure away these circumstances with counterfactual reasoning about what would be were things quite different than they are, and the situation changes. There is no residual determination of what would count as an instance of the practice, or what would have to happen for a rule to be applied in the same way, or for an action to be in accord with its normativity. What result would be reached were a measure applied under conditions which exclude the contingent history of its practice is as indeterminate as what would be expensive or cheap were there no market. The normativity which prevails in practice is incapable of sustaining the counterfactuals upon which the objection I have been considering relies. Nothing determines what would have to be done were a measure applied correctly or in the same way under the counterfactual condition of the nonexistence of its practice, nor does that practice in any way secure the "determination" of what would be were it not to have existed.[10]

My argument is that being same or different and being commensurable stand or fall together, that commensurability does not exist apart from actual practice, and that sameness and difference therefore have no determination and *are not* apart from that contingency. Take away the language-game where similarity first admits of evaluation, and there is no residual natural or purely physical determination of what is or what is the same. Being identical over time, or being similar or different to another, are as thoroughly conditioned by the historical circumstances of practice as anything you might call a sign, or an artifact, or a convention.

Here then is the objection to an account of truth in terms of correspondence. For what is meant by "correspondence"? One may expect to hear something about facts, about how truths correspond to them. The discussion then gets distracted by technicalities about these "facts"—their elements, structure, criteria of identity, and their relation to the vehicles of truth. What gets lost is why it should matter for truths to correspond to something that "is what it is." Why is a corresponding being so essential to truth? Greek onto-logic lives on in the intuition that it is, and that it, and it alone, "determines" whether what we say is true. The metaphor of correspondence owes its aptness to an older image of adequacy, of vicegerent fealty to sovereign being. As It is, so says truth, and never otherwise.

The problem is that how "it is" has no determination of its own apart from what can be said and taken seriously by historically contingent speakers like us. There is no being-in-itself to receive mimetic fealty. The "self-identical beings" it would take to make truths true in the sense of correspondence do not exist. There is nothing to correspond to because there is nothing whose own nature measures the adequacy of speech about it. Identity is history, indifferent to nature, which does not exist.

Sameness and Subjectivity

"To cognize anything a priori is to cognize it from its mere possibility."[11] Not just for Kant but for modern philosophy from Descartes to Husserl, when truth is cognized a priori it is not the presence of physical nature that comes into view, as it did for the Greeks. All that is strictly *given* according to the modern philosophy of truth is the "self-presence" of the *cogito*. This self-evidence proves the a priori possibility of truth. To meditate on *cogito, ergo sum* is to perform for yourself the demonstration that a true-making assimilation of thought (I am) and object (my being) is possible in principle. The question of limits to knowledge then moves to the center of attention, and epistemology becomes the modern *prote philosophia*.

Since early modern times, onto-logic has set down roots, as it were, in subjectivity. So a revisionary interpretation of subjectivity is to be expected from philosophers who deviate from onto-logic or question its guiding assumptions. Davidson speaks of the "the myth of the subjective."[12] For Derrida, "the subject . . . is inscribed in language, is a 'function' of language, becomes a *speaking* subject only . . . by conforming to the general law of *différance*" (M.14–15). Intentionality is as derived and secondary as a piece of writing. A "general law of *différance*," which is to say no general law, does not mean there is no rule or reason to the discourse with which we concoct our subjectivity, but only that what regularity there is escapes the will of the subject it constructs. As Foucault remarks, "it is not that the beautiful totality of the individual is amputated, repressed, altered by our social order; it is rather that the individual is carefully fabricated in it, according to a whole technique of forces and bodies. We are much less Greeks than we believe" (DP.217).

Wittgenstein too is drawn into this problematic. Where epistemology posits an original subjectivity, he discovers the derived and secondary character of mental states, with nothing *to* them apart from originally *inter*subjective language practices. This seems to me the chief point of Wittgenstein's celebrated "private language argument."[13]

The first thing Wittgenstein says to explain what would make a language "private" in the disputed sense is disappointing: "The individual words . . . refer to what can only be known to the person speaking; to his immediate private sensations. So another person cannot understand the language" (PI.243). The idea of something which necessarily just one person can use a sign to refer to is dubious enough. It becomes almost silly when it is added that this private sign with its private referent must be absolutely incomprehensible to others, though yet full of meaning. Why take this seriously? Wittgenstein's next eleven sections raise the obvious objections, but that merely increases the suspicion that this whole "private language argument," about which so much has been written, is superfluous ingenuity.

But then instead of having done with it, Wittgenstein reformulates the question: "Now, what about the language which describes my inner experiences and which only I can understand? *How* do I use words to stand for my sensations?—As we ordinarily do? Then are my words for sensations tied up with my natural expressions of sensation? In that case my language is not a 'private' one. Someone else might understand it as well as I" (*PI.256*). A language would therefore be "private" in the sense Wittgenstein now means to investigate when these regularities are missing. He goes on to make this explicit: "But suppose I did not have any natural expression for the sensation, but only had the sensation? And now I simply associate names with sensations and use these names in descriptions" (*PI.256*).

This provides another view of what is at stake and why in the otherwise seemingly pointless question of "private language." Say that a language is "private" when there is no intersubjectively salient relationship between the signs of this would-be language and the would-be speaker's behavior and environment. The question whether this is possible or impossible provides a focus for investigating claims both about "original" or "intrinsic" intentionality and about the "methodological solipsism" which holds it to be possible to think profitably about cognition without thinking about social practice. Is individual, subjective intentionality (your present thoughts and feelings, for instance) ever really original? That is, have we as subjects some native power to "determine the content" of thoughts, so that the culturally mediated contextual reactions of others to our behavior are external, secondary, accidental to the identity and existence of the occasional mental state?[14]

There is reason to think not. Under the conditions Wittgenstein stipulates as those of "privacy" in the sense he means to question, there would be no intersubjectively salient (interpretable) connection between behavior, environment, and the sounds or marks of would-be signs. This undermines the description of those sounds or marks as language, and of the body that emits them as a subject, as conscious, or intentional. So the conditions that would have to be satisfied for a private code are conditions under which no reference can occur. Conversely, *inter*subjective language practices are more original than subjective intentionality, which is *nothing* apart from the other and the exchange of speech and reply. Intentionality is not "originary," not a power to endow otherwise empty effects with content. Like reference and truth, intentionality is an effect rather than a source of signs.[15]

It would not be wrong to describe this as an argument *contra* Descartes for the resemblance between extension and consciousness. The relation of body (behavior) to mind or subjectivity is like that of a yardstick to the extension it measures. As only an extension can be longer or shorter and only in relation to another extension, so only in relation to other subjects is behavior subjective (yours, mine), and for the same reason. The standard commensurating extensive values applies only to an extension, while the standard for subjective determinations, for differences both of form (thought, sensation, intention) and of content (that *p*, of *q*), applies only to something recognizing and indeed at some point demanding the recognition of other subjects. To apply the standard, one must engage the other in the intersubjectivity of speech and reply. All questions concerning the existence, identity, and difference of mental states (to say nothing of their normality or mental pathology) pass through this intersubjective symbolic exchange, or what Lacan calls the defiles of the signifier.

There is one difference between extension and consciousness. The technique of the yardstick can be described and explained without using predicates of length, but in a typical first-person use of a vocabulary of subjective self-description there is no analogue to a ruler. For example, there is no *how you do it* when you "know your present sensation." This is the mildly anomalous result of a contingency in the language-game. It happens that behavior, above all verbal behavior semantically interpreted in terms of what is said when subjects speak, functions as a privileged means of determining the subjective quality of experience. One cannot say that this *had* to be. Furthermore, if a ruler can shrink, or have its graduations misprinted, or be otherwise discredited for standard determination, the same goes for a subject's privilege to describe present experience without reference to evidence everybody can see. This first-person privilege is highly conditional, circumscribed on all sides by norms of speech and comportment.

Wittgenstein's discussion of solipsism confirms this conclusion against original intentionality. He explains the solipsist's question in the *Blue Book:* "How *can* we believe that the other has pain; what does it mean to believe this? How can the expression of such a supposition makes sense?"[16] The force of these questions depends on a curious piece of reasoning. As similarity or difference in the length of things presupposes their commensurability in respect of extension, so similarity and difference among subjects presuppose the commensurability of their experience. But comparing what I feel with what I fail to feel seems worse than inconvenient. Like mass and motivation, felt and unfelt feelings seem strictly incommensurable. Now, I know that *I* exist; I know that it seems to me now that I am . . . and so on. If there were others out there, they would occasionally be the same as I am subjectively, thinking or feeling as I do. But sameness implies comparability. So if there is no intersubjective commensurability, there can be just one deduction: I am the unique subject of experience.

At one point in the *Philosophical Investigations* Wittgenstein introduces an interlocutor to dispute this conclusion:

> "But if I suppose that someone has a pain, then I am simply supposing that he has the same as I have so often had." (*PI.*350)

This would-be refutation of solipsism depends on the classical principle that being entails self-identity. The implicit argument is that merely because they exist, the solipsist's own experiences are identical to themselves; they have an identity or determination which is their own, their nature, what they are according to themselves. But just this ensures the possible existence of other minds. For if the solipsist's own experience exists, then it is identical to itself, and therefore has an identity which can repeat the same again, regardless of whether this sameness is felt or otherwise verified. Whether such a repetition happens to fall within the field of the solipsist's introspection would be accidental. Thus the very experience the solipsist calls his own guarantees the possible existence of the other's unfelt feelings and the logical significance of a reference to other minds.

In reply to this reasoning Wittgenstein elaborates and, to a point, defends the solipsist's argument. The interlocutor's assumption that the possibility of the other's experience is merely the possibility of something the same as my own yet not felt by me entirely misses the solipsist's strong point: How can two things be same or different *and* incommensurable?

> "But if I suppose that someone has a pain, then I am simply supposing that he has the same as I have so often had."—That gets us no further. It is as if I were to say, "You surely know what '5 o'clock here' means; so you also know what 'It's 5 o'clock on the sun' means. It means simply that it is just the same time there as it is here when it is 5 o'clock."

"The explanation by means of *sameness (Gleichheit)*," he adds, "does not work here."

> For I know well enough that one can call 5 o'clock here and 5 o'clock there "the same time," but what I do not know is in what cases one is to speak of its being the same time here and there.

"In exactly the same way," he continues,

> it is no explanation to say: The supposition that he has a pain is simply the supposition that he has the same as I. For *that* part of the grammar is quite clear to me; that is, that one will say that the stove has the same experience as I, *if* one says: It is in pain and I am in pain. (*PI*.350)

Wittgenstein defends the crux of the solipsist's sophism without solipsism or sophistry. That crux is the incoherence of same-but-incommensurable, which is absurd. This seems to be the point of his curious analogy. The sentence "It's afternoon on the sun" would be true just in case it was spoken when it was afternoon on the sun. That is not impossible; it calls for nothing more than an apposite stipulation. For example, since five o'clock Greenwich Mean Time anywhere on earth is five o'clock in Greenwich, one may stipulate that it shall be five o'clock GMT on the sun under the same condition.[17] Granted, this seems pointless; but the worst that can be said against this stipulation is that it remains unmotivated. If we want it, solar chronometry calls for nothing but the extension of a technique. By the same token, however, the sameness or difference of terrestrial and extraterrestrial places in respect of local time stands or falls with the technique and its extension. Wittgenstein's point in the analogy, therefore, must be that the identity and occasional sameness or difference of mental states are similarly circumscribed by practice. The solipsist is right to doubt the significance of a reference to something strictly incommensurable with "his own" experience, but wrong to think his title to subjectivity comes to him originally or by nature, wrong to overlook the passage through convention and ceremony, wrong to underestimate these vicissitudes as indifferent accidents in relation to what he is by nature.

The notion of a private subject with private mental states is on a par with that of a private commodity with a private price, or money "only I myself" can spend. Like commodities and prices, subjects and subjectivity do not exist apart from the signs of subjectivity in the intersubjective exchange of speech and reply. Take away the language-game, abstract from an intersubjective regard for the body and the signs it emits, ignore history, and bracket social practice, and *what it is like* (subjective similarity and difference) is as indeterminate as the time on the sun.

Aufhebung of Logic

Like a stitch or a fold in Wittgenstein's "album," referring back to earlier themes of understanding language and following rules and looking ahead to discussions of solipsism and private language, *Philosophical Investigations* §242 reads: "If we are to understand one another's language, there must be agreement not only in definitions but also (strange as this may sound) in judgments. This seems to abolish logic *(scheint die Logik aufzuheben),* but does not do so *(hebt sie aber nicht auf).*—It is one thing to describe methods of measurement, and another to obtain and state results of measurement. But, still, what we call 'measuring' is determined by a certain constancy in results of measurement."

In this last part of my look at Wittgenstein I shall consider three questions this passage raises. First, why is understanding another's language a matter of agreement not just in definitions but in judgments? Second, why might this seem strange, even like the *Aufhebung* (cancellation, destruction) of logic? Finally, how may one understand Wittgenstein's analogy to measurement? What reassurance does it offer against the queer feeling that logic has been relieved of something essential?

Gadamer has observed, "In situations in which understanding is disrupted or made difficult the conditions of all understanding emerge with the greatest clarity." Quine's idea of radical translation—a thought experiment in which he reflects on the situation of a field linguist compiling a dictionary and grammar for a language historically discontinuous (hence radically different) from his own—illustrates this. Quine believes this reflection should destroy certain received ideas about meaning by exposing the poverty of the ultimate data for their identification. The ultimate data are speakers' dispositions to assent or dissent from sequences (hypothetical sentences) proffered by the linguist under changing local conditions. These data, Quine argues, must fail to determine a unique translation of those sentences. There will always be multiple translations which satisfy all reasonable constraints yet provide nonequivalent interpretations. Rather than confirming what elusive things meanings are, Quine views this as an argument to show that "beyond what these fumbling procedures can come up with" there is nothing to get right or be true to, no meanings that are "present" and identical to themselves (at least), regardless of what interpretation can make of them.[18]

Thus Quine's thesis of the indeterminacy of translation: "rival systems of analytical hypotheses can conform to all speech dispositions . . . yet dictate . . . utterly disparate translations; not mere paraphrases, but translations each of which would be excluded by the other system of translation." To make this point is not to condemn translation, which "is fine and should go on." The point is to expose an "uncritical notion of meaning," namely, the idea that a "sentence has a meaning . . . and another sentence is its translation if it has the same meaning. This, we see, will not do . . . the old notion of separate and distinct

meanings . . . is better seen as a stumbling block cleared away
. . . What I have challenged is just an ill-conceived notion within traditional semantics, namely, sameness of meaning"—that is, *self*-same-
ness, *self*-identity of meanings. What Quine believes his argument
should "occasion, if grasped, is a change in prevalent attitudes toward
meaning, idea, proposition."

> A conviction persists, often unacknowledged, that our sentences
> express ideas, and express these ideas rather than those, even
> when behavioral criteria can never say which. There is the stub-
> born notion that we can tell intuitively which idea someone's
> sentence expresses, our sentence anyway, even when the intuition
> is irreducible to behavioral criteria. This is why one thinks that
> one's question "What did the native say?" has a right answer
> independent of choices among mutually incompatible manuals of
> translation.[19]

Anyone undertaking radical translation needs some kind of yardstick to go by in determining how to map informants' behavior onto
her or his home language. What can serve this function? Quine writes:
"Our radical translator would put his developing manual of translation continually to use, and go on revising it in the light of his successes
and failures of communication. And wherein do these successes and
failures consist, or how are they to be recognized? Successful negotia-
tion with natives is taken as evidence that the manual is progressing
well. Smooth conversation is further favorable evidence. Reactions of
astonishment or bewilderment on a native's part, or seemingly irrelevant responses, tend to suggest that the manual has gone wrong."[20]

Despite the empirical indeterminacy of translation, there is a kind of
normalizing pressure for an interpretation that maximizes intersubjective agreement. As Davidson remarks, "we damage the intelligibility of
our reading of the utterances of others when our method of reading
puts others into what we take to be broad error. We can make sense of
differences all right, but only against a background of shared belief."[21]
Wittgenstein made this point many times in his later work. At one
place he asks what it would be like to discover a group of people who
never agree in their judgments of color:

One man would say a flower was red which another called blue, and so on.—But what right should we have to call these people's words "red" and "blue" our color words?

"If human beings were not in general agreed about the colors of things, if discord were not exceptional, then our concept of color could not exist." No: our concept would not exist.

Calculating would lose its point if confusion supervened. Just as the use of the words "green" and "blue" would lose its point . . . the proposition that this room is 16 feet long would not become false if rulers and measuring fell into confusion. Its sense, not its truth, is founded on the regular working of measurement.

If people were (suddenly) to stop agreeing with each other in their judgments about tastes—would I still say: At any rate, each one knows what tastes he's having?—Wouldn't it then become clear that this is nonsensical?

Confusion of tastes: I say, "This is sweet," somebody else, "This is sour," and so on. Somebody comes along and says: "You have none of you any idea what you are talking about. You no longer know at all what you once called a taste." What would be the sign of our still knowing?

He answers this question in a variation on the passage with which this part of my discussion began:

We say that in order to understand one another's language people must agree about the meaning of words. But the criterion for this agreement is not just an agreement with respect to definitions, e.g. ostensive definitions—rather, also an agreement in judgments. It is essential for understanding that we agree in a great number of judgments.

"This peaceful agreement," he adds, "is the characteristic circumstance of the use of the word 'same.'"[22]

Here then is an answer to the first of the three questions I posed. If we are to understand one another when we speak, then perhaps we must agree in definitions, but that is nearly a tautology, like "If you are to repeat yourself, you have to say the same thing twice." The question is, how is sameness of definition measured? How is understanding evaluated, differentiated, determined in practice? The answer is that this is determined (to the extent that it is "determined" at all) by constant reference to a stabilizing, normative agreement in particular cases. This is the only yardstick by which to estimate problematic semantic values.

In a development of this thought, Davidson argues that "successful communication proves the existence of a shared, and largely true, view of the world," and that "belief is in its very nature veridical." This is not because Davidson has covertly redefined "true" as "agreed" or "believed." He is far from holding that agreement makes something true: "Agreement, no matter how widespread, does not guarantee truth." But this observation misses the point. "The basic claim is that much community of belief is needed to provide a basis for communication or understanding; the extended claim should then be that objective error can occur only in a setting of largely true belief. Agreement does not make for truth, but much of what is agreed must be true if some of what is agreed is false."[23]

This conclusion must seem too good to be true so long as one believes that where there is truth there has to be a being whose self-identity makes the truth true. Were the existence of truth in language subject to this onto-logic, there could be no reassuring inference to the existence of truth (the real thing) from the mere existence of a regular passing-for-true in practice. Yet this also shows that apart from the onto-logical presuppositions of truth-as-correspondence which I have criticized, there is no impressive philosophical difference between what passes for true and what really is true.

I address some of the difficulties that stand in the way of this claim in the next chapter. Here I shall only point out that differences of truth-value, like any other sort of difference, are subject to practical conditions which evade the dichotomies of logical/empirical, formal/material, or structure/content. Whether an occasional predication is true depends on more than the meaning of the sentence and the fact of the matter. To be true or false, to admit of evaluation in these terms, presupposes a practical context of standards and prescribed regimentation around norms apart from which symbolic values like truth, reference, or meaning do not exist.

This first came into view when considering the possibility of predicating color of a standard sepia. Suppose somebody points to that exemplary object, or picks it up and thrusts it out and says, "This concrete thing which you see, which reflects light to your eyes, which *looks* colored, is sepia." Here is a statement which, so far as logic and grammar go, certainly seems true or false. Yet it is neither. That the statement does not sustain evaluation in terms of true or false would become obvious as soon as one allows that the language of colors might have been misused or used nonstandardly, or that the speaker might have erred or lied. To settle doubts of this kind would take recourse to agreement about what is sepia. But since the subject term of the sentence ("this concrete thing") refers to the standard sepia, and since it is impossible to compare a thing with itself, it is not possible to evaluate the statement in terms of true or false. The statement *cannot possibly* be true or false, yet this depends on nothing but the utterly contingent fact that a certain object has a certain normative status in a local economy of symbolizing practice.

Like the truth-value of the occasional predication, the sameness or difference of what there is depends on everything that is presupposed by the evaluation of sameness in practice. Apart from this practice and the normativity it enforces and reproduces, there exist no two things in any respect the same or different. Certainly this includes doing the same again according to a rule. Wittgenstein writes:

> What, in a complicated surrounding, we call "following a rule" we should certainly not call that if it stood in isolation. Language, I should like to say, relates to a *way* of living *(Lebens w e i s e)*.
>
> In order to describe the phenomenon of language, one must describe a practice, not something that happens once, *no matter of what kind.*
>
> This is a very difficult thing to acknowledge *(sehr schwierige Erkenntnis)*. (RFM.335–336)

Perhaps this is a clue to Wittgenstein's strange expectation that the need for agreement not just in definitions but in judgments will seem strange, difficult, even the *Aufhebung* of logic.

In his use of the word *Logik,* Wittgenstein is closer to Heraclitus and Hegel than to Tarski or Quine. "Logic," he says in the *Tractatus,* "is not a doctrine *(Lehre),* but a mirror-image of the world. Logic is transcendental" (*TLP*.6.13). Logic belongs neither to the objective world nor to language exclusively, but informs and assimilates both, letting beings be what they are and letting language show what is. In the notebooks in which he worked out ideas for the *Tractatus,* Wittgenstein referred to this transcending and assimilating ordering as *das Logische.* He writes, "what is logical in what is signified *(das Logische des Bezeichneten)* should be completely determined just by what is logical in the sign and the method of symbolizing *(das Logische des Zeichens und der Bezeichnungsweise).* One might say: sign and method of symbolizing together must be logically identical with what is signified" (*NB*.19). Here is a singular sameness. The identity of symbol and situation is not of the $A = A$ sort, nor is it sameness in a respect which might be measured or evaluated. There being a logical possibility of truth-value and there being the facts in logical space are the same *being,* the same *that it is* or *happening to be*—but not the same entity, not entities at all. Wittgenstein was entirely capable of this distinction. "My *whole* task consists in explaining the nature of the proposition. That is to say, in giving the nature of all facts, whose picture the proposition *is.* In giving the nature of all being *(Sein).* (And here being does not mean existing [*existieren*]—in that case it would be nonsensical)" (*NB*.39).

"Logic must take care of itself." That is how Wittgenstein tried to think of its transcending priority, first in a notebook entry, 22 August 1914: "Logic must take care of itself. If syntactical rules for functions can be set up *at all,* then the whole theory of things, properties, etc., is superfluous . . . Once more: logic must take care of itself. A *possible* sign must also be capable of signifying." The next entry, the next week: "It must in a certain sense be impossible for us to go wrong in logic. This is already partly expressed by saying: Logic must take care of itself. This is an extremely profound and important insight" (NB.2). Then in the *Tractatus:* "Logic must take care of itself. If a sign is possible, then it is also capable of signifying . . . In a certain sense, we cannot make mistakes in logic" (TLP.5.473).

"Logic must take care of itself" says "What seems logical is logical." There is no distinction between *thinking* and *logical* (true-or-false) thinking, hence no "purely logical" mistakes. "We can think nothing unlogical *(nichts Unlogisches),* since, if we could, we would have to think unlogically" (TLP.3.03). If that is impossible it must be because to think is to operate logically with signs, combining them in a logical way, that is, in a way which models or mimics a situation in the logical space of the world. A thought *(Gedanke)* is the sign thus constructed; Wittgenstein defines a thought as "a propositional sign, applied and thought out" (TLP.3.5).[24] To apply or think-out signs is to project a logical combination of them toward the world as a model of what there is. "We use the perceptible sign of a proposition (spoken or written, etc.) as a projection of a possible situation. The method of projection is to think the proposition's sense *(Denken des Satz-Sinnes)* . . . And a proposition is a propositional sign in its projective relation to the world" (TLP.3.11–3.12). Thus "projected" or "thought-out," a logical configuration of signs "*shows* how things stand *if* it is true. And it *says that* they do so stand" (TLP.4.022).

This would be impossible apart from the onto-logic Wittgenstein unconsciously repeats, binding him to the oldest tradition in Western work on truth. A *syntactic* possibility of combining simple signs into a determinately true-or-false complex is the same as the *ontological* possibility of the situation which, if actual, makes the complex symbol true. A proposition shows what can be because the construction of propositional signs (thinking) is governed by the same ordering that informs what there is to get right or be true to, the *logos* that lets beings be what they are. "Propositions can present *(darstellen)* the whole of reality, but they cannot present what they must have in common with reality in order to be able to present it—logical form . . . Propositions *show* the logical form of reality . . . What *can* be shown *cannot* be said" (TLP.4.12–4.1212). A sameness that cannot be said but only shown is one absolutely unconditioned by anything contingent; for were it so conditioned, then it might not be, so it would be significant (and possible) to say that it is. Logic *(das Logische)*—the transcending ordering common to any language, any thinking, any fact or reality—looks as if it *had* to exist *if* truth is a reproductive, assimilating imitation of being.

"If sign and thing signified were *not* identical in respect of their total logical contents," Wittgenstein wrote in his notebook, "then there would have to be something still more fundamental than logic" (*NB*.4). It could not take care of itself. Yet that is exactly the implication of his later thinking. There is indeed something more fundamental than logic, yet it is something utterly contingent, something that does not *have to exist:* that "certain constancy" in the results of measurement he referred to in the passage with which this part of my discussion began. This constancy, the routine but still altogether contingent accommodation of speech to norms of intersubjective symbolizing practice, is all that *has to exist* if there is truth in signs or identity and difference in things.

This conclusion seems to abolish logic, yet Wittgenstein draws back from that implication. As if to explain why, he says, "It is one thing to describe methods of measurement, and another to obtain and state results of measurement. But, still, what we call 'measuring' is determined by a certain constancy in results of measurement." What we call measuring is the evaluation of things in dimensions of sameness and difference. To say this is determined by a certain constancy in results implies that identity has no more fixity than it receives from a normatively enforced predictability in the use of the signs.

The distinction between what "logically must" be true and what may or may not be is not abolished or destroyed, but it does have to be revised in a manner antithetical to the onto-logic of the *Tractatus*. The difference between empirical and logical determination becomes one between the use of a vocabulary or a move in a language-game (making a measurement, report, description, and so on), and the normativity which reigns in the practice. Someone computing the function $f(n) = n + 1$, for instance, "logically must" step from 4 to 5. That is not an empirical prediction of what calculators will do; rather, it belongs to what Wittgenstein called the description of methods of measurement (for instance, counting), in contrast to a use of language that states or records the result of a measurement. "If it is not supposed to be an empirical proposition that the rule leads from 4 to 5, then *this,* the result, must be taken as the criterion for one's having gone by the rule."

> Thus the truth of the proposition that 4 + 1 makes 5 is, so to speak, *overdetermined.* Overdetermined by this, that the result of the operation is defined to be the criterion that this operation has been carried out. The proposition rests on one too many feet to be an empirical proposition. It will be used as a determination of the concept "applying the operation + 1 to 4." For we now have a new way of judging whether someone has followed the rule. Hence 4 + 1 = 5 is now itself a rule, by which we judge proceedings. This rule is the result of a proceeding that we assume as *decisive (maßgebend)* for the judgement of other proceedings. (*RFM*.319–320)

"It is," he says, "as if we had hardened the empirical proposition into a rule. And now we have, not an hypothesis that gets tested by experience, but a paradigm with which experience is compared and judged. And so a new kind of judgement" (*RFM*.324). A "logical" judgment; adding 1 to 4 "must" give 5. The difference between this and what Wittgenstein calls an empirical proposition consists entirely in their application. The logical proposition is not put to the same use, not subjected to the same tests or expectations, as an empirical proposition. This implies, first, that the "must" of that so-called logical proposition has no determination independent of the normativity enforced and reproduced in symbolizing practice; second, there is nothing to prevent the modification or even revolution of such normativity— nothing, that is, beyond the interests or practice it sustains. There is no reason to suppose Wittgenstein would not say of the distinction between logical and empirical what Quine says of that between analytic and synthetic: "this difference is only one of degree, and . . . turns upon our vaguely pragmatic inclination to adjust one strand of the fabric [of knowledge] . . . rather than another in accommodating some particular recalcitrant experience." Indeed, Wittgenstein in one place says, "Sentences are often used on the borderline between logic and the empirical, so that their meaning changes back and forth and they count now as expressions of norms, now as expressions of experience"; and elsewhere, "the same proposition may be treated at one time as something to test by experience, at another as a rule of testing." So logic is not abolished, perhaps, but neither can it take care of itself. It is a historical precipitate and not a transcendental condition of symbolizing practices.[25]

Logic may not be abolished, but the onto-logic of the *Tractatus* is, precisely, *aufgehoben.* It is relieved of its reason. Its ontic postulates (objects, situations) and syntactic inventions (simple signs, complete analysis) lose their rationale, as does the logical form that would transcend their difference to let thoughts be thought and beings be. These were all supposed to be indispensable to the possibility of truth-value in signs. Wittgenstein took up this problem in a manner that can only be described as naive. His problem was to figure out what *has* to exist given something he merely assumed was given, namely, the onto-logic that subordinates truth in speech to beings whose identity and existence are unconditionally independent of contingent symbolizing practice. "What does the logical identity of sign and thing signified really consist in? This question is *(once again)* a main aspect of the whole philosophical problem" (*NB*.3). This was obvious, yet difficult. The need for a solution justified the theoretical postulate of a transcendental "logical" structure common to language and world. On the other hand, the discovery that the problem is factitious means it is less the details, more the whole onto-logical problematic from which they derived what theoretical justification they had, that the later work destroys. Back to the rough ground!

8 *Foucault, or Truth in Politics*

> If someone wanted to be a philosopher but didn't ask himself the question "What is knowledge?" or "What is truth?" in what sense could one say he was a philosopher? And for all that I may like to say that I am not a philosopher, nonetheless if my concern is with truth, then I am still a philosopher.
>
> Foucault, "Questions on Geography"

I have argued that the occasional truth and the identity or existence of beings stand or fall with the practice in which truth-values circulate and difference first acquires determinability. Apart from this, there exist no two things in any respect similar or different. Order is nowhere original. Nature does not exist.

This conclusion may seem to abolish truth, but it does not do so. It is one thing to deny a prior and autonomous order of self-identical beings to make truths true. It is something else to deny, absurdly, that nothing passes for true. And even though what passes for true is conditioned by nothing but the historically contingent normativity that prevails in practice, there is no impressive difference between what passes for true and the truth itself.

I shall return to this point later. For now, it is enough that the more indifferent truth's existence to anything that "is what it is" (by its own or another's nature), the less one should expect it to be a superior good whose value surpasses the differences that divide us. With this I return to Nietzsche's question concerning truth's value. I set this question at the head of my look at the work on truth in Foucault, who himself refers to it when, concluding a discussion entitled "Truth and Power," he writes: "The political question, to sum up, is not error, illusion, alienated consciousness, or ideology; it is truth itself. Hence the importance of Nietzsche" (*PK*.133).

This remark is directed against the assumption that it requires something external or accidental to bring truth into the play of political differences of power—as if one may speak of a politics of truth only where "truth" has slipped silently into quotation marks, to become a mere passing-for-true which is really false. Earlier in the same discussion, Foucault says: "The important thing is that truth isn't outside power, or lacking in power: contrary to a myth whose history and functions would repay further study, truth isn't the reward of free spirits, the child of protracted solitude, nor the privilege of those who have succeeded in liberating themselves. Truth is a thing of this world: it is produced only by virtue of multiple forms of constraint. And it induces regular effects of power" (*PK*.131).

Hence the importance of Nietzsche? To an interlocutor Foucault remarks, "My relation to Nietzsche, or what I owe Nietzsche, derives mostly from the texts of around 1880, where the question of truth, the history of truth, and the will to truth were central to his work" (*PPC*.32).[1] Certainly there is more to Nietzsche than this; for instance, there is everything that has to do with "will to power." But Foucault also observes "a perceptible displacement in Nietzsche's texts between those which are broadly preoccupied with the question of will to knowledge and those which are preoccupied with will to power" (*PPC*.33). This is an acute observation and a clue to the difference between these two philosophers. It is fitting that Foucault should associate Nietzsche with a number of critical questions concerning truth's claim to superior value. An interlocutor asks, "Doesn't science produce 'truths' to which we submit?"

> Of course. Indeed, truth is no doubt a form of power. And in saying that, I am only taking up one of the fundamental problems of Western philosophy when it poses these questions: Why, in fact, are we attached to the truth? Why the truth rather than lies? Why the truth rather than myth? Why the truth rather than illusion? And I think that, instead of trying to find out what

truth, as opposed to error, is, it might be more interesting to take up the problem posed by Nietzsche: how is it that, in our societies, "the truth" has been given this value, thus placing us absolutely under its thrall? (*PPC*.107)

These are indeed fundamental questions for the philosophy of truth, though they are not traditional ones. They do not appear prior to Nietzsche. It is this line of inquiry, more than any answer, that is his strong contribution to the philosophy of truth. To follow up on Nietzsche's question is not to repeat some dogma about will to power. It is to take up the question of truth's value, of its relation to practice and politics, where Nietzsche left it: "one of the fundamental problems of Western philosophy." But where Nietzsche forsakes the *askesis* of truth for the music of Dionysus, Foucault becomes austerely nominalistic. "One needs to be nominalistic, no doubt: power is not an institution, and not a structure; neither is it a certain strength we are endowed with; it is the name one attributes to a complex strategic relationship in a particular society" (*HS*.93). From this perspective, Nietzsche seems almost laughably to misunderstand what concretely there is to mean by the words "exercise of power" or "relationship of power." To speak of power apart from a dense texture of historically conditioned social relationships is a miserable abstraction.

What is at stake is not Nietzsche's influence or Foucault's originality. It is a question of how to understand the power whose exercise makes actions and relationships political. For this Nietzsche is of limited use. His work is useful for the new questions it raises more than for any answers it may suggest, and not at all for "the will to power," an idea which Foucault, for one, has the good sense to ignore.[2]

Political Government: Theory and Practice

Since medieval times, Western thinkers have represented political power on a juridical model: The act of power is to limit freedom (individual or corporate) by imposing a will, issuing a command, laying down the law, and exacting obedience. Modern politics would eventually appear to coincide with state action, while "political" philosophy becomes preoccupied with problems of sovereignty, framing its questions in terms of rights, obligations, procedures, and juridical persons. This theoretical architecture is the invention of medieval political thought, which was dominated by the question of sovereignty. Foucault claims that for all the difference in Western societies since then, "the representation of power has remained under the spell of monarchy. In political thought and analysis we still have not cut off the head of the king. Hence the importance that the theory of power gives to the problem of right and violence, law and illegality, freedom and will, and especially the state and sovereignty" (HS.88–89).[3]

His objection to this approach is practical, based on a historical analysis of contemporary practice. In his view, "we have been engaged for centuries in a type of society in which the juridical is increasingly incapable of coding power, of serving as its system of representation." We persist in a juridical representation of power at the price of a growing discrepancy between what thought can identify as political and a widening control of conduct by historically new instruments and relationships of power. These have altered the field of power relations, of government or the political control of conduct, in a way that undermines "a certain image of power-law, of power-sovereignty, which was traced out by the theoreticians of right and the monarchic institution." For "while many of its forms have persisted to the present, it has gradually been penetrated by quite new mechanisms of power that are probably irreducible to the representation of law" (HS.89–90).

What are these new mechanisms? Western societies have experienced a proliferation of new instruments and social relationships that work to individuate both persons and entire populations and make them objects of technical control: for instance, the technologies of economic forecasting and the assessment of risk, of psychiatry and forensic medicine, of advertising and opinion research. Foucault calls these configurations of knowledge and power "disciplines," and he has shown how since the late eighteenth century they have penetrated and profoundly reorganized Western justice, health, education, industry, warfare, and families. As a result, the political government of conduct now includes forms of control which make no threats and do not presume the right to legislate. Foucault remarks: "Our historical gradient carries us further and further away from a reign of law . . . I do not mean to say that the law fades into the background or that the institutions of justice tend to disappear," he explains; "but rather that the law operates more and more as a norm, and that the judicial institution is increasingly incorporated into a continuum of apparatuses (medical, administrative, and so on) whose functions are for the most part regulatory" (*HS*.144). In contrast to premodern sovereignty, where the power of the Prince would "display itself in its murderous splendor," modern disciplinary knowledge-power prefers "to qualify, measure, appraise, and hierarchize." It does not ostentatiously "draw the line that separates the enemies of the sovereign from his obedient subjects"; instead, it quietly "effects distributions around the norm" (*HS*.144).[4]

One result of this historical shift in the techniques and rationale of control is to establish a higher threshold of tolerance to intervention against anything that can be represented as abnormal in a constantly expanding range of conduct, experience, and organic functioning. Another result is the construction of what Foucault calls a disciplinary continuum: Transgressions of law and social danger are assimilated to and made continuous with deviations from a technically established norm. Spectacular and inhumane practices persisting well into the eighteenth century once made juridical punishment an extraordinary departure from everyday experience. Punishment today, however, even in the intense and compact form of the penitentiary, is continuous with disciplinary or normalizing interventions that form a routine part of everybody's experience. At the same time, crimes today are less actions to be punished according to the law than signals or symptoms of dangerous abnormalities in the social body. The objects of judicial attention are less the actions of agents in violation of law than abnormal individuals more or less dangerous. Legal punishment does not exact the price of illegality but tries to regulate a dangerous subpopulation. Foucault's analyses in *Discipline and Punish* show how close these developments bring juridical punishment to therapeutics, pedagogics, and public health. Abnormal conduct is assimilated to social danger, while, like more and more forms of governmental intervention, legal punishment becomes continuous with regulatory and therapeutic responses to a departure from the norm.

A further unintended effect is the appearance of historically new positions of power from which emanate judgments that do not claim to be sovereign but only true. Without making threats or presuming to legislate, disciplinary expertise does nonetheless contribute to the political government of conduct, inducing and sustaining complex, interconnected patterns of uncoerced submission to what might be called "the government of truth." By this I mean the power over conduct which Western societies have long extended to those authorized to speak from a position of knowledge and in the name of truth; but this is a power we experience today above all as the truth of norms and chances, the expert's truth concerning what is average or deviant, safe or dangerous, same or different. A massive discourse of disciplinary expertise contributes to the government of conduct as never before, yet not by contract, conquest, or divine right.

Marx was no doubt right to think that the circumstances under which we labor and produce surplus-values condition our consciousness. But the same should be said of the circumstances under which we acquire information, disseminate knowledge, and submit our conduct to what passes for true, probable, normal, and so on. Knowledge and truth are increasingly professionalized, commodified, and to an unprecedented degree made to enter into the control of belief, desire, and action.

For example, one sees this process at work in education, in what is taught, by whom, to whom and in how the whole experience is organized, teachers are trained and licensed, and schools administered. There is practically no man or woman in a modern society whose behavior and expectations are not shaped by this experience, the general conditions of which are determined by the diverse lines of disciplinary expertise which intersect at the public school.

In labor, large numbers of people now work at jobs which in one way or another are part of the production and use of knowledge for the government of conduct: in opinion research, advertising, and what calls itself "the media"; in medicine and everything associated with the health industry; in information services, data processing, and symbolic analysis.[5]

In the administration of justice, numerous complex relations between expertise and knowledge in psychology, medicine, psychiatry, criminology, and penology routinely and decisively enter into the disposition of those who come into the system of courts, police, and prisons.

In the postliterate audience for electronic media, there is a complex interaction among all sorts of expertise and knowledge, from the technology of satellite transmission to advertising, as well as the information, and the truth, we still expect from electronic journalism.

In global technoscience, even the most rigorously experimental practice contributes to the political control of behavior, by modifying what Joseph Rouse calls "the practical configuration within which our actions make sense, both to ourselves and to one another." This occurs most directly through the sciences' effects "upon the kinds of equipment available to us, the skills and procedures required to use that equipment, the related tasks and equipment that use imposes upon us, and the social roles available to us in performing these tasks." Through this, technoscience reconfigures "the *style* and interconnectedness of what we do," and the effect is precisely one of government.[6]

These are a few examples of how the government of conduct happens differently than it did before the age of scientific and democratic revolution. It is organized at sites neither strictly juridical nor strictly economic (hospitals, schools, laboratories, bureaucracies), and works by means more subtle than commands backed up by threats, lies, or ideological misrepresentations. There has to be a place for the productive work of advertising and media, the therapist and psychiatrist, the statistician, geneticist, pharmacologist, and forensic chemist. Here knowledge (of norms, averages, chances) and the technology which both produces and applies this knowledge reveal their capacity for political effects of government. Yet because they claim no sovereign legislative right but only the authority of knowledge and truth, this entire field of politically sensitive control slips through the interstices of a juridical, top-down analytic of power. The tactics, targets, instruments, and even the rationality of political control have changed. Foucault's revisionary interpretation of power is a response to this.

In a conversation shortly before his death in 1984, Foucault remarks, "I don't believe there can be a society without relations of power, if you understand them as means by which individuals try to conduct, to determine the behavior of others" (*PF*.18). Elsewhere he elaborates:

> In effect, what defines a relationship of power is that it is a mode of action that does not act directly or immediately upon others. Instead, it acts upon their actions: an action upon an action, on existing actions or on those which may arise in the present or the future . . . The exercise of power . . . is a total structure of actions brought to bear upon possible actions; it incites, it induces, it seduces, it makes easier or more difficult; in the extreme it constrains or forbids absolutely; it is nevertheless always a way of acting upon an acting subject or acting subjects by virtue of their acting or being capable of action. A set of actions upon other actions. (*SP*.220)

On this view, as Foucault says, "the exercise of power consists in guiding the possibilities of conduct and putting in order the possible outcomes." Viewed in this way, "power is less a confrontation between two adversaries or the linking of one to the other than a question of *government*." This idea of government is key to Foucault's later work, and his explanation deserves to be cited in full:

> This word must be allowed the very broad meaning which it had in the sixteenth century. "Government" did not refer only to political structures or the management of states; rather it designated the way in which the conduct of individuals or states might be directed: the government of children, of souls, of communities, of families, of the sick. It did not cover only the legitimately constituted forms of political or economic subjection, but also modes of action, more or less considered and calculated, which were designed to act upon the possibilities of action of other people. To govern, in this sense, is to structure the possible field of ac-

tions of others. The relationship proper to power would not therefore be sought on the side of violence or of struggle, nor on that of voluntary linking (all of which can, at best, be the instruments of power), but rather in the area of the singular mode of action, neither warlike nor juridical, which is government. (*SP*.221)

On this interpretation of government, the power that makes actions and relationships "political" is the power to modify the way individuals symbolize and interpret what they understand as their options or occasions for choice: liberties to be anticipated, repudiated, exercised, or denied. A "power relationship" is an asymmetry by virtue of which one subject is at liberty to act upon the significant space of possibilities in which another interpretively situates her or his future, thereby to a variable degree governing the latter's conduct. A "power structure" is any more or less solid complex of these asymmetrical relationships, producing a regular and reliable control of conduct over identifiable groups of people.

Understood in this way, "political" power has no original or essential relationship to the institutions of the modern state. Political power is exercised whenever one person acts with a view to the government of another or others, and this is not always or even usually the work of agents of the state. Nor can the acts of political government be accommodated by an exclusive alternative between coercion and consent. Nor are commands backed up by threats of violence especially exemplary of "political" power. Power can be violent, of course, or coercive, or repressive. But this is not the truth of power, not its essence or privileged instance. "In general terms, interdiction, the refusal, the prohibition, far from being essential forms of power, are only its limits, power in its frustrated or extreme forms. The relations of power are above all productive" (*PPC*.118). Foucault recommends that we therefore "cease once and for all to describe the effects of power in negative terms: it excludes, it represses, it censors, it abstracts, it masks, it conceals. In fact, power produces; it produces reality; it produces domains of objects and rituals of truth" (*DP*.194).

Passing for True

Before I pick up the thread of Foucault's work, I shall say something further about the idea of "passing for true." For this purpose I want to introduce a brief discussion of Davidson.

Nobody would believe in alternative conceptual schemes or flirt with conceptual relativity who did not distinguish these schemes from the content they supposedly organize. Theorists differ on what more precisely this content is. Is it nature or reality itself, or is it only *our* nature or consciousness or experience? One of Davidson's arguments against the very idea of a conceptual scheme relies on the principle that organization presupposes plurality. "We cannot attach a clear meaning to the notion of organizing a single object (the world, nature, etc.) unless that object is understood to contain or consist in other objects."[7] If one can organize only what is already understood to comprise a plurality, then a scheme of organization cannot be what first gives rise to our idea of what more particularly there is, nor is this particularity relative to a conceptual scheme.

An alternative account might say that a conceptual scheme does not organize an otherwise unorganized "reality," but helps us cope with stimuli already ordered by (our) nature as noxious, neutral, or nice. A conceptual scheme fits what we feel to an intellectual construction that links stimuli, making experience predictable. From this point of view, which is Quine's, "the totality of our so-called knowledge or beliefs, from the most casual matters of geography and history to the profoundest laws of atomic physics or even of pure mathematics and logic, is a man-made fabric which impinges on experience only along the edges," and we warp our "scientific heritage to fit . . . continuing sensory promptings."[8]

Davidson includes Quine among Whorf, Feyerabend, and Kuhn as proponents of the "third dogma of empiricism," the dogma of scheme and content. Note, however, that Quine did not mention truth in the passage I just cited, the *locus classicus* for his holism. He speaks of "our so-called knowledge or beliefs," of its links (mostly indirect and derivative) to sensory promptings, but he does not say that this relation is what makes our so-called knowledge true. Despite this Davidson claims, "the point is that for a theory to fit or face up to the totality of possible sensory evidence is for that theory to be true." He then argues that the difference between truth and falsity is not "made" by the presence or absence of anything, not even the totality of possible sensory evidence. "Nothing . . . no *thing*, makes sentences and theories true: not experience, not surface irritations, not the world, can make a sentence true . . . The sentence 'My skin is warm' is true if and only if my skin is warm. Here there is no reference to a fact, a world, an experience, or a piece of evidence."[9]

As I mentioned in Chapter 1, on a Tarskian approach to truth sentences are or are not satisfied, but they do not correspond, either singly or *en masse,* to anything whose being as it is makes them true. The conclusion Davidson draws, that nothing makes truths true, is an important one and coheres well with my antiontologic. The only problem (for Davidson) is that Quine accepts it too. In reply to Davidson, Quine says that while the evidence for a sentence or theory lies in the stimulation of our sensory surfaces, stimuli do not make truths true. Nothing does. "Truth is immanent," he says, meaning always "true-in-language-L," which Quine understands à la Tarski to mean "satisfied." As I pointed out, the Tarskian idea of satisfaction has nothing in common with the traditional conception of truth as a rightness of fit, positing no extra-linguistic entities to "make truths true" in the sense of corresponding differentially to each true sentence. "Truth is immanent, and there is no higher . . . The proper role of experience or surface irritation is as a basis not for truth but for warranted belief."[10]

So Davidson was wrong to saddle Quine with an "empiricist" ontology of truth-makers. Yet Quine does insist on an important relationship between the sentences of science and something that is not a sentence but empirical evidence for one (or lots). He says, "If empiricism is construed as a theory of truth, then what Davidson imputes to it as a third dogma is rightly imputed and rightly renounced. Empiricism as a theory of truth thereupon goes by the board, and good riddance. As a theory of evidence, however, empiricism remains with us . . . The third purported dogma, understood now in relation not to truth but to warranted belief, remains intact . . . It is what makes scientific method partly empirical rather than solely a quest for internal coherence."[11]

Properly scientific discourse is more and better than a coherent body of sentences. Science has a touchstone in something that is not just more sentences or beliefs, something natural, physical, antecedent to language, yet possessing the power to endow some of its sentences with the evidence of the senses. In *Pursuit of Truth,* Quine says, "my interest is epistemological, however naturalized. I am interested in the flow of evidence from the triggering of the senses to the pronouncements of science." Hence his privileged "observation sentences." Situated at the interface of symbol and sense, they are "directly and firmly associated with our stimulations," making "the link between language, scientific or not, and the real world that language is all about."[12]

Against this, Davidson has advanced a better argument, paradoxically reminiscent of Berkeley and Hume (canonical Empiricists), based on the principle that "nothing can count as a reason for holding a belief except another belief." In a variation on Berkeley's refutation of material substance, Davidson argues that a sensation "cannot serve as evidence unless it causes a belief. But how does one know that the belief was caused by a sensation? Only further beliefs can help." In a variation on Hume's argument against the idea that perceptions "represent" external beings, Davidson claims that experiment and observation bear no fruit except when they cause us "to add to, cling to, or abandon our beliefs. This causal relation cannot be a relation of *confirmation or disconfirmation,* since the cause is not a proposition or belief, but just an event in the world or in our sensory apparatus. Nor can such events be considered in themselves to be evidence, unless, of course, they cause us to believe something. And then it is the belief that is properly called the evidence, not the event." Not only is there no relation between a sentence or theory and the beings whose being would make it true; there is no "source of justification outside of other sentences held true." And not only is it "not clear that there is anything distinctive left to call empiricism"; there is an ignominious end to epistemology, naturalized or otherwise.[13]

Davidson's second argument succeeds in undermining Quine's distinction between observation sentences and the rest. Consider two remarks from Quine's reply to Davidson's first argument:

> Our typical sentences are about bodies and substances, assumed or known in varying degrees, out in the world. Typically they are not about sense data or experiences or, certainly, surface irritations. But *some of them are elicited by surface irritations,* and others are related to surface irritations in less direct and more tenuous ways.

> The fabric celebrated in my old metaphor is with us still. As before, it is a fabric of sentences accepted in science as true, however provisionally. The ones at the edges are occasion sentences. Moreover, they are occasion sentences of a special sort, namely, ones whose *acceptance as true on any given occasion is apt to be prompted by the firing of associated sets or patterns of receptors* on that occasion.[14]

These are "observation sentences," directly "elicited" by surface irritations. All other sentences have a less direct link to this ultimate, natural, purely physical source of evidence. But while sensory stimuli might cause me to do something you interpret as the utterance of a sentence, that or any cause is not a reason to believe my sentence is true, not a reason for you and not for me either. This is "the difficulty of transmuting a cause into a reason" which plagues even Quine's naturalized epistemology.[15] If there is a reason to believe something, the reason is another belief, not the "presence" of a thing (for example, the stimulation of an exterocepter) to which one sentence would be more adequate than another. Against Quine, then, Davidson's second argument implies that there is *no* interesting difference between science and a quest solely for internal coherence.

Rather than go into this further, consider instead one implication of the principle that nothing makes truths true. In a well-known passage, Wittgenstein writes: "We want . . . to quote the law of excluded middle and say: 'Either such an image is in his mind, or it is not; there is no third possibility!'—We encounter this queer argument also in other regions of philosophy. 'In the decimal expansion of π either the group 7777 occurs, or it does not—there is no third possibility.' That is to say: 'God sees—but we don't know.' But what does that mean?" (*PI.352*).

One tack some "antirealist" philosophers take is to say, heroically, that since the sentence:

(1) The sequence 7777 occurs in the expansion of π

is unproved, and so too its denial, then even though the logical product of these two sentences together has the classical form of Excluded Middle *(p or not-p)*—a supposed necessary truth of logic—sentence (1) lacks truth-value. Pending proof or disproof of the sevens, it is neither true nor false.

I favor a less heroic line. Let us agree that the sentence:

(2) Either the sequence 7777 occurs in the expansion of π, or it does not

is a true one. It is reasonable for practically anyone to agree that this sentence is true; for practically anyone can see that it is an instance of the logical form *p or not-p*, and practically anybody can agree that practically any instance of this is probably true. If you like, you can call it a "necessary" truth, although with Quine I doubt that there is anything useful to be said about the difference between necessary and contingent truth.[16]

The problem that divides realists and antirealists on the question of the four sevens depends entirely on the onto-logical assumption that if sentence (2) *is* true, there has to be something whose being *makes* it true, by making one disjunct true. If this onto-logic is suspended, however, the problem disappears. Sentence (2) is true, but it is not "determined" or "made" to be true by the being of any being whatsoever. To object, "But one disjunct or the other *must* be true!" is merely to repeat what is agreed: The sentence "Either 7777 occurs in π, or not" is no doubt a true one. But it is a further step to the existence of an entity whose being makes it true by making one disjunct true. It is not mere logic but the historical onto-logic of the metaphysical tradition that inspires this move from propositions to being via the vicegerent nature of truth.

It is finally in this context that I return to the idea of "passing for true." In the Prologue I said that a statement passes for true when it either formally sustains evaluation for truth or in any other way penetrates somebody's practical reasoning. The difference between this and a bare state of belief or holding-true is that passing for true is *dialogical* and therefore irreducibly intersubjective.[17] Passing for true is a dialogical interaction among speakers; there is an exchange, a passing of statements from one to another or others. Before there can be any question of monological holding-true, there has to be an intersubjective exchange: I take somebody's words seriously. They pass (by me) for true, penetrating my practical reasoning and contributing however slightly to the government of my conduct.

Davidson introduced the concept of what he calls *the occasions of truth*: "Truth is not a property of sentences; it is a relation between sentences, speakers, and dates. To view it thus is . . . to relate language to the occasions of truth."[18] Although he thinks of this in inadequate, monological terms, that does not deprive the idea of all interest. We may be sure of two things about the occasions of truth. First, they are mostly moments when one speaker successfully solicits the belief of another or others. The occasional truth is a motivated moment of social life, when somebody says something that not only solicits another's belief but is typically believed, thus passing for the truth in their dialogical exchange.

Second, much of what in this way passes for true really is true, the very truth itself. Let me not be misunderstood. Certainly *Sentence "S" is true* and *"S" passes for true* are logically independent propositions; the terms *is true* and *passes for true* are not interchangeable *salva veritate;* G. E. Moore's open question (Passing, but true?) remains open in any given case. The point, however, is that discrepancy cannot prevail in the relationship between opinion, or what passes for true, and reality, or being, or the very truth itself.

At least this much should be granted; namely, that while there is a logical difference of predicates between "passing" and "true," as far as anybody's practice or practical reasoning is concerned, there is no difference. Yet even this may seem wrong. Suppose I am innocent of crime, but it is passing for true among judge and jury that I am guilty. Surely it makes a difference to *my* practice that there is a difference between passing for true and really being true! Not really. It is not important to me that I *truly* am innocent, but only that I am innocent. The innocence is what matters, not the truth.

Wittgenstein made the point that although rules sometimes fail to be followed, this does not mean that what actually happens is simply indifferent to what ought to happen if rules are followed (*PI.*345). Similarly, while there is a notional difference between being true and passing, so that, for example, one can always say of what passes that it might be false, this does not mean that what passes for true might be mostly false. Just as not everything that circulates as currency in an economy of money is legal tender, so not everything authorities certify or everything a speaker may make pass for true need be true. But after one has considered everything that contributes to a statement's capacity to pass for true in a given context (the authorities and evidence which support it, and the presuppositions of those who solicit or otherwise receive it as the truth), there is nothing further to adduce which would explain, not the historical fact that that statement passed for true on that occasion, but the metaphysical fact that it really is true. The fact is factitious, its intuition an artifact. Where there is the occasional truth, it is not *made* to be true: it is made to pass. This is not the transcendental constitution of truth but a dialogical exchange among speakers. Sometimes this is aided by formal evaluation, when experts apply some technique of standard determination. Sometimes a seductive source suffices. And while what passes for true today may not tomorrow, this would be so only in light of what then passes for true. There is nothing more to the "being true" of the occasional truth than this currency, this dialogical passing for true. This is all the truth there is, the only truth to concern us, whether we are philosophers, or citizens, or subjects who want the truth.

The Political Economy of Truth

Occasions of truth are typically occasions of passing for true, and vice versa. Apart from that, however, these occasions can be very different. Consider the following examples.

A consultation with an expert. Perhaps with a physician, or anyone whose position in the production of knowledge gives her the power to determine what, provisionally but effectively, passes for the truth on the matter of the consultation.

Instruction in school, when a pupil is told what there is, or what happened, or why.

Reading or listening to speakers advance candidates for truth, soliciting belief, often successfully.

In conversation, when another says something and you accept it as a matter of course, that is, not from mere politeness and not with unexpressed skepticism but because it never occurs to you to doubt it.

A confession, whether the Easter duty of the Catholic or confessions solicited by and delivered over to therapists, lovers, parents, or police.

Bearing witness: testimony before a congregation, jury, inquisition, commission, hearing, etc.

All of these are situations of dialogical intersubjectivity. This is obvious in the case of conversation, consultation, pedagogy, and confession. Here others are present, listening, recording, interpreting what is said, and making no secret of their interest. Seemingly solitary solicitations of belief, as in reading or watching television alone, show that the intersubjectivity of the occasion can be highly imaginary, to use Lacan's term.[19] The dialogical relationship to the other (author, anchor, actor) may be an entirely unconscious imaginary overlay on the perceptual form of a human voice.

That there is a *logos* of dreaming, a dialogue or dialectic of censorship and desire reiterated in symptoms and slips, is for Lacan the true significance of Freud's "discovery of the unconscious." What Freud discovered is not merely the existence of unconscious contents (already postulated by Leibniz). More specifically and decisively it is that "at the level of the unconscious there is something at all points homologous with what occurs at the level of the subject—*this thing speaks (ça parle)*."[20] As a result, we are never without interlocutors, especially not when reading or asleep and dreaming. Considered from the psychological roots that have prepared the way for it, a disposition to acquiesce in a textual source of authority is the effect of the first dialogical relationships to others. Freud called this transference. As Harold Bloom writes, "A transference or metaphor takes place when we read . . . [These] echo or repeat earlier transferences, and what is transferred is our love for authority, our desire to be augmented by the authority." So Freud: "The credulity of love becomes an important, if not the most fundamental, source of authority."[21]

Contrast two occasions of truth passing:

(1) I consult an expert and receive an evaluation, which passes for true, penetrating my reasoning on the matter of the consultation.

(2) I read in a technical journal, believe what I read, and take it up (as true, probable, reasonable, etc.) in whatever inquiry I am pursuing.

The effect is the same. I submit uncoerced to a modification profound or slight of my subjective freedom to think or speak and choose to act. It would be wrong to insist on a sharp difference between these two cases solely because one is a conventionally solitary exchange between me and a text, the other an exchange between two subjects bodily present to each other. As far as power goes, these occasions are pretty close. The government-effect worked in (1) is not willful in a way that makes it closer to an exercise of power than the anonymous authority of the technical journal. Instead, the position of consultant, and indeed the individual herself, is as much an artifact as a text one might read. The position of consultant is an artifact of the discipline that authorizes somebody to hold it, that lets her be an effective producer of technical knowledge and gives her judgments currency, a reliable capacity to pass for true. Beyond that, the individual subject herself is like the rest of us: a solitary singularity, a historical artifact, a body made subjective by discipline and accident.

The individual that case (1) posits as an authority in some discipline or discourse of truth did not exercise power over me. She issues no command; she makes no demand on me to accept what she says "or else." It is in this sense that our relationship is noncoercive. The conclusion to draw, however, is not that this relationship is transparent and free, but that the power to control what passes in the most concrete contexts of truth's production is exercised without being held and is noncoercive, however irresistible it may be. The existence, or exercise, of this power is interstitial, relational, relative: not a property that someone simply has, but an asymmetrical relationship to another or others, producing effects of government.

In the Prologue, I said that the only sense in which truth is "determined" is when a given statement is evaluated for its truth and sustains that evaluation. In other words, what "determination" there is for truth is evaluation in actual practice. Since not every statement is critically contested or confirmed in its truth, there are lots of truths (lots of occasions of truth) that are not "determined" to be true, not by anything whatsoever, and their "being true" is none the worse for it.

To develop this idea further, I introduce the idea of the *production of truth*. This is an obvious extension of what the economist Fritz Machlup calls "the production of knowledge." Machlup argues that knowledge is produced whenever "someone learns of something *he* or *she* has not known before, even if others have." The production of knowledge is therefore not limited to the creation or discovery of historically new knowledge; discovery, in this sense, is properly just one major product (research and development) in the economy of knowledge. To produce knowledge means "not only discovering, inventing, designing, and planning but also disseminating and communication." I produce knowledge if I discover something nobody else knows, or if I tell you something you did not know, or only vaguely knew, or knew but had forgotten. This is why Machlup distinguishes "socially new" from "subjectively new" knowledge.[22] Yet perhaps it is clear that whatever effect socially new knowledge has on the government of conduct occurs at the level of the subjectively new. There is no truth, no occasions of truth, nothing to sustain evaluation in terms of truth, apart from the production of subjectively new knowing-that. Of course knowledge is not all or even mostly propositional knowledge that such and such is true. Still, new knowing-that is not nothing, and neither is the power to govern conduct through control of what passes for subjectively new knowledge on matters where it is believed that there is a technical truth to be had.

This understanding of the production of truth casts light on Foucault's idea of a "history of sexuality." In the first volume of his unfinished study Foucault argues against what he calls "the repressive hypothesis." This is partly the idea that there exists a Victorian regime of restrained, mute, hypocritical sexuality which continues to dominate us even today. But this is not the only idea Foucault's argument brings into question; the repressive hypothesis has as much to do with truth as with sex. The supposed good of liberating sexuality is more accurately the good of undoing what represses it, getting rid of the falsity, the error, the distortion of human nature this repression seems to entail. How could it not be good to be free of that? But if sexuality has come to be seen as something repressed, some piece of human nature that is falsified or distorted by civilization (or capitalism), this is because it has more fundamentally become established as something about which there is a truth in the first place—a truth at once elemental to our being or nature, yet difficult, elusive, protean. This combination of features rationalizes our uncoerced submission to those whose specialized position in the economy of knowledge empowers them to produce what passes for the psychological or medical truth about sexuality.

Foucault emphasized that the history of sexuality *would not* be "a history of sexual behaviors and practices, tracing their successive forms, their evolution, and their dissemination," nor would it "analyze the scientific, religious, or philosophical ideas through which these behaviors have been represented."[23] Instead, it would be a history of sexuality itself. The Lacanian psychoanalyst Jacques-Alain Miller put the obvious objection to Foucault: "Sexuality isn't historical . . . through and through from the start . . . There isn't a history of sexuality." Foucault replies: "There is one in the sense that there is a history of madness, I mean of madness as a question, posed in terms of truth, within a discourse in which human madness is held to signify something about the truth of what man, the subject, or reason is." Referring to his earlier work on the asylum, Foucault says: "my problem was to find out how the question of madness could have been made to operate in terms of discourses of truth, that is to say, discourses having the status and function of *true* discourses. In the West that means scientific discourse. That was also the angle from which I wanted to approach the question of sexuality . . . what I'm concerned with, what I'm talking about, is how it comes about that people are told that the secret of their truth lies in the region of their sex" (*PK.*210–214).

If there is a history of sexuality (of the thing itself) it is because a domain of knowledge has become unified (contingently, historically, not through the natural unity of the object) around the term *sexuality.* The history of sexuality is a history of how under this predicate a number of fairly recent disciplines (including psychoanalysis, sexology, gynecology, and the psychiatry and criminology of perversion), and correlated possibilities of making credible, effective statements productive of subjectively new knowledge, came to govern what passes for the truth on a range of questions concerning sensations, pleasures, desires, dreams, somatic functions, and public health. One cannot say that the subject—sexuality—was there all along, that it is one of nature's natural units. "It is precisely this idea of sex *in itself,*" the idea of something "with intrinsic properties and laws of its own," that Foucault's argument brings into question (*HS.*152–153). Sexuality "itself" is nothing but the dense pattern of discursive and interventionist power relations which knit together these heterogeneous circuits of knowledge production and practice (therapeutic, punitive, pedagogic, and so on). Sexuality is nothing—it does not exist—apart from this historically contingent assemblage.

Knowledge as product, as the production of subjectively and intersubjectively new knowledge, provides another perspective on the idea of "passing for true." A statement passes for true when it enters into a dialogical exchange productive of subjectively new propositional knowledge-that. This includes but is not limited to the production of standardly, expertly, critically, methodically, or scientifically determinable knowledge-that. Here we see disquotation through the other end of Quine's deflationary lens. Every case of the production of propositional knowing-that is a case of knowing "that such and such" is true. So the production of subjectively new knowledge of this sort is equivalent in extension to the occasions of dialogical passing for true.

"My general theme," Foucault says, "isn't society but the discourse of true and false, by which I mean the correlative formation of domains and objects and of the verifiable, falsifiable discourses that bear on them; and it's not just their formation that interests me, but the effects in the real to which they are linked." By the word "truth," he says, "I do not mean the ensemble of truths which are to be discovered and accepted, but rather the ensemble of rules according to which the true and the false are separated and specific effects of power attached to the true." It is here that we glimpse what is indispensable to the production of truth, "the mechanisms and instances which enable one to distinguish true and false statements, the means by which each is sanctioned; the techniques and procedures accorded value in the acquisition of truth; the status of those who are charged with saying what counts as true."[24]

To be able to produce truth, that is, to make a statement that passes for true in dialogical exchange, takes more than mere "linguistic competence." As Pierre Bourdieu observes, "The competence to produce sentences that are likely to be understood may be quite inadequate to produce sentences that are likely to be *listened to* . . . social acceptability is not reducible to mere grammaticality. Speakers lacking the legitimate competence are *de facto* excluded from the social domains in which this competence is required, or are condemned to silence." To say there are social conditions for the production of truth, he adds, "is to say there is a politics of truth, an action constantly exercised in order to defend and improve the functioning of the social universes in which . . . truth comes into being."[25] For some time now, more and more of the competence by which truth comes into being is governed by what Foucault calls a discipline or discourse of truth. This authorizes selected speakers for the production of new knowing-that which is technically certified, often with a high degree of equally technical evidence. And this production, no less than the production of commodities, presupposes demand for its product; for instance, demand for the kind of product that organized, disciplinary control over positions from which truth can be "determined," that is, warranted, certified, verified, or standardly evaluated, can supply. (Does the DNA in this bloodstain match the defendant's? Is this individual dangerous? What is the public opinion?)

A discourse of truth is a *practice*: the routine activity of many people whose intercommunication is governed by norms largely if not entirely internal to the activity they regulate. The practice is *discursive*: what they do is to operate on and with language, creating, analyzing, crediting, or discrediting symbols, including especially measurements and the signs of systematic differentiation. This activity is embedded in a wider political economy of knowledge production, where it contributes to the government of everyone whose social interaction is mediated by its discourse, that is, by the knowledge it produces and sets into circulation. Thus, as Foucault observes, truth acquires "a value . . . not only in the economy of discourse but, more generally, in the administration of scarce resources . . . as an asset—finite, limited, desirable, useful . . . an asset that consequently, *from the moment of its existence* (and not only in its 'practical applications'), poses the question of power; an asset that is, by nature, the object of a struggle, a political struggle."[26]

C. Wright Mills once defined intellectuals as "those who professionally create, destroy, [or] elaborate . . . symbols." He explains why this is a politically sensitive position: "ideas, beliefs, images—symbols in short—stand between men and the wider realities of their time, and . . . accordingly those who professionally create, destroy, elaborate these symbols are very much involved in all literate men's very images of reality. For now, of course, the live experience of men falls far short of the objects of their belief and action." This being so, it is all the more important, he thinks, for intellectuals to appreciate their special social responsibility. Since "much reality is now officially defined by those who hold power," the political task of the intellectual is "to find out as much of the truth as he can, and to tell it to the right people, at the right time, and in the right way." The work of "any man of knowledge, if he is the genuine article, [has] a distinct kind of political relevance: his politics, in the first instance, are the politics of truth." He must be "absorbed in the attempt to know what is real and what is unreal"; for "his job is the maintenance of an adequate definition of reality."[27]

Two assumptions stand out in this account of truth and politics. First, power prefers to hide; hidden, it is stronger. To show itself is a risk to be avoided wherever possible. Second, power does not only dissemble (when it can); it distorts reality, making error pass for truth and falsifying consciousness. The second point should be distinguished from the first. To hide is not the same thing as to lie. One might even guess that an asymmetry of power may be all the more invisible and stable without the liability of a lie.

Of the two assumptions, I suggest that Foucault would accept only the first. He says "power is tolerable only on condition that it mask a substantial part of itself. Its success is proportional to its ability to hide its own mechanisms" (HS.86). Yet he qualifies this statement in a way that contradicts Mills's second assumption; for truth can and regularly does have exactly this effect. "The history of the West cannot be dissociated from the way its 'truth' is produced and produces its effects. We are living in a society that . . . produces and circulates discourse having truth as its function, passing itself off as such and thus attaining specific powers" (PPC.112).

Western societies have struggled to make speech preeminent over other instruments of political power. The advantages of this are scarcely to be denied. But distinctive problems arise for a political culture that makes discourse the chief instrument of government. For instance, nothing about the nature of knowledge or the essence of truth precludes their being strategically aligned against select subject-positions or the bodies that labor there. Consider a historical example. In "The Study and Practice of Medicine by Women" (1872), the renowned physiologist Theodor von Bischoff explains how "impartial and certain science" reveals "the female sex to be incapable of cultivating knowledge, and this is especially true in the fields of natural sciences and medicine." In a treatise entitled *Medical Depictions of Female Life in Health and Sickness from Physiological, Intellectual, and Moral Standpoints: A Handbook for Germany's Women* (1830), another physician writes: "sexual differences are not restricted merely to the organs of reproduction but penetrate the entire organism . . . The male body expresses positive strength, sharpening male understanding and independence, and equipping men for life in the State, in the arts and sciences. The female body expresses womanly softness and feeling. The roomy pelvis determines women for motherhood. The weak, soft members and delicate skin are witness of woman's narrower sphere of activity, of home-bodiness and peaceful family life."[28]

That these statements are all false is unimportant. What is important is that there was once a political economy of knowledge in which they passed for true. Their currency contributed to the stability of a large pattern of asymmetrical differences of power between men and women. The key point though is that the statements did not have to be false to have this effect. It was enough that they passed for the truth. The fact that they now lack their former currency (the fact that they are false) should not be misunderstood as a necessary precondition for their having once done their part to sustain injustice. All that is important, then as now, is the currency they had; that they and others like them historically passed for the truth.

To acknowledge this is not to condemn everything that passes for true as a lie or a ruse; "neither is it a skeptical or relativistic refusal of all verified truth" (*SP*.212). Nor does it mean that one cannot sometimes merely dismiss or pointedly and successfully question what others claim to be true.[29] But it does cast doubt on the assumption of truth's intrinsic connection to freedom. The production and circulation of truth is as capable of complicity with tyranny, and all the more so with tutelage, as any instrument of government, and its products do not have to be *false* to have this effect. The distribution of truth-values over statements, their routine penetration of practical reasoning through private consultation and public communication, and the effects of this (whether global or carefully focused) on how people envision their options and choose and act are instruments and effects of political government. Without lapse or contamination, therefore, and without falsifying its nature or becoming what it essentially is not, truth is inextricably situated amid all the major asymmetries of social power.

Mills's discussion of truth and power first appeared in *Dissent* in

1955. In a presidential campaign speech the previous year, Adlai Stevenson said: "even the most fanatical ideology must adjust itself to revealed truth or perish. The job is to cling everlastingly to the truth: to try everlastingly to find it in the clatter and confusion of these times—and to find it even in the storm of words of a political campaign." F. G. Bailey reminds us that seven years later Stevenson "failed to cling hard enough to the truth when he talked to the United Nations about what his country was doing in the Bay of Pigs." In Bailey's view, "the only way in which we can understand 'truth' and 'untruth' is to see them as rhetoric, as concepts used primarily for persuasion. They are political words, weapons for use in competition for power. In that context, 'truth' and 'untruth' represent a tension, a tug of war, a dialogue between adversaries, who use these words in the contest, each striving to make their own ideas and values prevail."[30]

It may be that the disquotation property of the predicate "is true" makes the assertion of truth logically redundant, so that one might as well not speak of truth but just assert directly the sentence one wishes to affirm. Merely to make an assertion is to make a claim to truth. There is no logical difference of content between the bare assertion that p and the metalinguistic assertion that the sentence "p" is true or is the truth. Yet I suspect that this semantic insight has not penetrated widely or deeply. Most people probably perceive a difference between an unadorned assertion and the special kind of emphasis or rhetorical stance one can achieve by semantic ascent, when a speaker explicitly claims that what she says is the very truth. This rhetorical possibility depends not on any synchronic logical meaning for the word "true." Like the so-called correspondence intuition, it is instead a historical artifact of the Platonic and eventually traditional overestimation of truth's value.

"My problem," Foucault says, "is to see how men govern (themselves and others) by the production of truth . . . I would like in short to resituate the production of true and false at the heart of historical analysis and political critique."[31] It should be no more surprising that the production of truth can be used badly or be a source of political control than to hear the same said of money. This is because neither the truth-value of statements nor the exchange-value of commodities is measured by nature. According to some medieval numismatics, copper and silver are especially fit for minting and measuring value because they are naturally precious.[32] Value resides in them like weight or color in an Aristotelian substance. In theory, then, there could be as wide a discrepancy between the price goods actually fetch and their true value as between what somebody believes about a thing and the truth of the thing itself. Similarly, those who trust their "correspondence intuition" see a world of difference between opinion, or what passes for true, and the self-identical being of what is. But neither idea is tenable, and for the same reason. Nature does not prefer that bread should be cheaper than aircraft, nor does it prefer to be described with one more than another vocabulary or historical discourse (for instance, the language of chemistry rather than that of alchemy). Nor does nature itself see to the distribution of truth-values over statements.

These last considerations suggest a reply to Nietzsche's question that must seem anticlimactic to anyone who thinks as much hangs in the balance as Plato, Augustine, Condorcet, or Mills did. Considered in abstraction from *what* truth is in question, *for whom* it is passing true, and to *what effect,* truth "itself" has no more value than coins apart from their circulation.

The question "What good is truth?" can and must divide into many smaller, local questions, questions that directly touch the practice of all who (to recall Mills's description) professionally create, destroy, or elaborate symbols. Intellectuals are not the "bearers of universal values" but people who occupy specific positions in the production of knowledge, positions which are both local and (such is the political economy of knowledge) so intricately linked as to define what Foucault once called "the general functioning of an apparatus of truth." It is for this reason that their position "can take on a general significance and that [their] local, specific struggle can have effects and implications which are not simply professional or sectoral." Emphasizing that "what I am saying here is above all to be taken as a hypothesis," Foucault suggests that "it is necessary to think of the political problems of intellectuals not in terms of 'science' and 'ideology' but in terms of 'truth' and 'power.'"

The essential political problem for the intellectual is not to criticize the ideological contents supposedly linked to science, or to ensure that his own scientific practice is accompanied by a correct scientific ideology, but that of ascertaining the possibility of constituting a new politics of truth. The problem is not changing people's consciousnesses—or what's in their heads—but the political, economic, institutional regime of the production of truth.

It is not a matter of emancipating truth from every system of power (which would be a chimera, for truth is already power) but of detaching the power of truth from the forms of hegemony, social, economic, and cultural, within which it operates at the present time.

The political question, to sum up, is not error, illusion, alienated consciousness or ideology; it is truth itself. (*PK*.132–133)

Hence the importance of Foucault.

Epilogue

I have no desire to venture here a comparison
between agriculture and philosophy; it would not be
tolerated. I will ask merely, What is philosophy?
What do the writings of the best known philosophers
contain? What are the lessons of these friends of
wisdom? To listen to them, would one not take them
for a troop of charlatans, each crying from his own
place on a public square, "Come to me; I alone do not
deceive"?

Rousseau, *Discourse on the Origin of Inequality*

But, Truth is such a flyaway, such a slyboots, so
untransportable and unbarrelable a commodity, that
it is as bad to catch as light.

Emerson, "Literary Ethics"

To invest statements with a truth "determined" by beings serenely indifferent to the language and practice apart from which statements do
not exist is analogous to the "fetishism" that sees something in the
nature of goods which corresponds to and determines their fair market
price. Marx suspected that this "fetishism inherent in the commodity"
was responsible for "the dull and tedious quarrel over the part played
by Nature in the formation of exchange-values . . . Nature has no
more to do with it than it has in fixing the course of exchange."[1] The
same goes for the production of truth-values, and for being same or
different.

This is not the "usual objection" to correspondence theories of
truth. The usual objection is that it makes no sense to suggest that it is
somehow possible to compare words or beliefs with the world, since

the attempt to do so must employ words and cannot lead to anything but more perceptions and beliefs.[2] Berkeley argued somewhat in this way against material substance with his great principle that nothing but an idea can be like an idea. Hume made the more radical argument that, since there is nothing with which we may compare our perceptions except other perceptions, perceptions have no right to be called "representations" at all. We should simply drop the idea of external beings whose nature perception discloses. Except, as Hume allows, that we cannot just drop it. The best we can do is to regard this natural belief with Hume's ironic detachment, and follow our feelings.[3]

The argument is fine as far as it goes, but it is less an objection to truth-as-correspondence than to the "idea" idea in modern philosophy. How to get outside of our perceptions and estimate their adequacy to something that is not a perception is a "problem" only for a philosophy that relies on the Cartesian assumption that the act of the intellect is a representation whose subjective self-evidence is independent of the physical order it purports to represent. Against this, the usual objection to correspondence makes a point. But the onto-logic of correspondence does not stand or fall with a modern epistemology of representations.

If some philosophers have their "correspondence intuition," I too begin with a platitude: Nothing in the world would be true or false if there were no speakers or speech.[4] Truth would not then exist. My argument is that the same goes for being same or different, being identical, being one, determinately *this* or *that*. Identity and difference stand or fall with the their evaluation in an economy of knowledge, where, symbolized in language, the results pass for true. If "there are" determinate beings, it is because something is, in fact, determined, that is, evaluated, measured, differentiated. Take this away and "what there is" has no more "determination" than local time on the sun. This is why, recalling the definition by Boethius—Nature is that which informs each thing by a specific difference—I say that Nature does not exist.

Consider some of the reasons philosophers have found for their interest in truth:

1. Because it is sublime, divine (Parmenides, Plato, St. Augustine);
2. Because it is an essential part of the best kind of life (Heraclitus, Socrates, Aristotle, Stoics, St. Thomas, Peirce, Habermas);
3. Because it is useful, instrumental, empowering (Bacon, James, Dewey);
4. Because it distinguishes knowledge from opinion or mere belief and thus defines the problem of epistemology, which must circumscribe the scope and limits of true knowledge (Descartes, Locke, Kant, Russell).

Without onto-logic, (1) has no fresh interest. Without a Parmenidean discord between Opinion or the Way of Seeming (passing for true) and Being or the Way of Truth, there is no opening to skepticism; epistemology, and (4), lose their point. That leaves (2) and (3).

I suggested that Nietzsche and the Pragmatists might agree that nothing is noninstrumentally or finally good, least of all truth. Roughly speaking, this comes to agreement on (3). But Nietzsche does not link (3) with (2). On the contrary, his experiment was to break this link and follow up on the results of allowing "the value of truth . . . for once [to] be called experimentally into question." Peirce and James, in contrast, both assume that the more truth the better; in this they happily follow Bacon, Milton, Jefferson, and J. S. Mill. For Peirce, "truth, the conditions of which the logician endeavors to analyze, and which is the goal of the reasoner's aspirations, is nothing but a phase of the *summum bonum* which forms the content of pure ethics."[5] For James, "the possession of true thoughts means everywhere the possession of valuable instruments of action." Our "duty to gain truth . . . can account for itself by excellent practical reasons" (*P*.97). James knows this without having to take a closer look at what actually circulates as the truth, how it is produced or communicated, or to what effect. If it weren't good, it just wouldn't be true.

Bertrand Russell once suggested that "our preference for true beliefs rather than false ones . . . [is] explicable by taking account of the causal efficacy of beliefs, and of the greater appropriateness of the responses resulting from true beliefs."[6] James could not have said it better. Yet as Nietzsche had already observed, what is or is not "appropriate" depends on who more particularly you are, not on how "reality" is despite you. Appropriateness is perspectival; it is always a question of appropriate *for whom,* for what *style* of life. But what has that to do with truth?[7]

Peirce and James (and Dewey) also follow Bacon in conceiving of truth and knowledge as universally useful instruments for coping with a universal human plight, "nature" or "experience." But merely to know the truth-value of what passes for true is not yet to know anything about its value. We routinely submit to an anonymous government of truth, modifying our conduct in light of what passes for true, known, normal, average, probable, or risky. Whether this is good, or useful, or works depends on *what* truth and *for whom* it is passing true. Truth itself, just by itself and apart from such details, is worthless. Its value disappears into whatever more contestable good may be at stake in a demand for the truth.

Attempts like mine to speak philosophically about truth are often thought to come to grief on a self-referential paradox. If, for example, a philosopher is so incautious as to say "There is no truth," or "All truth is a lie," we can ask *Is that true?* If the claim is not true, must we not say that it is false and thus worthless in philosophy? But if it is true, then it implies its own falsity and lapses into self-contradiction. Again, if a philosopher claims that truth is relative (to a culture or a language-game, for instance), we can ask *Is that true?* If it is, then this truth too is relative, relative to the philosopher's culture or language-game. Another might deny its validity. If in that case or for that other it is not true, then the same proposition—that truth is relative—is true and false, contradicting itself.

What then of my claims? Am I on the brink of self-contradiction? I don't think so. Self-referential paradox is the fate of philosophers who wish to speak the onto-logical truth about truth, to disclose the truth of its being—even when on their account this being is not nature but something "relative," like a context, language-game, or tradition. If this is supposed to be the onto-logical truth of truth itself, then the claim possesses all the nonrelative validity it paradoxically denies. But while I claim that the determinability truth-value acquires in an economy of knowledge is all the "determination" there is for truth, neither this nor anything else on my account onto-logically makes true statements true. No thing or act corresponds differentially to each truth, making it to be the truth by its presence.

Is that true? Perhaps I merely believe it, when really it is false. *Do* I believe it is the truth, or am I merely trying to make it "pass" for true, and if so, to what purpose? These questions occasion no paradox. It should be clear by now why nothing would change, and how pointless it would be, if to the claims I have just summarized I add the words *It is true that.*

Richard Rorty imagines a "Reichenbach *redivivus*" casting his eye over our analytic philosophy. What would the author of *The Rise of Scientific Philosophy* (1951) find to his liking? "He would admire the style, the insistence on argument, the dialectical acuity. He would approve of the widespread distrust among philosophers of those who, as he put it, were 'trained in literature and history, who have never learned the precision methods of the mathematical sciences.' He would agree with a distinguished analytic philosopher who urged that 'intellectual hygiene' requires one not to read the books of Derrida and Foucault." The anecdote is true, and it got back to Foucault, who replied: "I'm very proud that some people think I'm a danger for the intellectual health of students. When people start thinking of health in intellectual activities, I think there is something wrong."[8]

Foucault writes well of philosophical practice. He says, "There is always something ludicrous in philosophical discourse when it tries, from the outside, to dictate to others, to tell them where their truth is and how to find it." This is Rorty's point too, when he dismisses philosophy's claim to know something about knowing which nobody else knows so well. If there is a difference between Foucault and Rorty at this point, it concerns their idea of what else philosophical activity might be. Rorty suggests conversation. Foucault suggests the alternative I have tried to illustrate in this book. Philosophy "is entitled to explore what might be changed in its own thought . . . to learn to what extent the effort to think [its] own history can free thought from what it silently thinks, and so enable it to think differently . . . instead of legitimating what is already known."[9]

Magna est veritas et praevalebit. "For all men, good and true are the same" (Democritus). "If a man violates against [nature] . . . he is not hurt on account of an opinion, but because of the truth" (Antiphon). "The disease of heresy can be cured, for truth has the power to cut away and burn up the false infection of heretical opinion" (Clement). "All knowledge is good" (St. Thomas). "And though all the windes of doctrin were loose to play upon the earth, so Truth be in the field, we do injuriously . . . to misdoubt her strength . . . For who knows not that truth is strong next to the Almighty" (Milton). "Truth is great and will prevail if left to herself . . . she is the proper and sufficient antagonist to error" (Jefferson). "Making the human soul perfect . . . consists solely in keeping it constantly striving after the truth" (Lessing). "Victory can only be gained by the truth" (Lukács). "The truth of statements is based on anticipating the realization of the good life" (Habermas). "Kindness and truth shall meet; justice and peace shall kiss. Truth shall spring out of the earth, and justice shall look down from heaven" (Psalm 85).[10]

This is an old faith. But truth has no value apart from whatever is built, destroyed, sustained, or impeded with what passes for true. Truth has no power of its own, no utopian potential, no affinity for good, and will not make us free.

Notes

Prologue

1. Heraclitus, XXXII/112. References to Heraclitus are from C. H. Kahn's edition of the fragments, *The Art and Thought of Heraclitus* (Cambridge: Cambridge University Press, 1979), with roman numerals for Kahn's arrangement and arabic for that of Diels. The citations of Plato are from *Gorgias* 526d–e, and *Republic* 490a. References to Plato are from *The Collected Dialogues,* ed. E. Hamilton and H. Cairns (Princeton: Princeton University Press, 1961).

   In a second century c.e. compendium of Platonic doctrine, Albinus writes: "Philosophy is a striving after wisdom . . . that occurs when we turn ourselves . . . to the things which truly are . . . the philosopher must have clung to the truth with desire, and he must in no way entertain falsehood." *The Platonic Doctrines of Albinus,* trans. Jeremiah Reedy (Grand Rapids: Phanes Press, 1991), p. 21. This Platonic association of wisdom, truth, and philosophy is confirmed for the later tradition in Macrobius, Boethius, Hugh of St. Victor, Thierry of Chartres, and John of Salisbury. Nor were "moderns" like Bacon inclined to think otherwise: "it is not merely calculations or predictions that I aim at, but philosophy . . . not what is accordant with the phenomena, but what is found in nature herself, and is actually and really true." In R. F. Jones, *Ancients and Moderns: A Study of the Rise of the Scientific Movement in Seventeenth-Century England* (1936; 2d ed. 1961) (New York: Dover, 1982), p. 52. Hobbes writes: "Wisdom, properly so called, is nothing else but this: *the perfect knowledge of the truth in all matters whatsoever.* Which . . . by the compendium of a word we call *philosophy.*" *Man and Citizen (De Cive),* ed. B. Gert (Indianapolis: Hackett, 1991), p. 90. For Locke, "Philosophy . . . is nothing but the true knowledge of things." *Essay Concerning Human Understanding,* ed. P. N. Nidditch (Oxford: Oxford University Press, 1975), p. 10. John Stuart Mill declares that it is "the business of a philosopher . . . to expose error, though it may happen to be accredited [and] to elicit and sustain truth, known or unknown, neglected or

185

obnoxious." *Works* (Toronto: University of Toronto Press, 1977), XIX, p. 642.

2. See Hans Blumenberg, *The Legitimacy of the Modern Age,* trans. Robert M. Wallace (Cambridge, Mass.: MIT Press, 1983), p. 449.

3. On this point I believe I am in agreement with Donald Davidson, *Inquiries Concerning Truth and Interpretation* (Oxford: Oxford University Press, 1984), p. 194; and with the "minimalist" interpretation of truth that Paul Horwich defends in *Truth* (Oxford: Blackwell, 1990). I have further discussion of Davidson in Chapter 8. The point was made more than a century and a half ago in a neglected work by the American banker Alexander Bryan Johnson: "I am speaking, I am standing, several persons are present. Each of these assertions is a truth; but if we seek among these truths for truth itself, believing it to be a unit, we are seeking in nature for what is merely a contrivance of language . . . [The] oneness of a thousand truths is verbal. The unit is a creation of language; hence the fallacy, ambiguity, and difficulty, when we seek in nature for a corresponding unit." *Treatise on Language* (1836), ed. David Rynin (Berkeley: University of California Press, 1959), p. 73.

1. Classical Philosophy of Truth

1. Aristotle, *Metaphysics,* in *The Basic Works of Aristotle,* ed. R. McKeon (New York: Random House, 1941), 1011b. Further references to Aristotle's works are parenthetically embedded. Also compare Plato, *Cratylus* 385b: "The statement which says of what is that it is, is true; the one that says that it is not is false."

   I add here a note on the Scholastic formula *veritas est adaequatio intellectus ad rem.* This formula is less common than is sometimes supposed; for instance neither Scotus nor Ockham use it, nor did it gain acceptance until comparatively late in the medieval period. St. Thomas and others credit it to Isaac Israeli's tenth-century *On Definitions,* although it seems to originate with Avicenna in the ninth century and did not gain currency in the West until after the twelfth century. See Steven Marrone, *Truth and Scientific Knowledge in the Thought of Henry of Ghent* (Cambridge, Mass.: Medieval Academy of America, 1985), p. 21n. Philotheus Boehner traces its first appearance to the early thirteenth century work of William of Auxerre and Philip the Chancellor; see Boehner, "Historical Notes on the Concept of Truth in Scholasticism," in *Collected Articles on Ockham* (St. Bonaventure, N.Y.: Franciscan Institute, 1958). An older and more common formula defines truth as "signifying that that which is is," while in the eleventh century Anselm defines truth as a "rightness *(rectitudo)* perceptible by the mind alone." *Dialogue on Truth* XI; in *Selections from the Medieval Philosophers,* ed. R. McKeon (New York: Charles Scribner's Sons, 1930), vol. 1, p. 172.

2. R. G. Collingwood, *The Idea of Nature* (Oxford: Oxford University Press, 1945), pp. 81–82.

3. Etienne Gilson, *Being and Some Philosophers,* 2d ed. (Toronto: Pontifical Institute of Medieval Studies, 1952), pp. 10–15, 21. Heidegger, *Identity and Difference,* trans. Joan Stambaugh (New York: Harper & Row, 1969), pp. 23–26. Plato describes the being of the entities he calls *eidos* or *idea* as *einai ti auto kath auto* (for example, *Phaedo* 78d, 100b; *Parmenides* 128e–129a; *Timaeus* 51d). The usage is analyzed in Gregory Vlastos, *Socrates, Ironist and Moral Philosopher* (Ithaca: Cornell University Press, 1991), pp. 72–76.

4. Plotinus, *Enneads* V.3.15; in Gilson, *Being,* p. 21. Augustine, *Soliloquies* II.8; in *The Basic Writings of St. Augustine,* ed. W. J. Oates (New York: Random House, 1948), vol. 1, p. 281. Anselm, *Dialogue on Truth* IV; in McKeon, *Selections,* vol. 1, p. 168. Matthew of Aquasparta, *Disputed Question on Knowledge* I.1; in McKeon, *Selections,* vol. 2, pp. 240–241.

5. St. Thomas, *Summa Theologica* I.xvi.1; in *Introduction to St. Thomas Aquinas,* ed. A. C. Pegis (New York: Random House, 1948), pp. 170–171.

6. See Norman Kretzmann, "Aristotle on Spoken Sound Significant by Convention," in *Ancient Logic and Its Modern Interpretations,* ed. J. Corcoran (Dordrecht: Reidel, 1974). Since Cratylus in Plato's dialogue of the same name, there has been dissent from the theme of the conventional sign. For instance Leibniz: "I know that the Scholastics and everyone else are given to saying that the significations of words are arbitrary *(ex instituto),* and it is true they are not settled by natural necessity; but they are settled by reasons—sometimes natural ones in which chance plays some part, sometimes moral ones which involve choice." *New Essays on Human Understanding,* trans. Peter Remnant and Jonathan Bennett (Cambridge: Cambridge University Press, 1981), p. 278.

7. C. H. Kahn, "Retrospect on the Verb 'To Be' and the Concept of

Being," in *The Logic of Being: Historical Studies,* ed. S. Knuuttila and J. Hintikka (Dordrecht: Reidel, 1986), pp. 21–22; and "Why Existence Does Not Emerge as a Distinct Concept in Greek Philosophy," *Archiv für Geschichte der Philosophie* 58 (1976), 333. Joseph Owens, *Doctrine of Being in the Aristotelian "Metaphysics,"* 3d ed. (Toronto: Pontifical Institute of Medieval Studies, 1978), p. 309.

8. Kahn, "Retrospect," pp. 8, 22; "Existence in Greek Philosophy," p. 329; and *The Verb "Be" in Ancient Greek* (Dordrecht: Reidel, 1973), pp. 313, 363. The idea of a veridical "be" has been questioned by Mohan Matthen, "Greek Ontology and the 'Is' of Truth," *Phronesis* 28 (1983).

9. Hume, *A Treatise of Human Understanding,* ed. P. H. Nidditch (Oxford: Oxford University Press, 1978), p. 634. Parmenides, fragment 3; in K. Freeman, *Ancilla to the Pre-Socratic Philosophers* (Cambridge, Mass.: Harvard University Press, 1948), p. 42.

10. Kahn, *The Verb "Be,"* p. 401, and p. 2, where Kahn cites A. C. Graham. On the "correspondence intuition," see Paul Horwich, *Truth* (Oxford: Blackwell, 1990), chap. 7. Horwich is concerned not to "deny that truths *do* correspond—in *some* sense—to the facts," and describes as "innocuous" the "idea that whenever a sentence or proposition is true, it is true because something in the world is a certain way . . . Thus we can be perfectly comfortable with the idea that each truth is made true by the existence of a corresponding fact" (pp. 110–112).

11. W. V. Quine, "Truth," in *Quiddities* (Cambridge, Mass.: Harvard University Press, 1987), p. 213. Even Davidson, while his enthusiasm for Tarski's work is well known, does not think it supports Quine's deflationary philosophy of truth: "Nothing in Tarski's truth definitions hint at what it is that these definitions have in common. Unless we are prepared to say that there is no single concept of truth (even as applied to sentences), but only a number of different concepts for which we use the same word, we have to conclude that there is more to the concept of truth—something absolutely basic, in fact—which Tarski's definitions do not touch." "The Structure and Content of Truth," *Journal of Philosophy* 87 (1990), 287–288.

Tarski regarded his semantic conception of truth as "grasping the intentions which are contained in the so-called *classical* conception of truth ('true—corresponding with reality')." *Logic, Semantics, Metamathematics* (Oxford: Oxford University Press, 1956), p. 153. There is now widespread agreement that this is not so. See Mary Hesse, *Revolutions and Reconstructions in the Philosophy of Science* (Bloomington: Indiana University Press, 1980), pp. 142–143; Alan White, *Truth* (Garden City, N.Y.: Anchor, 1970), p. 98; D. J. O'Connor, *The Correspondence Theory of Truth* (London: Hutchinson, 1975), pp. 91–111; and Hilary Putnam, "On Truth," in *How Many Questions?*, ed. L. S. Cauman et al. (Indianapolis: Hackett, 1983).

12. Tarski's method for defining a truth-predicate is informally explained by Quine in his *Philosophy of Logic* (Englewood Cliffs, N.J.: Prentice-Hall, 1970), chap. 3; and Steven Evnine, *Donald Davidson* (Stanford: Stanford University Press, 1991), §5.3. On the unnaturalness of "natural languages," see Roy Harris, *The Language Makers* (Ithaca: Cornell University Press, 1980), and *The Language Machine* (London: Duckworth, 1987). While Davidson emphasizes that a Tarski-style theory of truth posits no truth-makers, he does still think that it can have a role to play in understanding the relation between language and reality. See B. T. Ramberg, *Donald Davidson's Philosophy of Language* (Oxford: Blackwell, 1989), chap. 4.

13. Plato, *Laws* 730c; *Republic* 382b.

14. See Werner Jaeger, *Paideia*, 2d ed., trans. Gilbert Highet (Oxford: Oxford University Press, 1945), vol. 1, pp. 183–184; M. C. Stokes, *One and Many in Pre-Socratic Philosophy* (Washington, D.C.: Center for Hellenistic Studies, 1971), p. 89; and C. H. Kahn, *The Art and Thought of Heraclitus* (Cambridge: Cambridge University Press, 1979), pp. 21–22, 121. On the diversity of uses for the word *logos* in Greek at the time of Heraclitus, see W. K. C. Guthrie, *A History of Greek Philosophy* (Cambridge: Cambridge University Press, 1962), vol. 1, pp. 420–424.

15. Kant, *Critique of Pure Reason,* trans. N. Kemp Smith (London: Macmillan, 1933), A111; cp. A158/B197. Further references to the *Critique* are to the marginal pagination of this edition, which reproduces the standard German pagination.

16. Sextus Empiricus, *Adversus Mathematicos* VII.126–129; in Kahn, *Heraclitus*, pp. 293–294. Hegel, *Lectures on the History of Philosophy,* trans. E. S. Haldane and F. H. Simson (New York: Humanities Press, 1974), vol. 1, pp. 294–296. Kahn "see[s] no reason to doubt that down to the time of Plutarch and Clement, if not later, the little book of Heraclitus was available in its original form to any reader who chose to seek it out" (p. 5).

17. Parmenides, fragment 1; in Freeman, *Ancilla,* p. 42. Collingwood, *Idea of Nature,* p. 69. See also David Furley, "Truth as What Survives the *Elenchus:* An Idea in Parmenides," in *The Criterion of Truth,* ed. P. Huby and G. Neal (Liverpool: Liverpool University Press, 1989).

18. Demosthenes, quoted in Page DuBois, *Torture and Truth* (New York: Routledge, 1991), pp. 49–50.

19. The citations of Ulpian, Azo, and Bocer are from Edward Peters, *Torture* (Oxford: Blackwell, 1985), p. 1. Other citations in this paragraph are from Plato, *Sophist* 237b; and Diderot, *Pensées sur l'Interprétation de la Nature,* XLIV, in *The Irresistible Diderot,* ed. J. H. Mason (London: Quartet Books, 1982), p. 67.

   Ulpian also observes that "torture is a fragile and dangerous thing and the truth frequently is not obtained by it. For many defendants because of their patience and strength are able to spurn the torments, while others would rather lie than bear them, unfairly incriminating themselves and also others." Cited in John Teduschi, "Inquisitorial Law and the Witch," *Early Modern European Witchcraft,* ed. B. Ankarloo and G. Henningsen (Oxford: Oxford University Press, 1989), p. 100. Exactly the same argument will be repeated for centuries; see, for example, Beccaria, *On Crimes and Punishments* (1764), XII. Peters makes the point (pp. 162–164) that when after a hiatus of some one hundred years torture reappears in the West in the twentieth century, truth drops out of the rationale, while torture drops its former connection to the law and is now merely a device for terror.

20. Plato, *Phaedrus* 247d, *Republic* 490b. Isocrates, in George A. Kennedy, *The Art of Persuasion in Greece* (Princeton: Princeton University Press, 1963), pp. 8–9.

21. B. H. Streeter, *The Four Gospels* (New York: Macmillan, 1925), p. 367. The influence of Greek philosophy on this Gospel should not be exaggerated; see Jaroslav Pelikan, *The Christian Tradition* (Chicago: University of Chicago Press, 1971), vol. 1, pp. 186–187; P. Carrington, *The Early Christian Church* (Cambridge: Cambridge University Press, 1957), vol. 1, p. 354; and Etienne Gilson, *History of Christian Philosophy in the Middle Ages* (New York: Random House, 1955), p. 6. Throughout, biblical texts are cited from *The New American Bible* (Nashville: Thomas Nelson, 1983).

22. I draw on Pelikan, *Christian Tradition,* pp. 27–33; and Eric Osborn, *The Beginning of Christian Philosophy* (Cambridge: Cambridge University Press, 1971), pp. 265–271. Tertullian is cited in *Documents of*

the Christian Church, 2d ed., ed. Henry Bettenson (Oxford: Oxford University Press, 1963), p. 31. Citations of Justin are in Bettenson, *Documents,* p. 5, and E. Gilson, *History of Christian Philosophy,* p. 555, note 14. Clement is cited in Bettenson, *Documents,* p. 6. Tatian is cited in Etienne Gilson, *The Spirit of Mediaeval Philosophy* (1936) (Notre Dame: University of Notre Dame Press, 1991), p. 462.

23. Plato, *Euthydemus* 281e–282a; *Protagoras* 356d–e. Cicero, *Tusculan Disputations* (Cambridge, Mass.: Harvard University Press, 1966), IV.7; and *De Finibus Bonorum et Malorum* (New York: Macmillan, 1914), III.9, 22.

Of course not all schools of Hellenistic philosophy shared the Stoics' confidence in the relationship between truth and happiness. Skeptics, whether Academic or Pyrrhonian, attack the Stoic assumption that the search for truth (philosophy) is the path to wisdom and existential fulfillment. "Skepticism systemizes most resolutely the disappointment of the great pretension to truth that philosophy had introduced into the world. The signature of the epoch following Plato and Aristotle is the common possession of the characteristic Hellenistic idea of philosophy, which can be described as its *therapeutic* conception. Whereas for Plato and Aristotle, philosophy was supposed to provide fulfillment, through the truth it conveys, of the essential needs of the spirit, philosophical understanding now becomes the corrective of a mistaken orientation of man precisely in his theoretical endeavour." Pyrrhonian skepticism "neutralizes the value goal of truth by denying the dependence of happiness upon it . . . The methodological meaning of this skepticism . . . can only be to destroy every remanent of the suspicion that a relation of foundation could subsist between theory and eudaimonia." Hans Blumenberg, *The Legitimacy of the Modern Age,* trans. Robert M. Wallace (Cambridge, Mass.: MIT Press, 1983), pp. 269–274.

24. Augustine, *Enchiridion* LXXXI, XVII; *Sermons* 306.9; and *De Mendacio* XX.41; in *Basic Writings,* vol. 1, pp. 707, 666; and McKeon, *Selections,* vol. 1, p. 265.

25. Anselm, *De Veritate* III; McKeon, *Selections,* vol. 1, p. 157. Steven Marrone, *William of Auvergne and Robert Grosseteste: New Ideas of Truth in the Thirteenth Century* (Princeton: Princeton University Press, 1983), p. 9.

26. Tertullian, cited in Blumenberg, *Legitimacy of the Modern Age,* p. 301. Augustine, *Enarrationes in Psalmos* viii, and *De Moribus* I.38;

cp. *Confessions* X.35. Peter Damien, *Sermons 55*; in K. F. Morrison, "Incentives for Studying the Liberal Arts," in *The Seven Liberal Arts in the Middle Ages,* ed. D. L. Wagner (Bloomington: Indiana University Press, 1983), p. 36. Boethius of Dacia, *On the Supreme Good,* trans. J. F. Wippel (Toronto: Pontifical Institute for Medieval Studies, 1987), pp. 32–35. For the propositions condemned at Paris in 1277, see *Philosophy in the Middle Ages,* 2d ed., ed. A. Hyman and J. Walsh (Indianapolis: Hackett, 1987), pp. 582–591.

27. Bacon, "Truth," in *The Essayes or Counsels, Civill and Morall,* ed. M. Kiernan (Cambridge, Mass.: Harvard University Press, 1985), p. 8. Antoine Arnauld, *Art of Thinking* (Port Royal Logic), trans. James Dickoff and Patricia James (Indianapolis: Bobbs-Merrill, 1964), p. 78. Spinoza, *Ethics,* trans. Samuel Shirley (Indianapolis: Hackett, 1982), IV. Ap. 32.

28. Locke, letter to Molyneux, 1698; in John Dunn, *Locke* (Oxford: Oxford University Press, 1984), p. 87. Other citations in this paragraph are from John Balguy, *The Foundations of Moral Goodness* (1728), and Richard Price, *Review of the Principal Questions of Morals* (1758), in *British Moralists,* ed. L. A. Selby-Bigge (Indianapolis: Bobbs-Merrill, 1964), §§583, 647. Richard Price, *Discourse on the Love of Our Country* (1789), cited in Steven Schaffer, "States of Mind: Enlightenment and Natural Philosophy," in *The Languages of Psyche: Mind and Body in Enlightenment Thought,* ed. G. S. Rousseau (Berkeley: University of California Press, 1990), p. 247. Beccaria, *On Crimes and Punishment,* trans. H. Paolucci (New York: Macmillan, 1963), XVI. Condorcet, "Sketch of a Historical Outline of the Progress of the Human Spirit" (1793), cited in T. L. Hankins, *Science and the Enlightenment* (Cambridge: Cambridge University Press, 1985), pp. 189–190.

29. Bacon, cited in R. F. Jones, *Ancients and Moderns: A Study of the Rise of the Scientific Movement in Seventeenth-Century England* (New York: Dover, 1982), p. 55; and *Novum Organum,* ed. J. Devey (London: George Bell & Sons, 1911), I.cxxiv. Augustine, *The City of God,* trans. M. Dods (New York: Random House, 1950), VIII.3. *The Didascalion of Hugh of St. Victor,* trans. J. Taylor (New York: Columbia University Press, 1961), III.xii. Robert Boyle offers a variation on Bacon's famous aphorism: "in Man's knowledge of the nature of the Creatures does principally consist his Empire over them, his

Knowledge and his Power having generally the same limits" (Jones, *Ancients and Moderns,* p. 203).

30. Montaigne, "Apology for Raymond Sebond," in *The Complete Works of Montaigne,* trans. D. M. Frame (Stanford: Stanford University Press, 1958), p. 319. Hans Blumenberg, *Work on Myth,* trans. Robert M. Wallace (Cambridge, Mass.: MIT Press, 1985), pp. 231–233.

31. Bacon, in Jones, *Ancients and Moderns,* p. 52. On the value of truth, see also Hume, *Treatise,* pp. 449–451.

32. Kant, *Critique of Pure Reason,* A58/B82. See also A191/B236, A237/B296, A642/B670.

2. Modern Truth

1. Skepticism was better known to the medieval period than my remarks here suggest, most significantly by Nicholas of Autrecourt; see his *Letters to Bernard of Arezzo,* in *Philosophy in the Middle Ages,* 2d ed., ed. A. Hyman and J. Walsh (Indianapolis: Hackett, 1987). In a discussion of Nicholas, Michael Frede notes the existence of at least three fourteenth-century manuscripts of a Latin version of Sextus's *Outlines of Pyrrhonism;* see "A Medieval Source of Modern Scepticism," in *Gedankenzeichen: Festschrift für Klaus Oehler,* ed. R. Claussen and R. Daube-Schackat (Tübingen: Stauffenberg Verlag, 1988), p. 65. Democritus is supposed to have declared that "man is severed from reality," and that "it is impossible to understand how in reality each thing is." Fragments 6 and 8; in K. Freeman, *Ancilla to the Pre-Socratic Philosophers* (Cambridge, Mass.: Harvard University Press, 1948), pp. 92–93.

2. Martin Luther, "Final Answer to the Diet of Worms," in *Documents of the Christian Church,* 2d ed., ed. Henry Bettenson (Oxford: Oxford University Press, 1963), p. 201.

3. Richard H. Popkin, *The History of Skepticism from Erasmus to Spinoza* (Berkeley: University of California Press, 1979), pp. 5, 68.

4. Locke, *Essay Concerning Human Understanding,* ed. P. N. Nidditch (Oxford: Oxford University Press, 1975), IV.i.4.

5. Kant, *Critique of Pure Reason,* trans. N. Kemp Smith (London: Macmillan, 1933), A197/B243.

6. Edmund Husserl, *Logical Investigations,* trans. J. N. Findlay (New York: Humanities Press, 1970), vol. 1, p. 280.

7. John R. Searle, *Intentionality* (Cambridge: Cambridge University Press, 1983), p. vii.

8. Locke, *Essay,* IV.v.2, II.xxxii.26, and IV.i.2–7 (agreement of ideas).

9. Locke, *Essay,* IV.xi.8. On the corpuscular hypothesis, see Maurice Mandelbaum, "Locke's Realism," in *Philosophy, Science, and Sense Perception* (Baltimore: Johns Hopkins University Press, 1964); and Peter Alexander, "Boyle and Locke on Primary and Secondary Qualities," in *Locke on Human Understanding,* ed. I. C. Tipton (Oxford: Oxford University Press, 1977).

10. Locke, *Essay,* IV.v.5, I.viii.2. Berkeley, *Treatise Concerning the Principles of Human Knowledge,* I.8; in *Philosophical Works,* ed. M. R. Ayers (London: J. M. Dent & Sons, 1975), p. 79 (my emphasis). Elsewhere, Berkeley makes it clear that his argument is based on considerations of commensurability: "What can an Idea be like but another Idea, we can compare it with Nothing else, a sound like a Sound, a Colour like a Colour." *Philosophical Commentaries,* no. 861; *Works,* p. 334.

11. Some philosophers seek refuge from Berkeley's argument by saying that it is not ideas being "like" realities but propositions being "isomorphic" to facts which is the essence of truth, and isomorphism, being a "purely formal" relation, can hold between these otherwise heterogeneous items. In a justly famous argument, Hilary Putnam shows that if there is one isomorphism, there are infinitely many different ones, with no way to indicate which one we "mean." See "Models and Reality," in *Realism and Reason: Philosophical Papers,* vol. 3 (Cambridge: Cambridge University Press, 1983). Putnam discusses Berkeley's argument ("Berkeley's *tour de force*") in *Reason, Truth, and History* (Cambridge: Cambridge University Press, 1981), chap. 2.

12. Kant, *Critique of Pure Reason,* A111 and A158/B197.

13. Kant, *Prolegomenona to Any Future Metaphysics,* trans. P. Carus (Indianapolis: Hackett, 1977), §36.

3. Nietzsche, or A Scandal of the Truth

1. D'Holbach, *Le Bon Sens* (1772), in *The Enlightenment,* ed. Jack F. Lively (London: Longmans, 1966), pp. 61–62.

2. This paragraph combines passages from *B*.1 and *GM*3.24 and 27. For earlier work on truth see *Philosophy and Truth: A Selection from Nietzsche's Notebooks of the Early 1870s,* ed. Donald Breazeale (Atlantic Highlands, N.J.: Humanities Press, 1979).

Given a choice between "all truth" and "the everlasting striving after truth, so that I should always and everlastingly be mistaken," Lessing famously chose the latter. Yet this is far from Nietzsche's experience of the will to truth as a problem. The opening of Nietzsche's early essay "On Truth and Lie in an Extra-Moral Sense" (1873) demystifies Lessing's choice: "Once upon a time, in some out of the way corner of that universe which is dispersed into numberless twinkling solar systems, there was a star upon which clever beasts invented knowing. That was the most arrogant and mendacious moment of 'world history,' but nevertheless, it was only a moment. After nature had drawn a few breaths, the star cooled and congealed, and the clever beasts had to die.—One might invent such a fable, and yet he still would not have adequately illustrated how miserable, how shadowy and transient, how aimless and arbitrary the human intellect looks within nature" (*Philosophy and Truth*, p. 79). Not only can the search for truth never be everlasting; it comes to nothing but a vain conceit. As Walter Kaufmann observes, Nietzsche "lacked Lessing's and Kant's easy conviction that our ancient values could be salvaged after the ancient God had been banished from the realm of thought." *Nietzsche,* 4th ed. (Princeton: Princeton University Press, 1974), p. 128. Nietzsche briefly refers to Lessing's remark in *The Birth of Tragedy,* trans. Walter Kaufmann (New York: Vintage Books, 1967), p. 95.

3. Marx, "Theses on Feuerbach," in *The Marx-Engels Reader,* 2d ed., ed. Robert C. Tucker (New York: Norton, 1978), p. 144; also see Leszek Kolakowski, "Marx and the Classical Definition of Truth," in *Toward a Marxist Humanism* (New York: Grove Press, 1968). John Dewey, *Theory of Valuation, International Encyclopedia of Unified Science* II:4 (Chicago: University of Chicago Press, 1969), p. 56; *Human Nature and Conduct* (New York: Random House, 1957), pp. 209–215; and *Reconstruction in Philosophy* (Boston: Beacon, 1957), p. 156.

4. Atheism has always been advanced in the name of truth. Feuerbach is an example: "We need only . . . invert the religious relations—regard that as an end which religion supposes to be a means—exalt that into

primary which in religion is subordinate, [and] at once we have destroyed the illusion, and the unclouded light of truth streams in upon us." *Essence of Christianity* (New York: Harper, 1957), pp. 274–275. The atheist first claims to know that religion is bunk, and then, like one returned to Plato's cave from a sojourn in True Being, militantly seeks to disabuse the others in the name of enlightenment and the good of truth.

5. Augustine, *De Trinitate* VIII.1; Thomas, *Summa Theologica* I.16.8, and *Summa Contra Gentiles* I.lxi.6.

6. Augustine, *De Moribus* II, *Enchiridion* XVII, *Confessions* X.24.

7. Nietzsche, *Philosophy and Truth,* p. 92.

8. Heidegger, "Nietzsche's Word: God Is Dead," in *The Question Concerning Technology,* trans. William Lovitt (New York: Harper & Row, 1977), p. 61.

9. Heidegger, ibid., pp. 108, 74, 84.

10. Hannah Arendt, "Truth and Politics," in *Philosophy, Politics and Society,* 3d series, ed. P. Laslett and W. Runciman (Oxford: Oxford University Press, 1967), pp. 117, 120.

11. See H. D. Rankin, *Sophists, Socratics, and Cynics* (London: Croom Helm, 1983), chap. 13.

12. Strobaeus, *Florilegium* VIII.6; in Rankin, *Sophists, Socratics, and Cynics,* p. 233. I am using Goodman's concept of exemplification, which I explain in Chapter 7. Nietzsche alludes to Diogenes' performative *chreia* in an early statement of the "God is dead" formula (*Gay Science,* trans. Walter Kaufman, New York: Vintage, 1974, §125): "Have you not heard of that madman who lit a lantern in the bright morning hours, ran to the marketplace, and cried incessantly: 'I seek God! I seek God!'—As many of those who did not believe in God were standing around just then, he provoked much laughter . . . The madman jumped into their midst and pierced them with his eyes. 'Whither is God?' he cried: 'I will tell you. *We have killed him*—you and I." Plato is said to have described Diogenes as "Socrates gone mad," while for their part Cynics did not hesitate to denounce Plato's idealism as a betrayal of Socrates. See L. E. Navia, *Socrates* (Lanham, Md.: University Press of America, 1985), pp. 116, 222.

13. On the Cynic *askesis,* see Rankin, *Sophists, Socratics, and Cynics,* p. 229; also Foucault, "Technology of the Self," in *Technologies of the Self: A Seminar with Michel Foucault,* ed. L. H. Martin et al. (Amherst: University of Massachusetts Press, 1988); and T. Flynn,

"Foucault as Parrhesist," in *The Final Foucault,* ed. J. Bernauer and D. Rasmussen (Cambridge, Mass.: MIT Press, 1988). According to G. Reale, "the 'Cynic life' [*kynikós bios*] in the Imperial Age for a long time was a real and very strong attraction and stimuli" and "and continued to live or survive up to the end of the sixth century." The Cynic life "became an authentic mass phenomenon . . . It can safely be said that no philosophy of antiquity had a diffusion on the popular level even distantly comparable to that of the Cynics." *A History of Ancient Philosophy,* vol. 4 *Schools in the Imperial Age* (Albany: State University of New York Press, 1990), pp. 146–159.

14. Freud, *Introductory Lectures on Psychoanalysis* (Harmondsworth: Pelican Freud Library, 1973), vol. 1, pp. 485–486; and "Resistances to Psychoanalysis" (Harmondsworth: Pelican Freud Library, 1986), vol. 15, p. 271. Freud characterizes the analytic relationship as "based on a love of truth—that is, a recognition of reality—and . . . precludes any kind of sham or deceit." "Analysis Terminable and Interminable," in *The Standard Edition of the Complete Psychological Works of Sigmund Freud* (London: Hogarth Press, 1954–1976), vol. 23, p. 247. Morris Eagle notes that "the belief that under appropriate conditions the truth is not only enlightening but freeing is a value that has always informed psychoanalysis." *Recent Developments in Psychoanalysis* (Cambridge, Mass.: Harvard University Press, 1987), p. 171.

15. Freud and Breuer, *Studies on Hysteria* (Harmondsworth: Pelican Freud Library, 1974), vol. 3, p. 393. Freud, "Leonardo Da Vinci and a Memory of His Childhood" (Harmondsworth: Pelican Freud Library, 1985), vol. 14, p. 230.

4. William James, or Pragmatism

1. Richard Rorty, *Consequences of Pragmatism* (Minneapolis: University of Minnesota Press, 1982), p. 161; R. B. Perry, *The Thought and Character of William James* (Boston: Little, Brown, 1935), vol. 1, p. 409. For a concise and accurate survey of pragmatic philosophy, see J. P. Murphy, *Pragmatism from Peirce to Davidson* (Boulder: Westview Press, 1990).

2. Jefferson to Priestly, 21 March 1801, *The Life and Selected Writings of Thomas Jefferson,* ed. Adrienne Koch and William Peden (New York: Random House, 1944), p. 562. R. W. Emerson, *Essays and*

Lectures (New York: Library of America, 1983), pp. 71, 216–217, 270. George Santayana, "The Genteel Tradition in American Philosophy," in *The Genteel Tradition,* ed. D. L. Wilson (Cambridge, Mass.: Harvard University Press, 1967), pp. 54–58. This was originally a lecture at the University of California, Berkeley. Santayana was, however, more impressed with James's so-called radical empiricism than with the pragmatic philosophy of truth.

3. It is ironic that the opposition between finished and open worlds which James uses to define the pragmatic difference from European thought is a European thought. In a fragment on "Transcendental Philosophy," Friedrich Schlegel writes: "This proposition, that the world is still incomplete, is extraordinarily important in every respect. If we think of the world as complete, then all our doings are nothing. But if we know that the world is incomplete, than no doubt our vocation is to cooperate in completing it." Cited in Hans Blumenberg, *The Genesis of the Copernican World,* trans. Robert M. Wallace (Cambridge, Mass.: MIT Press, 1987), p. 65.

4. Emerson, "Experience," in *Essays,* pp. 474–475. Frank Lentricchia suggests that "the Emerson/James connection may constitute the most influential enhancement of intellectual force in American literary history." See "On the Ideology of Poetic Modernism, 1890–1913: The Example of William James," in *Restructuring American Literary History,* ed. Sacvan Bercovitch (Cambridge, Mass.: Harvard University Press, 1986), p. 230; also "The Return of William James," in Lentricchia, *Ariel and the Police* (Madison: University of Wisconsin Press, 1988). Cornel West underscores Emerson's importance for pragmatism; see *The American Evasion of Philosophy: A Genealogy of Pragmatism* (Madison: University of Wisconsin Press, 1989).

5. In psychology, James held that "the effort which [a man] is able to put forth to hold himself erect and keep his heart unshaken is the direct measure of his worth and function in the game of human life. He can *stand* this Universe. He can meet it and keep up his faith in it in [the] presence of those same features which lay his weaker brethren low." *The Principles of Psychology* (1890) (New York: Dover, 1950), vol. 2, pp. 578–579. On the prestige of psychology in America at the turn of the century, and on the reduction of political differences to psychological ones, see T. J. Lears, *No Place of Grace: Antimodernism and the Transformation of American Culture, 1880–1920* (New York: Pantheon, 1981), esp. p. 304. These trends had long been in prepara-

tion; see Perry Miller, *The Life of the Mind in America* (New York: Harcourt, Brace & World, 1965), p. 321.

6. A. J. Ayer writes of pragmatism, "Its standpoint is very closely akin to that which was later to be adopted by the logical positivists. Peirce's pragmatic maxim is indeed identical, for all practical purposes, with the physicalist interpretation of the verification principle." *The Origins of Pragmatism* (London: Macmillan, 1968), p. 55. Although he obviously did not share Ayer's experience with positivism, in "What Pragmatism Is" (1905), Peirce carefully distinguishes his position from that of Poincaré, Pearson, and other positivists of the time, remarking that while pragmatism "endeavors to define the rational purport" of terms, which "it finds in the purposive bearing of the word or proposition in question," it does not maintain that the pragmatic "purport of a word . . . [is] the only kind of meaning there is." *The Collected Papers of Charles Sanders Peirce*, ed. Charles Hartshorne and Paul Weiss (Cambridge, Mass.: Harvard University Press, 1934), vol. 5, pp. 285–289. See also Peirce's early "Critique of Positivism," in *Writings of Charles S. Peirce: A Chronological Edition* (Bloomington: Indiana University Press, 1984), vol. 2. Moritz Schlick also saw an important difference between his positivism and pragmatism; see *General Theory of Knowledge* (1918), trans. A. Blumberg (LaSalle, Ill.: Open Court, 1985), p. 165.

7. Peirce expects his pragmatic maxim to aid in attaining the "third degree" of logical apprehension of ideas (after clarity and distinctness), but he by no means supposes that it alone suffices for the determination of meaning. See "How to Make Our Ideas Clear," in *Collected Papers*, vol. 5, pp. 248–271.

8. For an example of the criticism I am rejecting, see Alan White, *Truth* (Garden City, N.Y.: Anchor, 1970), pp. 125–126. Paul Horwich also assumes that pragmatism asserts a logical synonymy between "true" and some predicate of practical value: "one might offer . . . a synonym that would permit us to eliminate the word 'true' in a uniform way from every context in which it appears . . . The pragmatists' identification of truth with utility has this character." *Truth* (Oxford: Blackwell, 1990), p. 34.

9. On Nietzsche and Emerson, see Sacvan Bercovitch, *The Puritan Origins of the American Self* (New Haven: Yale University Press, 1975), pp. 174–176; and Harold Bloom, *A Map of Misreading* (Oxford: Oxford University Press, 1975), p. 176. On Nietzsche and James, see M.

A. Weinstein, *The Wilderness and the City: American Classical Philosophy as a Moral Quest* (Amherst: University of Massachusetts Press, 1982), pp. 129–137. James was not much of a reader of Nietzsche, though he did know his work, to which I have found three references. In *The Variety of Religious Experience* he cites from the third essay of the *Genealogy* (a key text for the question of truth's value). *Writings, 1902–1910* (New York: Library of America, 1987), p. 336. In a review, he says of Benjamin Paul Blood's attitude that it "seems to resemble that of Nietzsche's *amor fati!*" *Writings,* p. 1312. Finally, a letter of 1905: "As for Nietzsche . . . I recall . . . a posthumous article in one of the French reviews a few months back. In his high and mighty way he was laying down the law about all the European countries." *The Letters of William James,* ed. Henry James (Boston: Atlantic Monthly Press, 1920), vol. 2, p. 233.

10. See Plato, *Theaetetus,* esp. 171a–e. James's friend and fellow pragmatist F. C. S. Schiller thought pragmatism had an affinity "with the great saying of Protagoras, that *Man is the Measure of all things.* Fairly interpreted, this is the truest and most important thing that any thinker ever has propounded." Yet he carefully distinguishes his interpretation of this from "travesties such as it suited Plato's dialectic purpose to circulate." *Humanism,* 2d ed. (London: Macmillan, 1912), p. xxi.

11. William James, *The Will to Believe and Other Essays in Popular Philosophy* (1897) (New York: Dover, 1956), p. 191.

12. R. B. Perry, *In the Spirit of William James* (Bloomington: Indiana University Press, 1958), p. 34, citing Royce, *Philosophy of Loyalty* (1908).

13. James had a long-standing interest in the cause of mental hygiene. He lent spiritual and financial support to the organization of the National Committee for Mental Hygiene, and when it was founded in 1909 he served as a trustee. *Writings,* pp. 1346–1347. Reviewing Henry Maudsley's *Responsibility in Mental Disease* thirty-five years earlier (1874), he judged a chapter on "the prevention of insanity" so "original" and "valuable" that "it should be reprinted as a tract, and dispersed gratis over the land." See H. M. Feinstein, *Becoming William James* (Ithaca: Cornell University Press, 1984), p. 311. Twelve years later, writing to Henry (then in Europe) of the Haymarket riot in Chicago (May 1886), he demonstrates a psychologist's confidence in judging maladaptive mental habits: "Don't be alarmed about the

labor troubles here. I am quite sure they are a most healthy phase of evolution, a little costly, but normal, and sure to do lots of good to all hands in the end. I don't speak of the senseless 'anarchist' riot in Chicago, which had nothing to do with 'Knights of Labor' but is the work of a lot of pathological Germans and Poles." *Letters,* vol. 1, p. 252. Addressing his audience at the Lowell Institute a decade later, the difference between pragmatist and antipragmatist becomes one between "healthy-minded and sick-minded" (*P.*141).

14. James, *Letters,* vol. 2, p. 90. The "Address on the Philippine Question" appears in *Writings;* I cite p. 1135.

5. Heidegger, or The Truth of Being

1. Heidegger, "Modern Natural Science and Technology," in *Radical Phenomenology: Essays in Honor of Martin Heidegger,* ed. John Sallis (Atlantic Highlands, N.J.: Humanities Press, 1978), p. 3. An editorial note states that "this text is reported to have been the last composed by him." Interview in *Heidegger and the Path of Thinking,* ed. John Sallis (Pittsburgh: Duquesne University Press, 1970), p. 10. For accuracy and consistency I often modify the published translations of Heidegger from which I cite.

2. Plato, *Republic* 585c. I discussed Hegel's statement concerning the *logos* of Heraclitus (*Lectures on the History of Philosophy,* vol. 1, p. 295) in Chapter 1. In an essay on Heraclitus, Heidegger writes: "The word *Logos* names that which gathers all present beings into presencing *(Jenes, das alles Anwesende ins Anwesen versammelt)* and thereby lets them lie before us" (*EGT.*76). Elsewhere in the same essay he says that "the authentic hearing of mortals is in a certain way the Same as the *Logos*" (*EGT.*67).

3. Citations of Heidegger in this paragraph are from *WT.*202, *WT.*228, *BW.*212, and *Grundbegriffe* (Freiburg Lectures, 1941), in *Gesamtausgabe* (Frankfurt: Klostermann, 1981), vol. 51, p. 43.

4. On the distinction between linguistic and temporal tense, and between tensed and tenseless time, see D. H. Mellor, *Real Time* (Cambridge: Cambridge University Press, 1981). Mellor is concerned with the question whether tense "exists" or is "real"; Heidegger would reject the question as oblivious to the distinction between time (which is not a being) and what is. Husserl's *Phenomenology of Internal Time Consciousness* (trans. J. Churchill, Bloomington: Indiana University Press,

1964) brackets the question whether tense "really exists" and is devoted instead to a phenomenological analysis of temporal consciousness. Heidegger would be unimpressed by Quine's argument that canonical notation can dispense with tense. *Word and Object* (Cambridge, Mass.: MIT Press, 1960), §36. In Heidegger's view, the very possibility of representing events in tenseless time or framing tenseless sentences presupposes an understanding of tensed temporality as reflected in the verbal tenses of historical languages.

5. On the unification of "to be" around the being of substance, see G. E. L. Owen, "Logic and Metaphysics in Some Earlier Works of Aristotle," in *Logic, Science, and Dialectic,* ed. Martha Nussbaum (London: Duckworth, 1986). The notion, popularized by Russell, that Plato and Aristotle failed to distinguish clearly the merely equivocal "is" of identity, predication, and existence is refuted by Benson Mates, "Identity and Predication in Plato," and Russell Dancy, "Aristotle and Existence," in *The Logic of Being: Historical Studies,* ed. S. Knuuttila and J. Hintikka (Dordrecht: Reidel, 1986). Note that for Aristotle to *be possible* is to be somewhere sometime actual: "evidently it cannot be true to say 'this is capable of being but will not be'" (1047b).

6. In *Being and Time* Heidegger distinguishes three modes of being: *Existenz, Vorhandenheit,* and the being peculiar to instruments or tools (*Zuhandenheit*). He repeats this three-part division in *Basic Problems,* although the simpler opposition of Dasein's existence and the extantness of nature or the mere thing is more prominent there, and I have chosen not to complicate the account. Derrida draws attention to the peculiar status of the (nonhuman) animal in Heidegger; see *Of Spirit: Heidegger and the Question,* trans. Geoffrey Bennington and Rachel Bowlby (Chicago: University of Chicago Press, 1989), pp. 52–57. Heidegger's pronouncements on this only become more extreme. In a lecture of 1927, he says: "we ourselves are not mere animals"; an animal "merely lives but does not exist" (*BP.*191). Twenty years later, in the "Letter on Humanism," he refers to "our appalling and scarcely conceivable bodily kinship with the beast." He says: "of all the beings that there are, presumably the most difficult to think about are living creatures, because on the one hand they are in a certain way most closely related to us, and on the other hand are at the same time separated from our ek-sistent essence by an abyss" (*BW.*206). The name of that abyss, as he goes on to say, is language, which is something else

whose essence has to be rethought from Heidegger's *Schritt zurück*. See the writings gathered in *On the Way to Language,* trans. Peter D. Hertz (New York: Harper & Row, 1971).

7. Husserl, *Ideas,* trans. W. R. Boyce Gibson (London: George Allen & Unwin, 1931), p. 310. Heidegger, *Kant and the Problem of Metaphysics,* trans. James S. Churchill (Bloomington: Indiana University Press, 1962), pp. 194, 200–201. Derrida acutely describes the idea of "time as the condition for the possibility of the appearance of beings in (finite) experience" as "that in Kant which will be repeated by Heidegger" (*M*.48). Heidegger's ontological difference and Kant's differentiation of transcendental and empirical both endeavor to specify a difference which conditions all intentional, meaningful, intelligent relation to an object. But to be, for Kant, is to be posited as an object of possible experience (A598/B626). The difference between being and beings is for him nothing but a difference between possible contents of experience on the one hand and the universal conditions of that experience on the other. From Heidegger's perspective, this remains oblivious to the ontological difference.

8. Heidegger, interview in *Listening* 6 (1971), 35. Elsewhere he says, "The oldest axioms of Western thought . . . already state this fact" (*WT*.80). He is referring to a fragment from the poem of Parmenides: "Thinking *(noein)* and being *(einai)* are the same *(to auto)*." Heidegger asks, "what does *to auto* mean?" It is "correctly translated with 'the same,'" but how should one interpret that? "*To auto* . . . means what belongs together . . . The two [thinking and being] belong together in this way, that the essential nature of *noein* . . . consists in its remaining focused on the presence of what is present. *Eon,* the presence of what is present, accordingly keeps and guards *noein* within itself as what belongs to it" (*WT*.240–242). "Parmenides' saying is an assertion neither about thinking nor about being . . . [but] about the essential belonging together of both in their difference . . . What is silently concealed in the enigmatic key word *to auto* is . . . the belonging-together of the duality" (*EGT*.85, 95).

9. Heidegger, "The Principle of Identity" (1957), in *Identity and Difference,* trans. Joan Stambaugh (New York: Harper & Row, 1969) pp. 25, 41.

10. Heidegger, "The Onto-Theo-Logical Constitution of Metaphysics" (1957), in *Identity and Difference,* pp. 47, 48, 50, 49; emphasis added.

11. Heidegger, *Logik: Die Frage nach der Wahrheit* (Marburg Lectures, 1925–26), in *Gesamtausgabe* (Frankfurt: Klostermann, 1976), vol. 21, p. 163; and *The Essence of Reasons,* trans. Terrence Malick (Evanston: Northwestern University Press, 1969), pp. 19–21. There is reason to think that Aristotle's auditors would have found his formula for truth as obvious as Heidegger fears his auditors will. In his study of the Greek verb "be," C. H. Kahn writes: "the classical formula given by Aristotle . . . merely articulates the pattern of the ordinary veridical idioms in Greek . . . As in the most contemporary idiom so in Homer and Sophocles: The man who speaks the truth 'tells it like it is,' and the liar tells it otherwise . . . this is the ordinary Greek notion of telling or knowing the truth, from Homer to Aristotle." *The Verb "Be" in Ancient Greek* (Dordrecht: Reidel, 1973), p. 363.

12. Heidegger, *Logik,* p. 6.

13. On the distinction between essence and existence, see G. Kopaczynski, *Linguistic Ramifications of the Essence-Existence Debate* (Lanham, Md.: University Press of America, 1979); and J. F. Wippel, "Essence and Existence," in *Cambridge History of Later Medieval Philosophy,* ed. Norman Kretzmann et al. (Cambridge: Cambridge University Press, 1982). Heidegger discusses this in *BP* §10. He repeats the banal criticism that the Thomistic "real distinction" between *esse* and *essentia* treats *esse* (existence) as if it were a thing *(res)*. Although formulations by Gilles of Rome suggest this, it is not plausible to make this objection against Thomas himself. See Etienne Gilson, *Being and Some Philosophers,* 2d ed. (Toronto: Pontifical Institute of Medieval Studies, 1952), chap. 5. It may also be worth pointing out here that Nietzsche was wrong to describe Christianity as "Platonism for the people" (*B.* Preface). It made a good aphorism, but we do not have that excuse for repeating it. Although for Plato being and truth are the same, this being is far from the infinite and fully actual God Who created finite being and conserves it through every moment of existence. Gilson argues that the essential Christian revision of Greek metaphysics is the idea that God, and God alone, is Being. Referring to the text of Exodus (3:14), *Ego sum qui sum,* he writes: "Exodus lays down the principle from which henceforth the whole of Christian philosophy will be suspended . . . There is but one God and this God is Being, that is the corner-stone of all Christian philosophy, and it was not Plato, it was not even Aristotle, it was Moses who put it in position." *The Spirit of Medieval Philosophy* (1936) (Notre Dame:

University of Notre Dame Press, 1991), p. 51. See also A. C. Pegis, *Saint Thomas and the Greeks* (Milwaukee: Marquette University Press, 1939), pp. 66–84.

6. Derrida, or Difference Unlimited

1. Aristotle defines the sign in *Prior Analytics* 70a; cp. *Rhetoric* 1357a–b. Stoic semiology is reconstructed by Theodor Ebert, "Origin of the Stoic Theory of Signs," in *Oxford Studies in Ancient Philosophy,* vol. 5, ed. Julia Annas (Oxford: Oxford University Press, 1987). For Augustine's influential definition of the sign, see *On Christian Doctrine,* trans. D. W. Robertson (Indianapolis: Bobbs-Merrill, 1958), II.1.1. On Locke, see Norman Kretzmann, "The Main Thesis of Locke's Semantic Theory," in *Locke on Human Understanding,* ed. I. C. Tipton (Oxford: Oxford University Press, 1977). On the theory of supposition, see M. M. Adams, *William Ockham* (Notre Dame: University of Notre Dame Press, 1987), pp. 327–351; and on this history generally, see John Deely, *Introducing Semiotic: Its History and Doctrine* (Bloomington: Indiana University Press, 1982). I say that syncategorematic signs, which do not themselves stand for anything, nonetheless confirm the rule according to which the essence of the sign is to stand for something else because syncategoremata do not signify save when in the context of a proposition they contribute to the determination of what a categorical term stands for.
2. F. de Saussure, *Course in General Linguistics,* trans. Roy Harris (LaSalle, Ill.: Open Court, 1986), pp. 65–67, 115–119; and a note cited in E. Benveniste, "Saussure after Half a Century," in Benveniste, *Problems in General Linguistics,* trans. Mary Elizabeth Meek (Coral Gables, Fla.: University of Miami Press, 1971), p. 36. On the objection to nomenclaturism, see Roy Harris, *Reading Saussure* (LaSalle, Ill.: Open Court, 1987), pp. 55–64.
3. Saussure, *Course,* pp. 114–115. On *semiotikē,* see Locke, *Essay,* IV.xxi.4.
4. Hans Aarsleff has observed that Taine's *De l'Intelligence* (1870) "contains all the elements of Saussure's doctrine of signs." This includes the distinctions between synchronic and diachronic, *langue* and *parole,* signifier and signified; the comparison of sound and sense in a language to recto and verso faces; and a concept of linguistic value. Aarsleff concludes that "Saussure was working within the conceptual

milieu of Taine's thought," and that "the concept of system or structure which a latter age found in Saussure was fully developed by Taine with the same broad implications and applications that have since been redeveloped from Saussure's linguistic thought." *From Locke to Saussure* (Minneapolis: University of Minnesota Press, 1982), pp. 358–361. But Aarsleff may underestimate the innovation entailed by thoroughgoing semiological difference. "It is this emphasis on *differences* which . . . [is] the distinctive signature of Saussurean structuralism." Roy Harris and T. J. Taylor, *Landmarks of Linguistic Thought* (London: Routledge, 1989), p. 190.

5. Plato, *Sophist* 255c–d.

6. Saussure, *Course,* pp. 14, 80, 99.

7. Citations of Saussure in this paragraph are from *Course,* pp. 15, 113; and from notebook material quoted in Jean Starobinski, *Words upon Words,* trans. Olivia Emmet (New Haven: Yale University Press, 1979), p. 5.

8. This criticism of Saussure is not the one Derrida advances in *Of Grammatology,* which focuses instead on Saussure's remarks apropos writing and its relation to what is assumed to be an originally spoken language. Derrida tries to convict Saussure of a "phonocentrism" and "logocentrism" that are supposedly abiding, unquestioned assumptions of Western science and metaphysics. "What Saussure saw without seeing, knew without being *able* to take into account, following in that the entire metaphysical tradition, is that a certain model of writing was necessarily but provisionally imposed . . . as instrument and technique of representation of a system of language . . . The system of language associated with phonetic-alphabetic writing is that within which logocentric metaphysics, determining the sense of being as presence, has been produced" (*G.*43).

My account of Saussure's place in the history of semiotic is not exactly Derrida's. At the same time, and contrary to his own self-commentary, the theme of phonocentrism is of little importance to my reading of Derrida, which does not depend on his version of this history or on his doubtful claim that Saussure no less than Aristotle privileges the voice over writing. This is worth emphasizing because this "myth of the voice" is probably the most implausible and untenable feature of Derrida's work. See J. Claude Evans, *Strategies of Deconstruction: Derrida and the Myth of the Voice* (Minneapolis: University of Minnesota Press, 1991), esp. chap. 10.

9. Derrida, "Sending: On Representation," *Social Research* 49 (1982), 324. Other citations in this paragraph are from Leonard Bloomfield, *Language* (New York: Holt, Rinehart, and Winston, 1933), p. 285; and Saussure, *Course,* pp. 24–25. Despite the authorities who can be cited, it is impossible to maintain seriously that writing is added to spoken language as an instrument for its representation; see Roy Harris, *The Origin of Writing* (London: Duckworth, 1986).

10. One indication of how badly Searle reads work he would criticize is that he does not consider whether Derrida might be less certain than he about the existence and nature of "types." In the patronizing tone of his entire discussion he says, "As Derrida is aware, any linguistic element . . . must be repeatable . . . To say this is just to say that the logician's type-token distinction must apply generally to all the . . . elements of language . . . Without this . . . there could not be the possibility of producing an infinite number of sentences with a finite list of elements; and this, as philosophers since Frege have recognized, is one of the crucial features of any language." "Reiterating the Difference: A Reply to Derrida," *Glyph* 1 (1977), 199. This is not a crucial feature; it is a tissue of dubious and unexamined presuppositions. Skepticism about this picture of language is a point on which Derrida can agree with Wittgenstein, Davidson, Bakhtin, Roy Harris, Pierre Bourdieu, and others. Nelson Goodman simply dismisses the type altogether and treats "the so-called tokens of a type as *replicas* of one another. An inscription need not be an exact duplicate of another to be a replica, or true copy, of it; indeed, there is in general no degree of similarity that is necessary or sufficient for replicahood." *Languages of Art,* 2d ed. (Indianapolis: Hackett, 1976), p. 131n.

11. This point has an interesting parallel with the criticism of Saussure from the circle around Bakhtin in the late 1920s. In a work Bakhtin may have written (published in 1929 under the name of his colleague Vološinov) it is argued that "the process of understanding is on no account to be confused with the process of recognition. These are thoroughly different processes . . . The basic task of understanding does not at all amount to recognizing the linguistic form used by the speaker as the familiar, 'that very same,' form." V. N. Vološinov, *Marxism and the Philosophy of Language,* trans. Ladislav Matejka and I. R. Titunik (Cambridge, Mass.: Harvard University Press, 1986), pp. 68–69, 77.

12. In a note from 1894 Saussure writes: "The object that serves as a sign

is never the same *(le même)* twice . . . therein lies its fundamental difference from an ordinary object." Cited in Roman Jakobson, "Development of Semiotics," in *Language in Literature* (Cambridge, Mass.: Harvard University Press, 1987), p. 448.

13. Heidegger, *On the Way to Language,* trans. Peter D. Hertz (New York: Harper & Row, 1971), p. 123.

14. In another place Derrida elaborates on the ambiguity of Heidegger's position in relation to metaphysics. Referring to Heidegger's 1933 Rectorship Address, he writes: "If its programme seems diabolical, it is because, *without there being anything fortuitous in this,* it capitalizes on the worst, that is on both evils at once: the sanctioning of nazism, and the gesture that is still metaphysical . . . Metaphysics returns . . . Is this not what Heidegger will never finally be able to avoid? . . . this awesome equivocality." *Of Spirit: Heidegger and the Question,* trans. Geoffrey Bennington and Rachel Bowlby (Chicago: University of Chicago Press, 1989), pp. 40–41.

15. Note that Derrida translates Hegel's *Aufhebung* as *la relève;* see "The Pit and Pyramid: Introduction to Hegel's Semiology," in Derrida, *Margins of Philosophy,* trans. Alan Bass (Chicago: University of Chicago Press, 1982).

16. One way to criticize Derrida would therefore be to criticize Saussure's principle of difference. Were this principle open to serious objections, the deconstructions might deconstruct. David Holdcroft argues that there are good reasons for rejecting Saussure's principle; see his *Saussure: Signs, System, and Arbitrariness* (Cambridge: Cambridge University Press, 1991), pp. 121–133. I examine this criticism in "Difference Unlimited," in *Working Through Derrida,* ed. G. B. Madison (Evanston: Northwestern University Press, 1993).

17. Donald Davidson, "The Structure and Content of Truth," *Journal of Philosophy* 87 (1990), 285; and "On the Very Idea of a Conceptual Scheme," in *Inquiries Concerning Truth and Interpretation* (Oxford: Oxford University Press, 1984), p. 194.

18. Of history, Michael Oakeshott writes: "an historical past . . . [is] composed entirely of contingently related differences which have no conceptual affinity; a continuity of heterogeneous and convergent tensions." He defines a historical event as "a by-product of a past composed of antecedent events which have no exclusive characters, no predetermined outcomes, and no inherent potentialities to issue in this rather than that, but which an historical enquiry may show that and

how they have in fact done so . . . Historical events are themselves circumstantial convergences of antecedent historical events; what they are is how they came to be woven." *On History and Other Essays* (Totowa, N.J.: Barnes and Noble Books, 1983), pp. 64–67, 94–117.

19. This point was not always entirely clear in earlier work. For example, it is not impossible to read the following passage as one in which the value of truth is at least contested if not destroyed: "I wished to reach the point of a certain exteriority in relation to the totality of the age of logocentrism. Starting from this point of exteriority, a certain deconstruction of that totality . . . might be broached. The first gesture of this departure and this deconstruction, although subject to a certain historical necessity, cannot be given methodological or logical intraorbitary assurances . . . It proceeds like a wandering thought on the possibility of itinerary and of method . . . an attempt to get out of the orbit, to think the entirety of the classical conceptual oppositions, particularly . . . the opposition of philosophy and nonphilosophy . . . being produced as truth at the moment when the value of truth is shattered" (G.161–162).

20. Richard Rorty, *Philosophical Papers,* vol. 1: *Objectivity, Relativism, and Truth* (Cambridge: Cambridge University Press, 1991), pp. 71–72.

7. Wittgenstein, or The Aufhebung of Logic

1. Plato, *Cratylus* 434a–b, my emphasis.

2. As evidence for this interpretation of Wittgenstein's enigmatic "objects," I cite the only two passages in which he says anything remotely informative about them:

> Space, time, and color (being colored) are forms of objects *(Gegenstände).* (*TLP.*2.0251)

> A spatial object must be situated in infinite space. (A spatial point is an argument-place.) A speck in the visual field, though it need not be red, must have some color: it is, so to speak, surrounded by color-space. Notes must have *some* pitch, objects of the sense of touch *some* degree of hardness, and so on. (*TLP.*2.0131)

3. See Nelson Goodman, "Routes of Reference," in *Of Mind and Other Matters* (Cambridge, Mass.: Harvard University Press, 1984), pp. 55–71. For more detail, see Goodman, *Languages of Art,* 2d ed. (Indianapolis: Hackett, 1976), chaps. 2–5. Goodman holds that what a sam-

ple refers to is not a property but a label, which denotes items that belong to a resemblance class that includes the sample. Goodman would therefore not allow that an exemplificational sign is the same as its referent in the referred-to respect, since that referent is not a property but a predicate. This is demanded by his nominalism, but Wittgenstein's theory depends on identifying properties (determinations of logical forms) with the objects of reference in signs.

4. Wittgenstein, *Wittgenstein's Lectures, Cambridge 1930–1932,* ed. Desmond Lee (Chicago: University of Chicago Press, 1982), p. 6; see also *Philosophical Remarks,* trans. Raymond Hargreaves and Roger White (Chicago: University of Chicago Press, 1975), pp. 78–79. Referring to *Tractatus* 2.1511, Wittgenstein says: "I have elsewhere said that a proposition 'reaches up to reality,' and by this I meant that the forms of the entities are contained in the form of the proposition which is about these entities." "Remarks on Logical Form," in *Essays on Wittgenstein's "Tractatus,"* ed. I. Copi and R. W. Beard (New York: Macmillan, 1966), p. 36.

5. Referring to "countless different kinds of use of what we call 'symbols,' 'words,' 'sentences,'" Wittgenstein says, "this multiplicity is not something fixed, given once for all; but new types of language, new language-games, as we may say, come into existence, and others become obsolete and get forgotten" (*PI*.23). Also, one should not regard language-games as narrowly linguistic but as broadly symbolic, involving signs other than those conventionally counted as language; for instance, samples or exemplary objects like a yardstick. See *PI*.16, and *Lectures and Conversations,* ed. Cyril Barrett (Oxford: Blackwell, 1978), where Wittgenstein remarks: "What belongs to a language-game is a whole culture" (p. 8).

6. On this point, compare Mary Douglas's thesis that "similarity is an institution." *How Institutions Think* (Syracuse: Syracuse University Press, 1986), chap. 5.

7. "*Australopithecus* is shorter than *Homo sapiens*" is true in English ≡ *Australopithecus* is shorter than *Homo sapiens*. This is the "disquotation" property of the truth-predicate discussed in Chapter 1. See W. V. Quine, *Pursuit of Truth,* rev. ed. (Cambridge, Mass.: Harvard University Press, 1992), §33.

8. Michael Dummett, "Wittgenstein's Philosophy of Mathematics," in *Truth and Other Enigmas* (Cambridge, Mass.: Harvard University Press, 1987), p. 175.

9. Especially in response to Saul Kripke's *Wittgenstein on Rules and Private Language* (Cambridge, Mass.: Harvard University Press, 1982). See the critical notice by G. E. M. Anscombe in *Canadian Journal of Philosophy* 15 (1985), 103–109. I discuss Kripke's argument in "Gruesome Arithmetic: Kripke's Skeptic Replies," *Dialogue* 28 (1989), 257–264.

10. I share Quine's distrust of claims about what would be under conditions that in fact never arise. "Everything is what it is, ask not what it may or must be." Quine, *Theories and Things* (Cambridge, Mass.: Harvard University Press, 1981), p. 174. Reasoning about what supposedly would be under counterfactual assumptions has always been deeply allied with the conviction that *what is* must be endowed with a nature or physical identity independent of the contingent circumstances under which it actually exists. In a sixth-century commentary on Aristotle's *Physics,* for example, Johannes Philopones writes: "We often assume the impossible, so as to understand the nature of things in and of themselves . . . And even though it is not possible that one of these assumptions become real, reasoning separates what is together according to nature in thought, so as to manifest how everything behaves in itself according to its specific nature." For a historical study of this style of reasoning, see Amos Funkenstein, *Theology and the Scientific Imagination* (Princeton: Princeton University Press, 1986), chap. 3. The citation from Philopones is on pp. 164–165.

11. Kant, *Metaphysical Foundations of Natural Science* (1786), trans. James W. Ellington (Indianapolis: Hackett, 1985), p. 7.

12. Donald Davidson, "The Myth of the Subjective," in *Relativism: Interpretation and Confrontation,* ed. M. Krausz (Notre Dame: University of Notre Dame Press, 1989).

13. For a sample of the large literature on the private language argument, see the papers collected in *The Private Language Argument,* ed. O. R. Jones (London: Macmillan, 1971). See also A. J. Ayer, "Can There Be a Private Language?" in *Wittgenstein: The "Philosophical Investigations,"* ed. George Pitcher (Notre Dame: University of Notre Dame Press, 1966); Richard Rorty, "Wittgenstein, Privileged Access, and Incommunicability," *American Philosophical Quarterly* 7 (1970), 192–205; Robert Fogelin, *Wittgenstein* (London: Routledge and Kegan Paul, 1976), chap. 8; and Stewart Candlish, "The Real Private Language Argument," *Philosophy* 55 (1980), 85–94.

14. I mentioned Searle's doctrine of original Intentionality in Chapter 2. Daniel Dennett explains original intentionality as "the claim that

whereas some of our artifacts may have intentionality derived from us, we have original (or intrinsic) intentionality, utterly underived . . . we are Unmeant Meaners." *The Intentional Stance* (Cambridge, Mass.: MIT Press, 1987), p. 288. He suspects that "the intuition that lies behind the belief in original intentionality" is "the idea that you are unlike the fledging cuckoo not only in having access, but in having privileged access to your meanings" (p. 313).

15. Some key references for this argument are *PI*.281–284, 357, and 377.

16. Wittgenstein, *The Blue and Brown Books* (Oxford: Blackwell, 1958), p. 48.

17. A more elaborate stipulation would allow for the relativity of simultaneity. See J. L. Mackie, "Five O'Clock on the Sun," *Analysis* 41:3 (1981), 113–114. Mackie's criticism of Wittgenstein in this article is, however, entirely misguided. Not only does Wittgenstein's argument not depend on the assumption, which Mackie attributes to him, that talk of time on the sun is irredeemable nonsense; Mackie also assumes that Wittgenstein's point in §350 is to dispute the "argument by analogy" for knowledge of other minds. This is not the argument Wittgenstein alludes to in the opening of §350. The interlocutor does not say that there is an analogy between the other's behavior and his own which provides a basis for inferring sameness of mental state, but that the possible truth of talk of the other's mental state is secured by the consideration that *what I mean* when I speak of this is just that the other's mental state is the same as mine.

18. Hans-Georg Gadamer, *Truth and Method* (New York: Continuum, 1975), p. 346. W. V. Quine, *Word and Object* (Cambridge, Mass.: MIT Press, 1960), chap. 2; and "Indeterminacy of Translation Again," *Journal of Philosophy* 84 (1987), 5–10. Although the problematic is quite different, Derrida discusses translation in "Des Tours de Babel," in *Difference in Translation,* ed. J. F. Graham (Ithaca: Cornell University Press, 1985), and in *The Ear of the Other,* ed. Christie V. McDonald (New York: Schocken Books, 1985). A basic reference for these discussions is Walter Benjamin, "The Task of the Translator," in *Illuminations,* ed. Hannah Arendt (New York: Schocken Books, 1969); see also Paul de Man, "Conclusions: Walter Benjamin's 'The Task of the Translator,'" in *The Resistance to Theory* (Minneapolis: University of Minnesota Press, 1986).

19. Citations in this paragraph are from Quine, *Word and Object,* p. 73; "Indeterminacy of Translation Again," pp. 8–10; and "Reply to Chomsky," in *Words and Objections: Essays on the Work of W. V.*

Quine, ed. Donald Davidson and Jaakko Hintikka (Dordrecht: Reidel, 1969), p. 304.

20. Quine, "Indeterminacy of Translation Again," pp. 7–8.
21. Donald Davidson, *Inquiries Concerning Truth and Interpretation* (Oxford: Oxford University Press, 1984), p. 200.
22. These citations are from Wittgenstein, *PI.* II.226; *Remarks on the Philosophy of Psychology,* trans. C. G. Luckhardt and M. A. E. Aue (Chicago: University of Chicago Press, 1980), vol. 2, §§347–348; *Zettel,* trans. G. E. M. Anscombe (Berkeley: University of California Press, 1970), §351; and *RFM.*200, 323, 343.
23. Davidson, *Inquiries,* pp. 199–200; and "A Coherence Theory of Truth and Knowledge," in *Reading Rorty,* ed. A. Malichowski (Oxford: Blackwell, 1990), p. 128.
24. "Thought," Wittgenstein is reported to have said in 1930, "is a symbolic process." All that matters is that "the symbolic process happens." "There is no mental process which cannot be symbolised; and if there were such a process which could not take place on the blackboard, it would not help. For I could still ask for a description of this process, and the description would be in symbols which would have a relation to reality. We are interested only in what can be symbolised." *Lectures,* pp. 25, 45; cp. *PG.*99.
25. W. V. Quine, *From a Logical Point of View,* 2d ed. (New York: Harper & Row, 1961), p. 46; Wittgenstein, *Remarks on Colour,* trans. Linda L. McAlister and Margarete Schättle (Berkeley: University of California Press, 1978), pp. 6–7, and *On Certainty,* trans. Denis Paul and G. E. M. Anscombe (New York: Harper & Row, 1972), §98.

8. Foucault, or Truth in Politics

1. As the third essay of the *Genealogy of Morals* (1887) demonstrates, the question of truth's value remained part of Nietzsche's work throughout the 1880s. Elsewhere, Foucault remarks, "What most struck me in Nietzsche is that for him the rationality of a science, a practice, or a discourse isn't measured by the truth that it is in a position to produce. Rather, truth itself has a share in the history of discourse, and in some ways has an internal effect on a discourse, or on a practice." *Remarks on Marx,* trans. R. James Goldstein and James Cascaito (New York: Semiotext(e), 1991), p. 62.
2. This is written against an unfortunate tendency to assimilate

Nietzsche and Foucault via the equivocal term "power." For instance, Habermas believes he has criticized Foucault when he says "Nietzsche's authority, from which this [Foucault's] utterly unsociological concept of power is borrowed, is not enough to justify its systematic usage." *The Philosophical Discourse of Modernity,* trans. Frederick Lawrence (Cambridge, Mass.: MIT Press, 1987), p. 249. Charles Taylor finds in Nietzsche "a doctrine which Foucault seems to have made his own"; namely, that "there is no order of human life, or way we are, or human nature, that one can appeal to in order to judge or evaluate between ways of life. There are only different orders imposed by men on primal chaos, following their will to power." "Foucault on Freedom and Truth," in *Foucault: A Critical Reader,* ed. D. C. Hoy (Oxford: Blackwell, 1986), p. 93. Here Taylor actually makes two points about Nietzsche. He notices Nietzsche's skepticism that nature or human nature prefers one ethos or practice more than another; he also notes a certain mythopoesis of primal chaos and will to power. But instead of observing their independence—for there is no compelling link between them—Taylor overlooks it, and then cannot see the difference between Nietzsche and Foucault.

One has to wonder at this determination to assimilate when differentiation is equally possible. It is entirely up to readers to perform this textual juxtaposition and make of it what they can, and, as Nietzsche observes, "Seeing things as similar and making things the same is the sign of weak eyes." *The Gay Science,* trans. Walter Kaufmann (New York: Vintage, 1974), §228.

3. See Walter Ullmann, *A History of Political Thought: The Middle Ages* (Harmondsworth: Penguin Books, 1965), pp. 15–18. Max Weber confirms the traditional centrality of the will in the definition of political power: "Power is the probability that one actor within a social relationship will be in a position to carry out his own will despite resistance, regardless of the basis on which this probability rests." *The Theory of Social and Economic Organizations,* ed. Talcott Parsons (New York: Free Press, 1964), p. 152. Even one of Foucault's critics on the Left confirms that Marxism cannot credibly claim to break with this traditional representation: "When all the recent complications of Marxist political theory are taken into account, the figure of the ruling class can still be discerned insistently playing the same unifying function with respect to what counts as political . . . [as the] Princes, Sovereigns, Legislators, etc. play in classical political theory."

Jeff Minson, "Strategies for Socialists? Foucault's Conception of Power," in *Towards a Critique of Foucault,* ed. Mike Gane (London: Routledge & Kegan Paul, 1986), p. 111.

4. The basic analysis of this history is in *Discipline and Punish* (DP.170–194, 293–308). The argument is elaborated in Part V of *The History of Sexuality,* where Foucault introduces the concept of bio-power. Significant details are examined in "The Politics of Health in the Eighteenth Century" (PK.166–182), and "The Political Technology of Individuals," in *Technologies of the Self: A Seminar with Michel Foucault,* ed. L. H. Martin et al. (Amherst: University of Massachusetts Press, 1988). See also Jacques Donzelot, *The Policing of Families,* trans. Robert Hurley (New York: Pantheon, 1979); and the studies, some by students and colleagues of Foucault, in *The Foucault Effect: Studies in Governmentality,* ed. Gorden Burchell et al. (Chicago: University of Chicago Press, 1991). Georges Canguilhem shows how from its beginning psychological research into reaction time, motivation, learning, and the measurement of aptitudes aimed at results useful for the management of individual differences in industry, military, and public administration. See "What is Psychology?," *Ideology and Consciousness* 7 (1980), 37–50. Ian Hacking shows how from the eighteenth to the nineteenth century the concept of "the normal state" wandered from pathology to populations in the work of Comte, Durkheim, and Galton. See *The Taming of Chance* (Cambridge: Cambridge University Press, 1990).

5. "In the United States, Canada, Western Europe, and Japan, the bulk of the labor force now works primarily at informational tasks, while wealth comes increasingly from informational goods such as microprocessors and from informational services such as data processing . . . [Information], embracing both goods and services . . . has come to dominate the world's largest and most advanced economies." J. R. Beniger, *The Control Revolution: Technological and Economic Origins of the Information Society* (Cambridge, Mass.: Harvard University Press, 1986), p. v. The economist Fritz Machlup writes, "There is evidence of a change in the composition of the labor force employed in the United States, in particular of an increase in the share of 'knowledge-producing' labor in total employment . . . the increase in the ratio of knowledge-producing labor to physical labor is strongly associated with the increase in productivity and thus with the rate of economic growth." In the United States, the total of what Machlup calls

"information activity, including both market and nonmarket transactions, accounted for 46% of GNP in 1967." *Knowledge: Its Creation, Distribution, and Economic Significance,* vol. 1: *Knowledge and Knowledge Production* (Princeton: Princeton University Press, 1980), pp. 10, 237n.

6. Joseph Rouse, *Knowledge and Power: Toward a Political Philosophy of Science* (Ithaca: Cornell University Press, 1987), pp. 246–247. See also Foucault, *Remarks on Marx,* pp. 165–166. The term "technoscience" is from Bruno Latour, *Science in Action* (Cambridge, Mass.: Harvard University Press, 1987).

7. Donald Davidson, "On the Very Idea of a Conceptual Scheme," in *Inquiries Concerning Truth and Interpretation* (Oxford: Oxford University Press, 1984), p. 192.

8. W. V. Quine, "Two Dogmas of Empiricism," in *From a Logical Point of View,* 2d ed. (New York: Harper & Row, 1961), pp. 42, 46. Elsewhere, Quine remarks: "Our talk of external things, our very notion of things, is just a conceptual apparatus that helps us to foresee and control the triggering of our sensory receptors in the light of previous triggering of our sensory receptors." *Theories and Things* (Cambridge, Mass.: Harvard University Press, 1981), p. 1.

9. Davidson, *Inquiries,* pp. 193–194.

10. W. V. Quine, *Theories and Things,* pp. 21–22, 39. Elsewhere, however, Quine does say: "What is it that makes one complete physical theory true and another false? I can only answer, with unhelpful realism, that it is the nature of the world." *Theories and Things,* p. 180.

11. Quine, *Theories and Things,* p. 39. Compare Hobbes's observation that "evidence is to truth, as the sap to the tree, which, so far as it creepeth along with the body and the branches, keepeth them alive; where it forsaketh them, they die: for this evidence . . . is the life of truth. Knowledge thereof, which we call science, I do define to be *evidence of truth,* from some beginning or principle of sense." *Human Nature,* VI.3; *English Works,* ed. William Molesworth (London, 1840), IV, p. 28.

12. W. V. Quine, *Pursuit of Truth,* rev. ed. (Cambridge, Mass.: Harvard University Press, 1992), pp. 41, 3, 5.

13. Davidson, "Empirical Content," in *Truth and Interpretation,* ed. Ernest Lepore (Oxford: Blackwell, 1986), pp. 324, 331; "A Coherence Theory of Truth and Knowledge," in *Reading Rorty,* ed. A. Malichowski (Oxford: Blackwell, 1990), p. 126; and *Inquiries,*

p. 189. On "naturalized epistemology," see Quine's essay "Epistemology Naturalized," in *Ontological Relativity and Other Essays* (New York: Columbia University Press, 1969), pp. 69–90.

14. Quine, *Theories and Things,* p. 40; my emphasis.

15. Davidson, "Coherence Theory," in *Reading Rorty,* p. 125.

16. See W. V. Quine, *Word and Object* (Cambridge, Mass.: MIT Press, 1960), p. 199. See also Christopher Hookway, *Quine* (Stanford: Stanford University Press, 1988), pp. 83–84.

17. When we speak we not only anticipate a reply, but also reply to, repeat, or revise the memorable words of others. The identity of utterances as speech or as language and their effectiveness as verbal meaning are artifacts of the dialogical history that embeds them. On dialogic, see V. N. Vološinov, *Marxism and the Philosophy of Language,* trans. Ladislav Matejka and I. R. Titunik (Cambridge, Mass.: Harvard University Press, 1986); and Tzvetan Todorov, *Mikhail Bakhtin: The Dialogical Principle,* trans. Wlad Godzich (Minneapolis: University of Minnesota Press, 1984). Vološinov remarks: "The real unit of language that is implemented in speech is not the individual, isolated monologic utterance, but the interaction of at least two utterances—in a word, *dialogue*" (p. 117). It was for this reason that Julia Kristeva introduced the term *intertextuality.* See *Desire in Language,* ed. Leon S. Roudiez (New York: Columbia University Press, 1980), pp. 65–69.

18. Davidson, *Inquiries,* pp. 43–44. Likewise Quine: "Truth cannot on the whole be viewed as a trait, even a passing trait, of a sentence merely; it is a passing trait of a sentence for a man." *Word and Object,* p. 191.

19. See the article "Imaginary" in Jean Laplanche and J.-B. Pontalis, *The Language of Psychoanalysis,* trans. Donald Nicholson-Smith (New York: W. W. Norton, 1973); and Fredric Jameson, "Imaginary and Symbolic in Lacan," *Yale French Studies* 55/56 (1977).

20. Jacques Lacan, *The Four Fundamental Concepts of Psychoanalysis,* trans. Alan Sheridan (New York: W. W. Norton, 1978), p. 24; my emphasis. Note that *ça* = *Es* = id.

21. Harold Bloom, *Ruin the Sacred Truths* (Cambridge, Mass.: Harvard University Press, 1989), p. 8. Freud, *Three Essays on the Theory of Sexuality* (Harmondsworth: Pelican Freud Library, 1977), vol. 7, pp. 62–63.

22. Fritz Machlup, *Knowledge: Its Creation, Distribution, and Economic*

Significance, vol. 1: *Knowledge and Knowledge Production* (Princeton: Princeton University Press, 1980), pp. 7–8. For the distinction between subjectively and socially new knowledge, see p. 22. On the production of knowledge and truth, see also my "Demonology, Styles of Reasoning, and Truth," *International Journal of Moral and Social Studies* 8 (1993).

23. Foucault, *The Use of Pleasure,* trans. Robert Hurley (New York: Pantheon, 1985), p. 3.

24. Citations in this paragraph are from "Questions of Method," in *Foucault Effect,* p. 85; and *PK*.131–132. On the idea of discourse and its distinction both from language and from speech, see *HS*.100–102; *Archaeology of Knowledge,* trans. A. M. Sheridan Smith (New York: Pantheon Books, 1972), pp. 80, 107; and Todorov, *Mikhail Bakhtin.*

25. Pierre Bourdieu, *Language and Symbolic Power,* ed. John B. Thompson (Cambridge, Mass.: Harvard University Press, 1991), p. 55; and *In Other Words,* trans. Matthew Adamson (Stanford: Stanford University Press, 1990), p. 32.

26. Foucault, *Archaeology of Knowledge,* p. 120; my emphasis.

27. C. Wright Mills, "On Knowledge and Power," in *Power, Politics, and People,* ed. I. L. Horowitz (Oxford: Oxford University Press, 1963), p. 611.

28. These quotations are from Londa Schiebinger, "Skeletons in the Closet: The First Illustrations of the Female Skeleton in Eighteenth-Century Anatomy," in *The Making of the Modern Body: Sexuality and Society in the Nineteenth Century,* ed. Catherine Gallagher and Thomas Laqueur (Berkeley: University of California Press, 1987), pp. 51, 67–72. See also Schiebinger, *The Mind Has No Sex?* (Cambridge, Mass.: Harvard University Press, 1989).

29. As Foucault observes, "what has always characterized our society, since the time of the Greeks, is the fact that we do not have a complete and peremptory definition of the games of truth which would be allowed, to the exclusion of all others. There is always a possibility, in a given game of truth, to discover something else and to more or less change such and such a rule and sometimes even the totality of the game of truth. No doubt that is what has given the West, in relationship to other societies, possibilities of development that we find no where else" (*PF*.17).

It is possible to speculate that this may owe something to the history of writing in the West. Jack Goody points out that in Greece writing was from the beginning "unrestricted by centralized religious, political or scribal interests [and] penetrated into most areas of culture

... Writing was never an esoteric craft, being open to a large segment of the population, and this constituted one of the most significant contributions to the Greek achievement." *The Interface between the Written and the Oral* (Cambridge: Cambridge University Press, 1987), pp. 107–108. In a related observation, Charles Segal writes: "The increasing literacy of the late fifth century, at least in Athens, is one of several interrelated influences that tend to cut the discourse of truth loose from the communal, performative, and agonistic context of the archaic period and thereby to require the poet to reflect consciously on the source of truth or, in other words, on the kind of story he has, implicitly, to tell about himself." "Greek Tragedy: Writing, Truth, and the Representation of Self," cited in Page DuBois, *Torture and Truth* (New York: Routledge, 1991), p. 104.

30. F. G. Bailey, *The Prevalence of Deceit* (Ithaca: Cornell University Press, 1991), p. 128. Adlai Stevenson is quoted on p. ix.

31. Foucault, "Questions of Method," in *Foucault Effect*, p. 79. He continues: "Of course this is a problem of philosophy to which the historian is entitled to remain indifferent. But if I am posing it as a problem within historical analysis, I'm not demanding that history answer it ... it's a matter of ... a nominalist critique itself arrived at by way of a historical analysis" (p. 86).

32. See Foucault, *The Order of Things* (New York: Random House, 1970), chap. 6. An anonymous sixteenth-century *Compendieux* contains the remark, "neither copper, nor gold, nor silver were minted, but only valued according to their weight" (pp. 169–170). A seventeenth-century author can still say, "The essential value of gold and silver coins is based upon the precious metal they contain" (p. 211). Foucault argues that mercantilism "freed money from the postulate of the intrinsic value of metal ... [and] established between it and wealth a strict relation of representation" (pp. 176–177). The interpretation is confirmed in Pierre Vilar, *A History of Gold and Money*, trans. Judith White (London: Verso, 1991). But compare Jacques Le Goff: "money was appreciated because of its value, not as a symbol but as merchandise. It was not worth the theoretical value written on its face ... but the real value of the precious metal which it contained. People weighed coins to find out how much they were worth. As Marc Bloch has said, 'a coin which one has to put in the scales looks very much like an ingot.' It was only just at the very end of the thirteenth century that French civil lawyers began to distinguish its intrinsic value—its weight in gold—from its extrinsic value, that is to say its

transformation into a monetary symbol, an instrument of exchange." *Medieval Civilization,* trans. Julia Barrow (Oxford: Blackwell, 1988), p. 248.

Epilogue

1. Marx, *Capital,* trans. Samuel Moore and Edward Aveling (Moscow: Progress Publishers, 1977), vol. 1, p. 86.

2. On the "usual objection," see Donald Davidson's "Afterthoughts, 1987" to his "Coherence Theory of Truth and Knowledge," in *Reading Rorty,* ed. A. Malichowski (Oxford: Blackwell, 1990), p. 135; and Davidson, "The Structure and Content of Truth," *Journal of Philosophy* 87 (1990), esp. pp. 302–304. Variations on this objection can be found in most critics of correspondence (for example, Goodman, Rorty, Putnam), although it is not their only argument. Etienne Gilson observes its irrelevance to medieval realism; see *The Spirit of Medieval Philosophy* (1936) (Notre Dame: University of Notre Dame Press, 1991), p. 236. I discuss Davidson's objection to correspondence in "The Historical Discourse of Philosophy," *Reconstructing Philosophy: New Essays in Metaphilosophy, Canadian Journal of Philosophy,* supple. vol. 18 (1992).

3. Hume writes: "It is a question of fact, whether the perceptions of the senses be produced by external objects, resembling them: How shall this question be determined? By experience surely; as all other questions of a like nature. But here experience is, and must be, entirely silent. The mind has never any thing present to it but the perceptions, and cannot possibly reach any experience with their connection with objects. The supposition of such a connection is, therefore, without any foundation in reasoning." *Enquiry Concerning Human Understanding,* §XII (Part I).

Hume does not explicitly discuss truth in this argument, which he uses against the assumption that perceptions resemble beings without the mind. It was turned into an objection to correspondence by Kant's first readers. For instance, Karl Leonhard Reinhold: "For Hume, representations consist originally in mere *impressions* and their *reproductions;* hence he was able to show from the very nature of *representation,* as the source of all knowledge, that knowledge in general and philosophical knowledge in particular is merely the product of the imagination, and that all *objective truth,* i.e., any *real* conformity of representations to their objects, lacks foundation and is quite undemonstrable . . . Being *more consistent* than Locke, Hume confronted this crucial issue about *conformity* of impressions to their objects; this was what everybody had taken for granted without proof before his time, and he demonstrated that no proof can be offered that is without contradiction. Every possible demonstration of objective truth would call for a *comparison* between a *representation* and an *object* different from it; but at the same time this comparison could only take place through representations, and indeed it would have to be between the one representation that consists in the impression itself, and the other through which this impression is represented; consequently, the comparison would never be set up between a representation and an object that is not already a representation." *The Foundations of Philosophical Knowledge* (Jena, 1791); *Between Kant and Hegel,* ed. George di Giovanni and H. S. Harris (Albany: State University of New York Press, 1985), pp. 56–57.

4. Several philosophers have thought this worth remarking on; for instance Davidson: "Nothing in the world, no object or event, would be true or false if there were not thinking creatures." "Structure and Content of Truth," p. 279. Heidegger: "There is truth only insofar and for so long as Dasein is" (*SZ.*226). William Ockham: "If no intellect existed, still man would not be a stone, and yet the proposition 'man is not a stone' would not be true then, because no proposition would exist then." Cited in M. M. Adams, *William Ockham* (Notre Dame: University of Notre Dame Press, 1987), p. 412.

5. C. S. Peirce, *The Collected Papers of Charles Sanders Peirce,* ed. Charles Hartshorne and Paul Weiss (Cambridge, Mass.: Harvard University Press, 1931), vol. 1, paragraph 575.

6. Bertrand Russell, *The Analysis of Mind* (London: George Allen & Unwin, 1921), p. 278. In an earlier writing Russell worried whether the preference for truth might not be "a mere unaccountable prejudice." "As for the preference which most people—so long as they are not annoyed by instances—feel in favor of true propositions, this must be based, apparently, upon an ultimate ethical proposition: 'It is good to believe true propositions and bad to believe false ones.' This proposition, it is to be hoped, is true; but if not, there is no reason to think that we will do ill in believing it." See "Meinong's Theory of Complexes and Assumptions" (1904), in Russell, *Essays in Analysis,* ed. D. Lackay (New York: Brazillier, 1973), pp. 75–76.

7. In *The Philosophy of Money,* Georg Simmel elaborates on this

Nietzschean perspectivism: "The difference in organization requires that each species, in order to survive and attain its essential aims in life, must behave in a way that is distinctive and different from that of other species. Whether an action guided by a representation will have useful consequences cannot be determined by the content of this representation, even though it might correspond with absolute objectivity. The result will depend entirely upon what this representation can accomplish as a real process within the organism, allied with other physical and psychological forces and with reference to the specific needs of life. If we assert that man sustains and supports life only on the basis of true representations, and destroys it by false ones, what does this 'truth'—the content of which is different for each species and which never reflects the true object—mean except that some representation associated with a particular organization and its powers and needs leads to useful results? . . . We dignify with the name of 'truth' those representations that, active within us as real forces and motions, incite us to useful behavior." Georg Simmel, *The Philosophy of Money*, 2d ed., ed. David Frisby (London: Routledge, 1990), p. 107.

James referred to Simmel as "a humanist of the most radical sort" (*M*.44). In a letter of 1905 he says that although he has not read Simmel's longer works, he did read "his original pragmatistic article (which seemed to me rather crude, though essentially correct)" (editorial note to *M*.44).

8. Richard Rorty, *Consequences of Pragmatism* (Minneapolis: University of Minnesota Press, 1982), pp. 223–224. Michel Foucault, "Truth, Power, Self," interview in *Technologies of the Self: A Seminar with Michel Foucault*, ed. L. H. Martin et al. (Amherst: University of Massachusetts Press, 1988), p. 13.

9. Foucault, *The Use of Pleasure*, trans. Robert Hurley (New York: Pantheon, 1985), pp. 8–9. Richard Rorty, *Philosophy and the Mirror of Nature* (Princeton: Princeton University Press, 1979), p. 392.

10. "Truth is great and will prevail"—anonymous. Democritus, fragment 69, and Antiphon, fragment 44; in K. Freeman, *Ancilla to the Pre-Socratic Philosophers* (Cambridge, Mass.: Harvard University Press, 1948), pp. 101, 147. Clement, in Eric Osborn, *The Beginning of Christian Philosophy* (Cambridge: Cambridge University Press, 1971), p. 269. Milton, *Areopagitica*, ed. J. W. Hales (Oxford: Oxford University Press, 1932), pp. 51–52. Jefferson, Prologue to the Virginia Statute, *The Life and Selected Writings of Thomas Jefferson*, ed. Adri-

enne Koch and William Peden (New York: Random House, 1944), p. 313. G. Lukács, *History and Class Consciousness,* trans. Rodney Livingstone (Cambridge, Mass.: MIT Press, 1971), p. 81; Jürgen Habermas, *Knowledge and Human Interests,* trans. Jeremy J. Shapiro (Boston: Beacon Press, 1971), p. 314. The citations from St. Thomas and Lessing are in Hans Blumenberg, *The Legitimacy of the Modern Age,* trans. Robert M. Wallace (Cambridge, Mass.: MIT Press, 1983), pp. 331, 423.

Acknowledgments

I thank Michael Frede, Calvin Normore, Ron Yoshida, and Shelley Tremain, with whom I have discussed some of the questions I touch on this book.

Parts of several chapters were read at meetings of the Canadian and American Philosophical Associations, 1987–1992. I thank my commentators and audiences.

Chapters 1 and 3 use material from "Nietzsche's Question, What Good is Truth?," *History of Philosophy Quarterly* 9 (1992). Chapter 4 began as a contribution to Sacvan Bercovitch's seminar on American dissent at the School of Criticism and Theory, Dartmouth College, 1987; I draw on my contribution to a volume from the seminar, "Work on Truth in America: The Example of William James," in *Cohesion and Dissent in America,* edited by Joseph Alkana and Carol Colatrella (Albany: State University of New York Press, 1993). This essay first appeared in *Studies in Puritan American Spirituality* 3 (1992). Chapter 6 reworks some pages from "Difference Unlimited," in *Working Through Derrida,* edited by G. B. Madison (Evanston: Northwestern University Press, 1993). Chapter 7 draws a page from "The Lesson of Solipsism," *Idealistic Studies* 44 (1991). Chapter 8 takes some pages from "Government in Foucault," *Canadian Journal of Philosophy* 21 (1991), and "The Historical Discourse of Philosophy," in *Reconstructing Philosophy: New Essays in Metaphilosophy, Canadian Journal of Philosophy* suppl. vol. 18 (1992). I thank the editors and publishers for their permission to use this material in revised form here.

Citations from translations of Wittgenstein published by Basil Blackwell and published by Routledge appear by kind permission of the Wittgenstein Trustees and the publishers. Citations from William James, *Pragmatism* and *The Meaning of Truth* © 1975, 1978 by the

President and Fellows of Harvard College, appear by permission of Harvard University Press. Excerpts from *Being and Time* by Martin Heidegger, translated by J. Macquarrie and E. Robinson, copyright © 1962 by SCM Press, Ltd.; from *What Is Called Thinking* by Martin Heidegger, translated by F. Wieck and J. G. Gray, English translation copyright © 1968 by Harper & Row, Publishers, Inc.; from *Early Greek Thinking* by Martin Heidegger, English translation by David Farrell Krell and Frank A. Capuzzi, English translation copyright © 1975, 1985 by Harper & Row, Publishers, Inc.; and from *Basic Writings* by Martin Heidegger, copyright © 1977 by Harper & Row, Publishers, Inc., copyright © 1977 by David Farrell Krell are all reprinted by permission of HarperCollins Publishers. Excerpts from *Beyond Good and Evil* by Friedrich Nietzsche, translated by Walter Kaufmann, copyright © 1966 by Random House, Inc.; from *The Will to Power* by Friedrich Nietzsche, translated by Walter Kaufmann and R. J. Hollingdale, copyright © 1967 by Walter Kaufmann; from *On the Genealogy of Morals and Ecce Homo* by Friedrich Nietzsche, translated by Walter Kaufmann, copyright © 1967 by Random House, Inc.; and from *The Gay Science* by Friedrich Nietzsche, translated by Walter Kaufmann, copyright © 1974 by Random House, Inc., are all reprinted by permission of the publisher. Lines from "The Skaters" by John Ashbery are reprinted from the volume *Rivers and Mountains,* copyright © 1962, 1963, 1964, 1966 by John Ashbery (New York: Ecco Press, 1966), p. 39.

Index

227